MORALITIES ON THE GOSPELS

A NEW SOURCE OF *ANCRENE WISSE*

MORALITIES ON THE GOSPELS

A NEW SOURCE OF
ANCRENE WISSE

BY

E. J. DOBSON

OXFORD
AT THE CLARENDON PRESS
1975

Oxford University Press, Ely House, London W. 1

GLASGOW   NEW YORK   TORONTO   MELBOURNE   WELLINGTON
CAPE TOWN   IBADAN   NAIROBI   DAR ES SALAAM   LUSAKA   ADDIS ABABA
DELHI   BOMBAY   CALCUTTA   MADRAS   KARACHI   LAHORE   DACCA
KUALA LUMPUR   SINGAPORE   HONG KONG   TOKYO

ISBN 0 19 812056 7

*Printed in Great Britain
at the University Press, Oxford
by Vivian Ridler
Printer to the University*

IN MEMORIAM

T. P. DUNNING

ACKNOWLEDGEMENTS

My chief debt in writing this book is made clear by its opening sentences, but I have also to thank Dr. Anne Hudson for her continuing interest and help as what seemed at first a straightforward investigation turned into one much longer and more complicated. I was also greatly helped, from beginning to end, by Dr. R. W. Hunt, who made freely available, as he always does, both his skill as a palaeographer and his detailed knowledge of the Latin literature of the period. Dr. A. B. Emden, *magister magistrorum*, among other kindnesses first pointed out to me that there was a Magister Alexander who had been dean of Wells about the right time, and Miss D. E. Greenway at a later stage was most generous in supplementing and correcting the information that I had gathered about him and his immediate successors. Miss A. C. de la Mare, Mrs. Sonia Patterson, Mr. N. R. Ker, and Mr. M. B. Parkes gave welcome—and by no means unsolicited—advice on various matters of palaeography; and Professor Norman Davis and Dr. Pamela Gradon are other friends to whom I am obliged for encouragement and help. The members of my family whom I have pestered with questions about Latin will no doubt regard it as an inescapable domestic hazard, but I should at least put on record that they did what they could to save me from error and that any errors are mine. And since we are sometimes too apt to take it for granted, I should like also to record my appreciation of the courtesy and helpfulness of the library staffs of the Bodleian, of Balliol College, and of Cambridge University

Library. To the staff of the Clarendon Press I am indebted for the care and learning with which they have read my proofs and for most helpful suggestions which I have been glad to follow.

E. J. D.

Jesus College
Oxford

CONTENTS

I

ANCRENE WISSE AND THE
MORALIA SUPER EVANGELIA

IN the spring of 1972 Dr. Anne Hudson, reading the unprinted *Moralia super Evangelia*[1] commonly attributed to
Robert Grosseteste in the hope of finding parallels to the
writings of Wyclif and his followers, found instead two clear
and important parallels to *Ancrene Wisse* (*The Ancrene Riwle*):
one, in *Moralia* III. 3, a passage concerning the symbolism of
the shield which corresponds to *Ancrene Wisse* (Corpus MS.),
f. 106a/19–26,[2] and the second, in *Moralia* III. 47, a much
more concise version of the passage concerning the four chief
loves in *Ancrene Wisse* ff. 106b/2–107b/4, for which no exact
early parallel had hitherto been known.[3] Miss Hudson,

[1] Modern scholars usually refer to the work as the *Moralitates super
Evangelia*, but this form of the title lacks authority in the early manu-
scripts; MS. Lincoln College Oxford Lat. 79 has, in the hand of the
original scribe, the title *Moralia super evangelia* (f. 11), and MS. Trinity
College Oxford 50 calls it *Omili*[*e*] . . . *super hystoriam euuangelicam* (f. 2)
and *Moralis tractatus secundum ordinem quatuor euangelistarum* (f. 7).
In view of the earlier date and greater authority of the Lincoln College
MS. (see below), I follow its title.

[2] My references to the *Moralia* are by part and chapter, thus III. 3
is Part III, chapter 3; those to *Ancrene Wisse* are to folio and line of the
Corpus MS. (ed. J. R. R. Tolkien, E.E.T.S. 249, 1962). References to
the pages of Morton's edition (Camden Society lvii, 1853) are given in
the margins of the E.E.T.S. editions, preceded by the abbreviation 'M.'

[3] See Geoffrey Shepherd (ed.), *Ancrene Wisse: Parts Six and Seven*
(London and Edinburgh, 1959), p. 59 (note to p. 23, ll. 9 ff.), who comments, 'This classification of loves is apparently the author's own.'

Edward Wilson, 'The Four Loves in *Ancrene Wisse*', *RES* N.S. xix
(1968), 41–7, prints the text of a fifteenth-century sermon (in MS. Lincoln

recognizing the relevance of her discovery to work on which I was engaged, kindly informed me of it, saying that she thought there might well be other parallels to *Ancrene Wisse* in the *Moralia*; and so it proved when, with her consent, I continued the search. There are, by my count, over a hundred passages in the *Moralia* which offer parallels to *Ancrene Wisse*, and there may be others that I have missed. In many cases, admittedly, the resemblance is imperfect or general, and in others it could easily be the result of a common tradition of exegesis (e.g. when the same citations from scripture or from other authorities are used in similar contexts); but in at least half of the instances, in my judgement, the parallels are close enough to leave no doubt of the interdependence of the two texts, and in some there is almost word-for-word agreement—so close, indeed, in a few special cases, as to form a reliable basis for argument concerning the textual affiliations of *Ancrene Wisse* and the manuscripts of the *Moralia*. Even the minor or imperfect resemblances gain significance from the demonstration, from the major or close agreements, of the relationship between the two works, for if

Cathedral 50, ff. 40–7, and MS. Gloucester Cathedral 22, Press No. 1, pp. 88–101) on the theme. But though Mr. Wilson thinks that there is 'no evidence of any dependence on *Ancrene Wisse*' (p. 41) and that the sermon represents an independent tradition, I cannot agree. The sermon is extensively and thoroughly rewritten, with suppression of some of the details in *Ancrene Wisse* and the introduction of much new material (in part probably from elsewhere in *Ancrene Wisse*, in part from a passage by St. Bernard which is used as the theme of a thirteenth-century vernacular sermon written into MS. Cleopatra C. vi, f. 57ᵛ, but mostly from other sources); nevertheless it is essentially based on *Ancrene Wisse*'s account. The order of the loves is the same (and different from that in *Moralia* III. 47), and there is the distinctive detail, in the discussion of the love of mother for child, of the reference to a child which might be a 'fowle leper' and 'myȝte not be helyd but if he had an hote baþe of his moders bloode', which no mother would be willing to suffer death to supply (p. 46). This is merely an elaboration of *Ancrene Wisse* f. 107a/3–5, which in turn is based on, but significantly different from, the *Moralia*'s sentence, 'Mater filium in aquis balneat, Cristus in sanguine.'

the one author had read the other the likelihood that the lesser resemblances are the chance result of a common tradition is much reduced.

It will not be possible to give a full account of the parallels in this study, which must largely be concerned with the *Moralia* itself, but I cite illustrative passages in the course of my discussion of the relationship between the two works and of the textual tradition of the *Moralia*, and I print in an appendix the text of those passages in the Latin work which I take to be parallel, or at least in some way comparable, to the English. These are varied in nature: some are extensive, others brief and particular. An example of the latter type, which I choose because it is both distinctive and complex in its relations, is the remark in *Ancrene Wisse* Part VII (f. 107b/10–11)

swa me seið bi large mon þe ne con nawt edhalden, þet he haueð þe honden, as mine beoð, iþurlet,

on which Professor Shepherd comments that 'no proverbial expression of this type . . . has been found', though he cites a partial parallel (*manus perforatas ad largiendum*) from a Latin note written on the final page of MS. Cotton Nero A. xiv;[1] but a close parallel comes in *Moralia* I. 49,

Et sicut manus domini erant affixe, perforate, extente, sanguine irrigate, ita sacerdotes et prelati ecclesie debent habere manus extentas ad pauperes perforatas largitate. Qui enim dapsilis est, dicitur habere manus perforatas.[2]

[1] Op. cit., p. 62. This is of course the manuscript of the 'Nero version' of the *Ancrene Riwle*; the Latin note is cited on p. xxii of Miss Day's edition (E.E.T.S. 225, 1952), where *perforatos* is presumably an error for *perforatas*.

[2] My quotations from the *Moralia* are edited texts, based on collation of the Lincoln College MS. (L) and the Trinity College MS. (T), with preference given to the readings of the former in case of doubt; but I normally adopt the spelling of whichever manuscript agrees more closely with classical usage. I expand the *nomen sacrum* abbreviation as *Cristus*, conformably to the practice of the time. Conjectural emendations lacking

But this is not the only analogue; another comes in a sermon of Stephen Langton's for Passion Sunday ('Sermon 81c'):[1]

Nonne solet dici quod manus habet perforatas qui omnia dat et pauca retinet? Hoc etiam modo Dominus manus mistice perforatas habuit, quia se ipsum pro nobis donauit et obtulit, qui uno verbo nos liberare potuit.

But we do not have to choose between these two sources, each of which contributed something to the sentence in *Ancrene Wisse*.[2] The author of the English work had certainly read the *Moralia*, as it is my main purpose to show; but he had independent knowledge of at least some of Langton's sermons, and in particular of this one.[3] But there can also be no doubt

the authority of either of the early manuscripts are enclosed in square brackets.

[1] Quoted in Phyllis Barzillay Roberts, *Studies in the Sermons of Stephen Langton* (Toronto, 1968), p. 105; but I have modified her text by collation of MS. Magdalen College Oxford Lat. 168, f. 88. I owe this reference, and my acquaintance with Mrs. Roberts's important book, to Miss Hudson.

[2] The *Moralia*'s *dapsilis* (and *largitate*) correspond more closely to *Ancrene Wisse*'s *large mon* than Langton's *qui omnia dat*, but Langton's *qui . . . pauca retinet* is a close, though not an exact, parallel to *þe ne con nawt edhalden*.

[3] There are three further indications that the author of *Ancrene Wisse* had read this sermon, the first a general parallelism of idea, the others verbally more precise. (i) Langton, in the context of confession, says that Christ at the raising of Lazarus did not shrink from opening the tomb because of the stench; so the sinner should not shrink from revealing his sins to God through confession because of their stench (Magdalen MS., f. 87). Cf. *Ancrene Wisse* f. 88b/15–21. (ii) Immediately afterwards, Langton says 'Ipse [*sc.* deus] enim medicus est et infirmitates uult uidere . . . Si medicus uulnus non uidet, medicamen non apponit', with a passing reference, between these sentences, to the *puluerem peccatorum tuorum* (ibid., f. 87$^{\text{r-v}}$). Cf. *Ancrene Wisse*, f. 85b/14, 19–22 (though the main source is in the *Moralia*). (iii) A little later (f. 87^{v}) Langton says:

'Crucifixio hec fit in nobis per macerationem carnis et per pugnam contra pestes mentis. Sic portatur a nobis crux Cristi. Non possumus autem conregnare ei nisi uelimus compati. Scire ergo debetis quomodo a nobis portari oporteat crucem domini.'

Cf. the beginning of Part VII of *Ancrene Wisse* (f. 94a/13 ff.), with its *si*

that the author of the *Moralia* himself made use of a collection of Langton's sermons,[1] and in this instance the similitude has come to *Ancrene Wisse* both directly from Langton and indirectly.

Parallels to *Ancrene Wisse* are found in all four parts of the *Moralia*, from the first chapter[2] to the last,[3] but rather more than two-thirds of them come in Parts III and IV, which means, even allowing for the fact that these two parts constitute almost three-fifths of the whole book, that in them the parallels are more frequent; the greatest proportion is in Part III. In *Ancrene Wisse* parallels to the *Moralia* are found in all the parts (II–VII) of the Inner Rule, but not in the Outer Rule (Parts I and VIII), whose sources, as well as

---

compatimur, conregnabimus, a similar reminiscence of 2 Tim. 2: 12. (*Moralia* III. 88 also cites the text in the form *Si enim ipsi non compatimur, non conregnabimus*, but the context there is different.)

Ancrene Wisse is probably influenced by others of Langton's sermons. Roberts, op. cit., p. 94, cites from 'Sermon 1a' the similitude

'Sicut enim expugnatores castri alicuius ferventibus aquis exscaturizantur, sic diabolus lacrima penitentis conficitur',

which corresponds to *Ancrene Wisse* f. 66b/1–5, and on p. 109, n. 3, the *exemplum* in 'Sermon 115a'

'Vir absens si per nuntium audierit de uxore quod contristetur de absentia viri, et quod defleat eum absentem, multum placet ei, quia hoc est certum argumentum magne et firme dilectionis quam illa habet erga maritum suum',

which corresponds to *Ancrene Wisse* f. 99b/3–8. I did not notice parallels to either of these passages in the *Moralia*, though I was looking for them; the nearest is a passage in IV. 42 which tells how a wife separated from her husband would hurry to meet him if his journeyings brought him to a place near his home.

[1] See below, pp. 97–100.
[2] Christ's poverty as a remedy (*medela*) for pride (I. 1), as in *Ancrene Wisse* f. 67a/22–4.
[3] A similitude in IV. 64 comparing the wings of a bird extended in flight (of which one was justice and the other mercy) to the arms of Christ spread on the cross, which (like a passage in IV. 38) offers a partial parallel to *Ancrene Wisse* f. 36a/4–9.

purpose, are quite different; and though there are a couple of possible parallels to the *Moralia* in the Preface of *Ancrene Wisse*, I do not think them significant. If account is taken of the varying lengths of the parts of *Ancrene Wisse*, there are relatively fewer parallels in Parts II, IV, and VI, though some of those that occur are distinctive and important;[1] they are about twice as frequent in Parts III and V, and most frequent of all (allowing for its brevity) in Part VII. But it is misleading to talk of the number or even the frequency of the parallels, especially in the case of Part V (Confession), for the whole outline and much of the detail of the discussion of the qualities that confession ought to have (ff. 82b–92b), which constitutes most of the Part, follows, though with greater elaboration, a single lengthy chapter of the *Moralia* (IV. 18) on the same topic; and some of the additional material used in Part V is to be found elsewhere in the *Moralia* in widely dispersed chapters.[2]

More characteristic of the way in which *Ancrene Wisse* uses material also found in the *Moralia* is Part VII (Love), the climax of the Inner Rule and justly one of the most admired sections of the work. It is really no detraction from the author's achievement that more of his material than was hitherto thought turns out to occur elsewhere, especially as he uses it to much greater advantage. The parallels to the *Moralia* begin at f. 104b/26, with the account of God's wooing of the world by gifts and by sealed and open letters, which corresponds (though with differences, including some

---

[1] Thus in Part VI (Penance), which has the smallest absolute number of parallels, the discussion of the symbolism of Nicodemus and the three Marys (ff. 100b/16–101b/19) is derived from *Moralia* IV. 44 and IV. 46, with some further detail from IV. 50; and there are other important parallels in Part VI.

[2] I. 43; II. 11, 35; III. 11, 16, 26, 54, 96, 98; IV. 9, 22, 29, 50, 62. The parallels in these chapters vary in extent and significance; some are minor, others important.

well-judged pruning of the citation of authorities) to a similar narrative at the beginning of *Moralia* III. 47. There follows, in *Ancrene Wisse*, the famous *exemplum* of the lady besieged in an earthen castle, which seems to be the author's own invention; but there are similar passages in the *Moralia*, in particular one in III. 21 in which mankind beset by sin is likened to a castle surrounded by its enemies.[1] In any case the extended allegory in *Ancrene Wisse* is introduced at the point where, in the first section of *Moralia* III. 47, its author writes of Christ:

Homo factus ad arma recurrit, quibus strenuitatem suam fidelibus propalaret, et nouo pugnandi modo usus de hostibus suis triumphauit. Iudicum: 'Noua bella elegit dominus sibi, portas hostium ipse subuertit.' Ad strenuitatis ipsius euidentiam, scutum ipsius, id est corpus, quinque locis perforatum est, et manibus cruci affixis de demonibus palmam quam affectauerat assecutus est. Mortuus est ergo Cristus in cruce ut quem uiuum mundus non dilexerat, saltem mortuum diligeret.

This whole prose passage is summed up in 'memorial' verses at the end of the chapter:

> Munera dat, breue mittit, ad arma recurrit; in hostes
> Deseuit. Clipeus Cristi penetratur, obitque,
> Vt qui uiuus erat odio, defunctus ametur.

In *Ancrene Wisse* the allegory of the king who lost his life in warfare to rid the lady of her foes corresponds to Christ's resort to warfare against the devils in the Latin, and towards the end of the English allegory the last phrase of the Latin prose passage, or its verse equivalent, is echoed by the king's request to the lady

þet tu luuie me . . . dead hwen þu naldest liues.

[1] Cf. *Ancrene Wisse* f. 105b/22, 'ure sawle þe deoflen hefden biset'.

This is closely followed (ff. 105b/24–106a/1) by another similitude, of Christ as a champion in a tournament whose shield, which was his body, was pierced 'on each side'; this is partly suggested by the same passage in *Moralia* III. 47, in which Christ, taking up arms to show his vigour (*strenuitas*), has his shield, i.e. his body, pierced in five places,[1] and partly by two others, in III. 5 and IV. 17, where Christ is specifically referred to as a champion (*athleta*), especially by the first,

Athleta etiam Cristus est, qui scutum, id est carnem in cruce habuit perforatam,

and there is yet another passage (in III. 1) where his body is described as a shield pierced in five places. *Ancrene Wisse* immediately goes on to elaborate this by saying that as a shield is broad above and narrow beneath, so was Christ's body on the cross, with spread arms and 'the one foot, after many a man's opinion, set upon the other'; in the *Moralia* there are two passages (in III. 61 and III. 66) in which it is explicitly stated that Christ's feet were placed one above the other and fastened by a single nail and in which there are similar comparisons to material objects—in the first passage to a *comptus*, in the second to a door.[2] Then, after two Biblical citations

[1] Both the allegory of the lady and the king, and the similitude of a knight in the tournament, seem suggested by the same passage in *Moralia* III. 47; and I think it possible that the allegory was a slightly later insertion and that in a first draft there was a direct transition from *ant hire luue wealden* (f. 105a/17) to *þes king is iesu godes sune* (f. 105b/21). There would be no discontinuity in sense, and without the extended allegory of the lady in the earthen castle there would be a more equal correspondence between *Ancrene Wisse* and *Moralia* III. 47. But if so, the addition must have been made almost immediately; it is still influenced in part by III. 47.

[2] The context shows that by *comptus* is meant some sort of rack or frame from which to hang kitchen utensils, fastened to a post by two nails at the top and one at the bottom, and hanging out from the post at the top. The basis of the comparison to a door (*hostium*, i.e. *ostium*) is less

concerning shields,¹ *Ancrene Wisse* proceeds (f. 106a/13–19)
to consider whether Christ could not have redeemed mankind
with less pain; this closely follows a passage in *Moralia* III.
56, and in particular the phrase

Non enim multum solet diligi qui dat quod non multum constat
sibi

corresponds to, but in the context is more logical than,

Me buð lihtliche þing þet me luueð lutel

('one pays a low price for a thing that one loves little'),
where the English author momentarily shifts the argument to
emphasize Christ's great love for us, rather than how much
he deserves our love (though he returns to this—'forte
ofdrahen of us ure luue toward him, þet costnede him se
sare').² He then resumes the treatment of the symbolism of
the shield, first of its component elements, then of the fact
that a dead knight's shield is hung high in the church, as

clear to me. The author says that a door opens in three parts, above,
below, and to the side; likewise Christ hanging on the cross was 'opened'
(*reseratus*) by the fastenings (*fixuras*) of the nails driven into his hands,
and below was also open (*apertus*) to the impression of the single nail
transfixing his feet. Perhaps he has in mind a door like a modern stable
door, with two leaves at the top which can be opened wide and fastened
on either side, and a single leaf at the bottom. Even so, the similitude is
forced.

¹ Both of these, it is fair to say (in view of my subsequent argument),
occur in Grosseteste's *Dictum* 95, on the symbolism of the shield; but it
has no other resemblance to the passage in *Ancrene Wisse*.

² This passage, which interrupts the treatment of the 'shield' *motif*
and comes from a different chapter of the *Moralia*, again may well have
been an afterthought, inserted after the author had written his first draft
but before any form of *Ancrene Wisse* was 'published' by the making of
a fair copy. It is interesting that Dr. Gradon, in her perceptive discussion
of the imagery of this 'shield' passage in *Ancrene Wisse* (Pamela Gradon,
Form and Style in Early English Literature (London, 1971), pp. 51–2),
omits the sentences which I suppose may have been a later insertion.

Christ's 'shield', the crucifix, is;[1] this passage closely agrees with one in *Moralia* III. 3 (the first of Miss Hudson's parallels). It is significant that the latter ends

Nouo pugnandi modo usus est dominus cum, manibus cruci affixis, de diabolo triumphauit; unde in Iudicum dicitur, 'Noua bella sibi elegit dominus',

which provides a very obvious link with the passage from III. 47 cited above; and at this point *Ancrene Wisse* (f. 106b/2 ff.) reverts to *Moralia* III. 47, where, immediately after the passage referred to, there is a concise treatment of the theme of the superiority of Christ's love to what *Ancrene Wisse* calls 'the four chief loves which are found in this world', a theme developed much more expansively and effectively, though also sometimes more popularly, in the English work. This is the second of the parallels noted by Miss Hudson, and one of the most significant of all; despite the difference of scale, there can be no question of the direct link between the two treatments.[2] Thereafter *Ancrene Wisse* diverges from the *Moralia*, but there is still some material in common. In *Ancrene Wisse* (f. 107b/4–10) Christ asks: if your love is to be given, where can it be better bestowed than on me, who am the fairest, richest, highest-born, wisest, most gracious (*hendest*), and most liberal (*freoest*)? Here are six qualities (of which the last two are not easily distinguishable); *Moralia* III. 52 says (in the better text given by L) that Christ has

---

[1] *Ancrene Wisse* f. 106a/19–26. In this passage the phrase 'Eft þe þridde reisun' has troubled commentators, perhaps because the intervention of the discussion of why Christ redeemed us with such pain obscures the line of argument. In my view the author is giving three 'reasons' or justifications for equating Christ's 'leoue licome þet wes ispread on rode' with his shield (ff. 105b/27–106a/1), namely (1) because of the shape, broad above and narrow beneath, (2) because of the symbolism of the three materials of which a shield is made, and now (3) because of the symbolism of a memorial shield hung in a church.

[2] For the text of the Latin see Appendix, entry no. 72 (second paragraph, p. 175).

four qualities sought in a carnal bridegroom—riches, power, beauty, and high birth—but in the elaboration of the theme, chiefly by scriptural citations, mentions wisdom (which in T's text is added to the list of qualities) and uses both the adjectives *nobilis* and *generosus*. The two passages do not exactly correspond, but have much in common. In *Ancrene Wisse* there immediately follows (f. 107b/10–11) the saying, already cited, that a generous man has pierced hands, which in the *Moralia* comes in a widely separated place (I. 49) and a different context (the qualities required of priests and prelates). It is, I think, not very significant that *Ancrene Wisse*, at f. 108a/28–108b/1, cites the text 'Ignem veni mittere in terram' (Luke 12: 49), also cited in *Moralia* I. 30 and II. 4 (and indeed elsewhere), and at f. 108b/5–6 'Utinam frigidus esses aut calidus' (Rev. 3: 15–16), cited in *Moralia* III. 48 and III. 94; these citations could easily be independent. Nor does it seem significant that *Ancrene Wisse* at f. 108b/18–20 expresses the conception that Christ 'spreads his arms towards you and bows down his head as if to offer a kiss', which in different forms occurs in *Moralia* III. 45 and IV. 16; the idea was a commonplace at the time. But it is more remarkable that at f. 108b/25 there begins an extensive discussion based on the properties of Greek fire, which, it is said, can be put out only by urine, sand, and vinegar, and that in *Moralia* III. 18 there is the brief similitude

Sicut igitur ignis grecus aceto, sic et recordatione sanguinis Iesu Cristi luxurie flamma extinguitur;

for though the scale, the details, and the application are different, references to Greek fire at this time are rare.[1]

---

[1] Cf. Shepherd, op. cit., p. 65. Alexander Nequam, in *De Laudibus Divinæ Sapientiæ*, IV. 504–5 (ed. T. Wright, Rolls Series 34, London 1863, p. 432), has a reference to Greek fire very similar to that in the *Moralia*:

> Non aqua sed penetrans virtus extinguit aceti
> Ignem cui nomen Græcia nota dedit.

It has been difficult, in the preceding discussion, to avoid the use of expressions which imply that *Ancrene Wisse* is adopting material from the *Moralia*, and indeed I have not always succeeded. But in view of the problem of dating that is involved, it was necessary to consider carefully, on internal evidence alone, which text had priority. I am convinced that, as one might expect, it belongs to the Latin text; the English is the borrower. The instances cited below (pp. 54–8), in which *Ancrene Wisse* has readings superior to those of the two thirteenth-century Latin manuscripts L and T, do not establish its priority; there has been early corruption of the Latin text, but we are free to assume that the English author used an independent manuscript of the *Moralia* which avoided at least these errors. Other evidence is in favour of the priority of the Latin. *Ancrene Wisse* repeatedly blends in a single passage, or treats successively in a connected discussion, ideas which in the *Moralia* are dispersed in two or more chapters, often widely separated;[1] it is easy to see how the English author, carefully using the Latin work, could have combined what in it is separate (especially if his copy included, as it almost certainly would have done, the classified subject-index found in the Lincoln College MS.), much harder to see how or why the Latin author could or should have separated what in the English is unified.[2]

[1] A striking example, in addition to those given elsewhere, is in Part V (f. 70b/15 ff.), where Christ's poverty is set up as a 'remedy' for covetousness; here *Ancrene Wisse* is combining details from *Moralia* IV. 30 and IV. 51, and perhaps I. 39 (which differs little from IV. 51); in III. 95 there is also the sentence 'Omnem reuoluite uitam saluatoris ab utero uirginis usque ad patibulum crucis, non inuenietis in eo nisi stigmata paupertatis', which has a general resemblance to the introductory sentence (f. 70b/15–16) of the passage in *Ancrene Wisse*.

[2] There is, however, a minority of instances in which the reverse applies, and *Ancrene Wisse* treats separately material which occurs in a single chapter of the *Moralia*, but this is unusual. It may also be admitted that a writer so ill organized and repetitive as the author of the *Moralia* might from time to time treat, in more places than one, part of

There are also more particular arguments. In Part II of *Ancrene Wisse* (ff. 30b/9–31a/15) the discussion of the tenderness of Christ's flesh and his bloodletting on the cross corresponds to two passages in the *Moralia*, a brief sentence in IV. 17 and a more detailed treatment in IV. 38, of which the second (quoted below, p. 56) is in quantitative hexameters; the interdependence of the prose of *Ancrene Wisse* and the verses of the *Moralia* is clear. It is of course possible to translate English prose into Latin verse, but it is a sophisticated academic exercise unlikely to have been practised by a medieval theologian; the normal assumption, when of two versions one is in verse and the other in prose, is that priority belongs to the verse. In *Ancrene Wisse* Part IV (f. 66a/24–8) the author cites the Latin tag 'Oratio lenit, lacrima cogit; hec ungit, illa pungit', but in translating it he renders the first phrase 'Eadi bone softeð ant paieð *ure lauerd*'. In *Moralia* I. 62 the tag is also cited, in the form 'Oratio autem *dominum delinit*, lacrima cogit; illa ungit, ista pungit'. *Ancrene Wisse*'s text of the Latin is obviously better at the beginning, but its translation seems affected by the version of the *Moralia*. Sometimes what is clear or normal in the Latin is obscure or abnormal in the English. I have already pointed out an instance in Part V (f. 106a/16–17) where the English, deliberately as it seems varying from the Latin, diverts the logical progression of the argument. In Part II (f. 28a/15–16) there is a sentence ('He himself wept thrice with his fair eyes') which comes in so abruptly that Miss Salu in her translation, mistaking the syntax, adds it to the preceding sentence;[1] in fact it corresponds to *Moralia* IV. 2 ('Legimus de triplici aque effusione per Cristum facta'), where the occasions are

the material which he had found in a single source. But this would not explain the regular tendency of *Ancrene Wisse* to unify what in the *Moralia* is dispersed.

[1] *The Ancrene Riwle*, translated by M. B. Salu (London, 1955), p. 46.

specified: when he wept at the sight of the city of Jerusalem and at the raising of Lazarus, and when he poured water into the basin.[1] Here it is clear that the third 'effusion of water' was not a shedding of tears, as the author of *Ancrene Wisse*, reading carelessly, seems to have supposed. In Part III (f. 40a/6 ff.), in a passage arguing that good deeds lose their virtue if they are boasted of publicly, the English author develops at some length the symbolism to be derived from the Biblical account of how Moses' right hand, withdrawn from his bosom, appeared leprous; the germ of this is in *Moralia* III. 84. But he ends with an apparent inconsequence (f. 40b/9–12):

For þi, ȝef ei deð eani god, ne drahe ha hit nawt utward ne ȝelpe nawiht þrof, for wið a lutel puf, wið a wordes wind, hit mei beon al toweauet.

Obviously a hand, withdrawn from the bosom, cannot be carried away by the wind; but what then is the image? The answer is probably in *Moralia* I. 61, which deals with hypocrisy, and which, commenting on Job 8: 14, says

Tela aranearum studiose texitur, flatu uenti dissipatur.[2]

---

[1] 'tercia cum aquam misit in peluim'; cf. John 13: 5.

[2] There is an undoubted link between the passage in *Ancrene Wisse* and *Moralia* I. 61. The latter is on the text 'Cum facis elemosinam, noli tuba canere ante te sicut hypocrite faciunt', from Matt. 6: 2, the latter part of which ('Amen dico vobis, receperunt mercedem suam') is cited by *Ancrene Wisse* (f. 40a/17). Shortly before its remark that 'tela aranearum . . . flatu uenti dissipatur' the *Moralia* cites from, or rather paraphrases, Gregory's *Moralia in Job*, viii. 43 (*P.L.* lxxv, col. 844): 'Uecordia est magnam rem uili precio uendere, id est bona laboriosa agere pro fauore' (perhaps with scribal omission of *humano* after *fauore*). *Ancrene Wisse* also paraphrases the same passage in Gregory (Corpus f. 40a/19–22; cf. Cleopatra f. 61ᵛ/8–10, which avoids the corruption *uerecundia* for *uecordia*) before its first introduction of the phrase *windes puf* (Corpus f. 40a/24) and the puzzling image at f. 40b/9–12. The combination of the citation of Matt. 6: 2 and of Gregory and the use of the phrase *flatu uenti* (*windes puf*) in both *Moralia* I. 61 and *Ancrene Wisse* cannot be accidental.

In Part IV (f. 79b/4–6), *Ancrene Wisse* reads:

To unwreast mid alle ha is þe mei, wið to heouen up hire þreo fingres, ouercumen hire fa, ant ne luste for slawðe,

in which the phrase *wið to heouen up hire þreo fingres* must in the context mean 'by lifting up her three fingers' but is so unidiomatic[1] that it has been suggested that the author may have been translating from or thinking in French. He may indeed have been thinking in French, but he was translating from the Latin of *Moralia* II. 30:

Item miserrimo maius miser censendus esset siquis in bello hosti subcumberet, de quo *trium digitorum motu* triumphare posset. Pro miserrimis ergo habendi sumus qui, cum tribus digitis nobis signaculum fidei imprimere possumus, hosti nobis noxio et pernicioso subcumbimus, cum ad crucis signaculum, fide cooperante, omnes uersutie eius euanescunt.

But the most conclusive instance is, I think, in Part V, at f. 85b/8–9, in the sentence which in the Corpus MS. is punctuated

Schrift schal beon ihal. þ is. iseid al to a mon ut of childhade.

The Latin version of the *Ancrene Riwle*[2] renders this

Confessio debet esse integra, id est, vni homini dicta ab infancia,

and the Trinity French version,[3] after a similar translation

---

[1] In normal Middle English idiom it should mean 'to lift up her three fingers with'. The Cleopatra and Caius MSS. support Corpus, but Titus and Nero substitute *for to* (*uorto*) for *wið to*, and Vernon and Pepys omit *wið to* (or *for to*) and recast the sentence (thus Vernon '. . . þat may heuen vp his þreo fingres and ouer comen his fo', and similarly Pepys, though with more drastic attendant revision). The later scribes, even in the thirteenth century, found the idiom unacceptable.

[2] Ed. Charlotte D'Evelyn (E.E.T.S. 216, 1944), p. 119, ll. 27–8.

[3] Ed. W. H. Trethewey (E.E.T.S. 240, 1958), p. 68, ll. 14–19. We need not suppose that the translator of the Trinity version had independent knowledge of the *Moralia*, but he knew some work that expressed

(different in word-order but not in sense), adds the explanation that the sinner must say all his sins to a single priest and not parcel them out among various priests, 'for the Lord God . . . spares [*garit*] a man wholly or not at all'. This is essentially right, but Miss Salu[1] is so troubled by the passage that she deliberately omits 'to one man' from her translation and gives in her text the rendering 'it must cover all sins from childhood onward', which is not what her author wrote. We should in fact punctuate and translate slightly differently from the medieval versions:

Schrift schal beon ihal (þet is, iseid al to a mon) ut of childhade.

'Confession must be complete (that is, made all to a single man) beyond childhood.'

This is shown by the sources in the *Moralia*. The more direct is the corresponding paragraph of the systematic discussion of the necessary qualities of confession in IV. 18:

[*Side-heading*] Integra debet esse confessio. [*Text*] Satagendum est homini ut *integre et plene et uni omnia* peccata confiteatur. Peccant enim quidam qui, ut innocentes uideantur, non *omnia uni*, sed eadem diuisim pluribus confitentur, sperantes se per particularem confessionem plenam indulgentiam assequi posse; et falluntur . . . Non enim particulariter remittit deus, [atqui] simul aut omnia peccata mortalia aut nulla.

But there is an important secondary source in I. 43, from which *Ancrene Wisse* takes two of its examples of the ill effects of incomplete confession—a ship holed in various

the same doctrine. Some years ago Mr. J. A. Burrow pointed out to me a parallel in *Cursor Mundi* ll. 26380–3, in the discussion of the 'points' of confession:

> Hale agh shrift to be alsqua
> & noȝt for to be delt in twa
> as to prestis twin or þrin
> agh þou noȝt to-dele þi synne.

[1] Op. cit., p. 139 and n. 1.

places, all of which are stopped except one, which may endanger the ship, and a man with several wounds, of which all are cured but one, which suffices for his destruction (*interemptionem*); and this passage in *Moralia* I. 43 begins:

illi soli (adulte etatis dico) secuntur Cristum et sunt de familia eius . . . qui conteruntur de peccatis et confitentur.

Here *adulte etatis dico* 'I mean of adult age' is a parenthetical qualification; the obligation to confess, and to confess fully, does not apply to children. The author of *Ancrene Wisse* had certainly read the passage, and his phrase *ut of childhade* must have the same force; it qualifies *Schrift schal beon ihal*, not *iseid al to a mon*. Again the Latin is clear where the English is difficult; and the difficulty results from combining in one passage the two separate discussions of the Latin.

It was also necessary to consider the possibility, remote though it may seem, that the two works were written by the same man; for they have much in common in material, in point of view, and in methods of exposition. It may, I am sure, be confidently rejected. I doubt whether the vernacular language of the author of the *Moralia* was English; the only two vernacular phrases that I have noted him citing are French.[1] It is unlikely, if the same man had written both works, that the English would have shown the obscurities and (in one place) the misunderstanding of the Latin discussed in the previous paragraph. There are also, despite the many resemblances of the two works in their Biblical scholarship and in their expositions, some clear discrepancies. Both use animal symbolism for vices and virtues, but it more often

---

[1] In IV. 17 he writes of boys before Christmas crying 'Noel, Noel', which if not very distinctive is French and not English, and in III. 2 he says that a whore, when she has run through all her lover's money, derides him, exclaiming 'Deiheit lechur quant burse li faut' (against which T, in the margin, has the note 'Gall[ice]').

differs than agrees: thus in *Moralia* III. 23 it is said that a man is transformed into a beast,

sus si in libidine, leo si in crudelitate, uulpecula si in astutia delectetur,

and in IV. 16 there is a similar passage,

Quidam enim habent formam suis per inmundiciam, quidam lupi per rapacitatem, quidam auium per leuitatem, quidam leonum per ferocitatem.

But in *Ancrene Wisse* Part IV (ff. 52a ff.) the lion represents pride, the fox covetousness, and the sow greed; there is no agreement. There are also differences in the application of texts. In *Moralia* IV. 50 the text 'Quantum glorificauit se et in deliciis fuit' (Rev. 18: 7) is cited against the proud 'in temporalibus gloriantes', in *Ancrene Wisse* f. 58a/20–1 against the glutton. In *Moralia* II. 45 the text 'Ingredere in petram' (Isa. 2: 10) is explained from the similitude of a substance 'aspectu uilis' which, included in a crystal, is made beautiful; likewise those

in Cristo inclusi, licet mundo sint contemptibiles, deo patri fiunt perspicui et uisu affectabiles.

In *Ancrene Wisse* f. 79b/14 it is cited in connection with the advice to 'creep into' Christ's wounds.[1] More striking still is the difference in the interpretation of the text 'Onager assuetus in solitudine' (Jer. 2: 24). In *Moralia* II. 9 it is rationally explained by saying that the wild ass is so lascivious that it can smell and seek out the female over long distances, and is cited in a discussion of lechery (*luxuria*).

[1] A little later in this passage, *Ancrene Wisse*'s application of the text 'Columba mea in foraminibus petre' (S. of S. 2: 14), and its statement (f. 79b/27) that the dove is without gall, are paralleled in Alexander Nequam's *De Naturis Rerum* I. 56 (ed. T. Wright, Rolls Series 34, London 1863, p. 106). There can be little doubt that the author of *Ancrene Wisse* had read the *De Naturis Rerum*.

Even allowing for the willingness of medieval writers to apply the same text, as occasion seemed to require, in very different ways,[1] it is hard to believe that the same man could have used this text as it is in *Ancrene Wisse* f. 57a/12–14, where it is applied to the proud trumpeters in the devil's court, with the comment

'Of þe wind drahinde in for luue of hereword' seið as ich seide,

' "drawing in wind for love of praise" means what I said',

as if the author had taken *uentum amoris sui* as meaning 'the wind of self-love'. An interesting if minor divergence is that *Moralia* IV. 40 says that

via que ducit ad uitam uiridis, que ducit ad infernum trita est,

from which it is clear that the author means by a 'green way' a little-used path, narrow and overgrown,[2] as in *Poema Morale* (Trinity MS.), l. 343; by contrast *Ancrene Wisse* (f. 50b/21) speaks of the *grene wei* to hell, meaning a road through pleasant lowland country, as in the version of the *Poema Morale* in MS. Jesus College Oxford 29 and in Milton's Sonnet IX,

> Lady that in the prime of earliest youth
> Wisely hath shun'd the broad way and the green . . .

But the chief reason for believing that the *Moralia* and *Ancrene Wisse* cannot be by the same author is the very different literary qualities which the two works display. The author of the *Moralia* is the more learned and scholarly, and more logical within a narrow compass (though perfectly

---

[1] The *Moralia* itself provides examples enough, notably the inconsistent accounts of the symbolism of the three Marys in IV. 46 and IV. 50. It does not seem likely that these two contradictory chapters represent lectures delivered within a few days of each other.

[2] Cf. *Moralia* II. 28, 'Arta est uia que ducit ad uitam', following Matt. 7: 14.

capable of inconsistency). He has some facility in writing quantitative hexameters, and his Latin prose is clear, straightforward, and correct; he shows skill in using the rhetorical devices of antithesis and parallelism, can be neatly and effectively concise, and at times achieves real eloquence in short passages. He is ingenious and fertile in his *exempla* and similitudes, but has little ability to develop them; they are usually brief, and sometimes he seems intent merely on demonstrating how many different similitudes can be drawn from a single object, even if they are inconsistent with each other. He has little power of organization: long connected discussions, like that in IV. 18 of the qualities that confession should have, are rare, and it is more characteristic of him to jump from one topic to another within a single chapter (hence the need for subheadings); and in the book generally there is no coherent arrangement of subject-matter, one and the same topic being repeatedly discussed in widely separated chapters (hence the need for a subject-index, itself compiled very competently). Though he sometimes avoids unnecessary repetition by a (correct) cross-reference, he much more often repeats himself, sometimes almost word for word, without any apparent awareness that he is doing so. His is essentially an academic book with academic virtues, but though it is interesting in extracts and in brief passages, as a whole it is dull. It is no wonder that it has never been printed, despite the ascription to Grosseteste, and that it seems to have been little read in the Middle Ages themselves; and I am tempted to suspect that in modern times only I have read it, doggedly and reluctantly and not always closely, from beginning to end. The author of *Ancrene Wisse* is less precise, less logical, less consistent in his writing in short passages; he can obscure the line of argument within a paragraph or a subsection. But his book is well organized, with the Parts and the sections within them coherently arranged; when he repeats himself, he hardly ever fails to refer back ('as was said above' or even 'as was said far above'); he develops his themes well, is more selective in his *exempla* and similitudes, but makes much more of them; he has a far wider range of stylistic skills, and is altogether a more effective writer. His book, despite its limited purpose and its being in the vernacular, achieved wide influence in the Middle Ages and has been the subject of admiring and close study in modern times. I doubt whether the author of *Ancrene Wisse* could or would have written the *Moralia*, though he read it evidently with interest and certainly with profit; I am sure that the author of the *Moralia* could never have written *Ancrene Wisse*.

One must conclude, then, that the *Moralia* was written by a different man, that it was earlier than *Ancrene Wisse*, and that it was a major source of the English work—perhaps the most important single source yet discovered, and the only one (apart from Langton's sermons, the extent of whose influence is yet to be determined, and probably Nequam's *De Naturis Rerum*) which was at all closely contemporary.

II

ROBERT GROSSETESTE AND THE *MORALIA*

Professor Harrison Thomson[1] clearly regards the *Moralia super Evangelia* as representing Grosseteste's lectures delivered to the Franciscans of Oxford shortly after the completion of their lecture-hall, which is dated about 1229–30, and other historians have more cautiously approached or less explicitly stated the same view.[2] Miss Smalley stresses that

---

[1] S. Harrison Thomson, *The Writings of Robert Grosseteste* (Cambridge, 1940), p. 134.

[2] A. G. Little, to whom Thomson, loc. cit., attributes the suggestion that 'the Trinity MS. was a copy of the work referred to by Thomas of Eccleston', did not make it. In his 'The Franciscan School at Oxford in the Thirteenth Century', *Archivum Franciscanum Historicum*, xix (1926), 808 n. 3, to which Thomson refers, he says only that the *Moralia* 'possibly ... may represent a course of *lectiones ordinariae*', and in a footnote to his edition of Thomas of Eccleston's *De Adventu Minorum* (Manchester, 1951), p. 48, though he cites the *Moralia* as a book which (in contrast to Grosseteste's sermons and *dicta*) illustrates the qualities described by Thomas, he stops well short of claiming that it represents Grosseteste's lectures to the Franciscans, even though he knew and quotes from Thomson's discussion. D. A. Callus, 'The Oxford Career of Robert Grosseteste', *Oxoniensia*, x (1945), p. 60, says that the contents of the *Moralia* corroborate Little's surmise that it may possibly represent a course of *lectiones ordinariae* and adds that they 'fit in fairly well with Eccleston's description'; after 'fairly well' it is a little surprising to find that he goes on to say, 'It would accordingly be justifiable to propose for its date the year about 1229–30', which is Thomson's view without acknowledgement to Thomson. Beryl Smalley, *The Study of the Bible in the Middle Ages* (2nd edition, Oxford, 1952), p. 266, who refers to Callus, implies but does not say that the *Moralia* represents the lectures to the Franciscans; she comes nearer to saying it in *Robert Grosseteste, Scholar and*

the book 'consists of lectures, not sermons',[1] but this needs some qualification. There are in all 301 chapters,[2] which, if each represents a lecture (and each has the *form* of a lecture), would make up a course as intolerable to deliver as to attend. But there are indications that some of the chapters were originally independent. The last of all (IV. 64), on the Ascension, must originally have been delivered on Ascension Day:

Sic et uos uoluntatem dei, sicut dictum est, facere debetis, quos Cristus ascendendo *hodie* honorauit, ut ad eum ascendatis.

It would be a remarkable coincidence if a course of 301 lectures were so timed as to end on Ascension Day. Some chapters, separated in the *Moralia*, evidently once belonged more closely together. Thus IV. 23 is on the festivals of the Church, and IV. 61 on ecclesiastical processions, and in these two chapters (and, as far as I have noticed, only in them) the author directly addresses his audience as 'fratres' and 'fratres karissimi'; they appear to be taken from a series of lectures or homilies on the ceremonies of the Church, delivered to a group of clergy of which the author was himself a member. The repeated but scattered discussions of prelates (of which the Indexes in L list thirty-one) often intrude uncomfortably among incompatible material; they could well, however, have formed originally a coherent separate lecture-course, and the same is probably though less obviously true

Bishop, ed. D. A. Callus (Oxford, 1955), pp. 71–4, in which she again cites Dr. Callus. Her account of the *Moralia* in this book (pp. 71–2) is a travesty. If one wishes to guy the *Moralia*, the best instance that I have noticed is in III. 92, where the flesh of virgins is compared to that of elephants: the latter is impenetrable by material arms, the former by spiritual weapons.

[1] *Robert Grosseteste*, p. 72.

[2] Not 311 as stated in the final colophon; there are 79 in Part I, 60 in Part II, 98 in Part III, 64 in Part IV. The chapters differ more in length, and most are shorter, than one would expect of lectures, even allowing for the fact that published *moralitates* were only part of the lectures as delivered (cf. Miss Smalley, loc. cit.).

C

of certain other topics repeatedly discussed, such as *Peccatum* (thirty-five entries in the Index) or *Passio Cristi* (twenty-six) or *Humilitas* (fifteen), especially as there are often verbal links between what are now widely separated chapters. Indeed, the list at the beginning of the Index of major topics not arranged in alphabetical order might be, at least in part, an indication of the subjects of a number of once-distinct courses of lectures or homilies which were broken up when the *Moralia* as we have it was compiled. What I suspect may have happened is that the author decided to make a collection of his discourses, and hit on the ingenious but somewhat perverse device of giving them an artificial appearance of unity by basing each on a gospel text (but the connection between text and subject-matter is often exiguous) and by arranging the texts in the chronological sequence of the events of Christ's life, from before the Annunciation to the Ascension.[1] But this externally imposed order does not correspond to any internal order of subject-matter, and related discussions which in content belong together are usually widely separated because the gospel texts on which they are based do not belong together. If this hypothesis is correct, the *Moralia* as published is essentially a literary production, and though most of its materials doubtless come (and some very obviously do) from delivered discourses, a good deal was probably specially written for the work as published (though still in the form of lectures) and was never actually delivered. This is suggested by the relative infrequency with which we are allowed glimpses of an audience which is being addressed (*fratres, uos, nos*); more often the address is to a reader in the singular, as in the repeated formulae 'Dictis adicias quod...' and 'Nota quod...', or more distinctively 'Ad... rubricam recurras' (III. 88).

---

[1] But the first chapter, on Pride, stands outside the scheme, for there is no text; it is really a sort of introduction, though numbered as a chapter.

But even if the *Moralia* were based on a single protracted course of ill-arranged and discursive lectures, it has certainly been written up for publication; the text seldom reads like lectures as delivered, and the style has been carefully polished. The division into four parts, which Miss Smalley tentatively suggested may have been due to an 'editor',[1] is in fact authorial; it is announced in the Preface,[2] there are some ten places within the text where there are cross-references by part and chapter, and three[3] others where there are cross-references by 'rubric' as well (meaning thereby a subheading indicating a particular section of a chapter). It follows that even the subheadings are authorial. But these are closely linked with the classified index of which two copies are preserved in L, and many of the subheadings are specifically 'index-headings' (those of the type 'Peccatum i', 'Peccatum ii', etc.) which could only have been supplied while the index was being made and the various discussions of each subject were being listed. So the index too must have been compiled by the author or under his supervision, and indeed it is difficult to imagine that anyone else could or would have made it. The *Moralia* as published is very far from being lectures as delivered. Moreover it is clear that the author, even after he had prepared his text for publication, kept it by him for a while, adding notes to it; both of the surviving early manuscripts have many footnotes, usually short, in the hands of the text-scribes and therefore derived from their exemplar, and many of these are found in both manuscripts, similarly or even identically placed. They are characteristically of three types: the citation of additional authorities, further notes on the 'interpretation' of Biblical names (of which there are very numerous examples in the text), and additional verses

---

[1] *Robert Grosseteste*, p. 72.
[2] 'Ipsum uero opusculum quadrifaria sectioni parciemur' (L f. 11, T f. 7).   [3] III. 88 (twice) and IV. 47.

summarizing or illustrating the text (themselves often with interlined explanations) which in style, metre (quantitative hexameters), and purpose are exactly comparable with the 'memorial verses' (explicitly so termed) which are frequent in the text and which are there sometimes made the basis of detailed exposition. There can be no doubt that these footnotes are authorial.[1] The case is different with the longer notes, which in L are written in the margins (though they may spread across the feet of the pages) but in T are also written if possible as footnotes (though sometimes part at least of the margins has to be used as well).[2] These longer notes are usually different in content from the shorter notes (L's footnotes) and are differently treated by the two scribes;[3] and though most of them were probably copied from the exemplar, as a class they are unlikely to be authorial. But even

---

[1] Dr. R. W. Hunt reminds me that Nequam was also in the habit of adding marginal notes or footnotes to his works. He cannot be accepted as the author of the *Moralia* (see below, pp. 90–3), but the similarity of method is interesting.

[2] Cf. the descriptions of the manuscripts, pp. 36–7 and 42 below.

[3] Whereas L and T often agree in copying the shorter notes, the scribe of T copies comparatively few of the longer notes and the text-scribe of L copied none; those now in L (as marginal notes) are in other hands, chiefly that of the scribe who acted as rubricator of the second subject-index (Index B). The two text-scribes must have had some reason, apart from length, for their tendency to include the short notes and to exclude the longer ones; probably they could tell from the appearance of the exemplar (i.e. from the hands that occurred in it) that the short notes (L's footnotes) were part of the transmitted text, the others mostly additions of less authority. Both scribes probably erred, in opposite directions— the L scribe in omitting some notes that were, and the T scribe in including more that were not, authorial; but in general they followed similar policies. Even the scribe who added most of the marginal notes in L made distinctions: the two complementary notes on ff. 15 and 192^{r-v}, with their cross-references to the text, are fully rubricated, in contrast to the others, which have no such obvious connection with the text and were left without the intended rubricated initial capitals. None of the longer notes occurs in both manuscripts, which seems very significant when in other respects they are so close.

among them there are exceptions: thus L, at I. 6 (f. 15), has a long marginal note which ends with a rubricated cross-reference to IV. 9; and the reference, when checked, not only proves to be correct but leads to another long marginal note, of similar form, against IV. 9 (f. 192^{r-v}) which again ends with a rubricated cross-reference, this time back to I. 23. The two notes were obviously composed at the same time, probably during the compilation of the index. It is likely that the lost manuscript used by the author of *Ancrene Wisse* included some at least of these notes, for T at f. 112^v has a footnote (not in L) to II. 16 which reads:

Nota quod tripliciter [*so MS.*] formantur vasa, scilicet manu, flatu, fusione, malleactione. Sic et dominus quos uult reformat tamquam bonus artifex, quandoque manu . . . quandoque flatu . . . quandoque per modulum . . . quandoque per malleum aspere tribulacionis;

this has a marked resemblance to, though it does not correspond verbally with, *Ancrene Wisse* f. 77b/19–27. All this editorial work on the *Moralia* must have taken time, and the copying still more; if the basic lectures were indeed (as I do not believe) those given by Grosseteste to the Franciscans, which cannot well be dated before 1229, it is hard to see how the author of *Ancrene Wisse* could have acquired a copy of the published text—and the detailed evidence is clear that he worked from the published text, not from memory or from notes of the lectures—much before 1231.

This presents obvious difficulties for the dating of *Ancrene Wisse*. If its author did not begin to write the Inner Rule before 1231—and many of the passages derived from the *Moralia* are so essential to the text that they cannot have been grafted on later—he is unlikely to have finished it before, at earliest, 1233, for he tells us that he had spent a 'great while' (*muchele hwile*) writing it, and two years is not really a great while. Even so, on this reckoning the Cleopatra MS. could not well be earlier than 1240,[1] the 'Corpus revision' and the Corpus MS. itself would be a year or two later, and the Nero and Titus MSS., which are comparatively low in the *stemma codicum*, could hardly be earlier than 1250.[2] Now it may not seem a grave matter to revise the datings, which are largely on palaeographical and linguistic grounds, of four vernacular manuscripts by a dozen years or so, but in this case it would present serious difficulty.[3] The only recent scholars who have contemplated a dating for the composition of *Ancrene Wisse* after 1230 are the late Vincent McNabb, O.P., who wished to ascribe the work to the Dominican Robert Bacon, and his disciple Miss Kirchberger; but McNabb's arguments, though they deserved more respect than was paid to them, have rightly not convinced scholars. I myself have argued for a later date than has been fashionable ('after 1215, and even possibly after 1222');[4] but I must add that I do not really believe that it was after 1222, and I certainly do not believe that it was after 1230. There is a particular reason against such an assumption. It is well known that though the revised

[1] It is removed by two intervening copies from the autograph, the main reference to the original 'three sisters' had been deleted from its exemplar, and it was evidently produced to meet some urgent need for additional copies, probably because of an increase in the number of anchoresses towards the 'twenty now or more' mentioned in an addition in the Corpus MS. See my edition of Cotton MS. Cleopatra C. vi (E.E.T.S. 267, 1972), pp. ix–xi.

[2] Especially as the Titus MS. gives the 'generalized' text, and is not the manuscript in which this text was first formed.

[3] The accepted datings of the manuscripts are 'about 1228 or a little later' for the Cleopatra MS., 'about 1230 or a little later' for the Corpus MS., and 'about 1240–50' for the Nero and Titus MSS. The intervals between them, and between the earliest (Cleopatra) and the date of composition, would have to be kept essentially the same; therefore if the date of composition were altered by some twelve years, so also would the datings of the manuscripts have to be.

[4] 'The Date and Composition of *Ancrene Wisse*', *Proceedings of the British Academy*, lii (1966), 181–208.

Corpus text includes two very friendly references to the friars of both orders—but written in such terms as to show, *pace* McNabb, that the author himself was not a friar, but a well-disposed outsider—there is no mention of friars in the original text. This is easy to explain if *Ancrene Wisse* was written before 1221, when the Dominicans arrived in England, or 1224, when the Franciscans came, or even before 1227, the probable date of the founding of their first houses in the West Midlands; but it would be very hard indeed to explain if the *Moralia*, of which we now know that the author of *Ancrene Wisse* made such extensive use, had originated as lectures given to the Franciscans in Oxford, and still more difficult if, to save a year or two, we assumed, against all probability, that he did not work from the published text but had attended the lectures himself.

But the hypothesis that the *Moralia* represents the lectures given to the Franciscans in 1229–30 creates difficulties also for the biographers of Grosseteste. Miss Smalley implies the old-fashioned nature of the work when she speaks of 'his loyalty to the methods used at Paris in the late twelfth and early thirteenth centuries', and is led to suppose that it is based on materials brought back from Paris, presumably on his return about 1214.[1] And as the *Moralia* shows virtually no interest in or knowledge of Greek,[2] and none at all of the

---

[1] *The Study of the Bible*, p. 266.

[2] Greek words, or corruptions of them, are occasionally cited, sometimes explicitly stated to be Greek, sometimes not. Examples are *artocopus* (II. 16), derived from *arthos* and *scopos*, the former interpreted as 'panis' and the latter as 'labor'; *scenophegia*, i.e. *scenopegia*, derived in III. 21 from '*phegos* quod est fixio, *scenos* uero interpretatur umbraculum', but in III. 6 more accurately interpreted as 'fixio tabernaculorum'; *agyos* (III. 27) given as synonym of *sanctus* but 'interpreted' etymologically as 'sine terra'; *agyos* again cited in III. 36, with a 'word' *otheos*, presumably ὁ θεός; and in IV. 63, where it is said that '*Theos* grece "deus" uel "timor" latine interpretatur.' The general effect is to show that the author had no first-hand knowledge of Greek. Grosseteste's *Dictum* 109 (Thomson, op. cit., p. 228) is distinctly more competent.

Greek Fathers, we are compelled to assume that Grosseteste's Greek studies were a new development of his last years in Oxford, after 1230. It is unfortunately not at all impossible that a man nearing the end of a career as a university teacher should deliver very old-fashioned lectures, though more surprising that they should be well received; and it is, I suppose, not altogether impossible that the same man, a year or two later, should take up an entirely new subject and, when his election to a bishopric gave him the means to do so, should initiate and energetically direct a bold and far-reaching programme of Greek studies. But it is not a convincing picture of an intellectual development; things happen in historians' accounts which seldom occur in life.

It is, however, only an assumption, and a somewhat romantic one, that the surviving *Moralia* and the lectures to the Franciscans are to be identified. It is based on Thomas of Eccleston's words in his *De Adventu Minorum*:[1]

... fecit frater Agnellus scholam satis honestam ædificari in loco fratrum, et impetravit a sanctæ memoriæ magistro Roberto Grosseteste ut legeret ibi fratribus. Sub quo inæstimabiliter infra breve tempus tam in quæstionibus quam prædicationi congruis subtilibus moralitatibus profecerunt.

But it is important to distinguish what Thomas says from what he does not say. He says that Grosseteste lectured to the Franciscans in their new lecture-hall, and clearly implies that the lectures included, or consisted of, *moralitates*. But he does not say that Grosseteste lectured on the Gospels, or that they were new lectures, or that they were published, least of all that they were circulating in his own day under the title *Moralia super Evangelia*. Only the ascription of the *Moralia* to Grosseteste in three of the four extant manuscripts, and in acknowledged citations in Alexander Carpenter's early-

---

[1] Ed. A. G. Little (Manchester, 1951), p. 48.

fifteenth-century *Destructorium Viciorum*,[1] connects the work with him, and even so it might represent lectures given at any time after he began to teach divinity, which is assumed to have been when the Oxford schools reopened in 1214. It would be risky to identify the *Moralia* with the lectures of 1229–30 even if there were no contrary evidence. But if Index A of the Lincoln College MS. (on which see below) is correctly dated to the first quarter of the century, a copy of the *Moralia*, itself containing errors and therefore not the autograph,[2] was already in circulation before the Franciscans had even arrived in England.

Indeed, I find it surprising that scholars as learned as Miss Smalley and the late Dr. Callus have accepted the ascription of the *Moralia* to Grosseteste. He and its author had had the same sort of training in divinity, and they have much in common in their methods of exposition and in their conceptions and interests. Nevertheless the style of the *Moralia* seems to me to be markedly different—cleaner, neater, less pretentious—from that of Grosseteste's sermons and *Dicta*, of which some are known to be earlier than February 1231–2 because versions of them are included in MS. Durham

[1] That Carpenter's work cites the *Moralia* (as 'Linconiensis super evangelia') was pointed out by Miss Smalley (*Robert Grosseteste*, p. 74 and n. 2); she refers only to a single instance, but there are in fact many (see pp. 74–5 below). Her observation was of great importance, but unfortunately she was gravely misleading in saying (n. 2) that after the beginning 'the rest of the quotation is verbal', which I assume to mean 'word for word'. Carpenter is incapable of perfectly accurate quotation, but the instance cited by Miss Smalley is exceptionally loose; though it is obvious that his version of the *exemplum* in question is directly based on the *Moralia* (which was her main point), it is so extensively rewritten that less than half of the original words are exactly reproduced, in form and order, and even the details of the story are altered, presumably to make them more acceptable to fifteenth-century taste.

[2] That the text of the *Moralia* in this copy contained errors is a deduction, though a certain one; that its index contains copying errors is an observable fact. On both points see further below, pp. 45–58, 64–5.

Cathedral Library A. III. 12;[1] Grosseteste's style is more
self-conscious, tortuous, and inclined ruthlessly to hunt the
word. The author of the *Moralia* is fond of citing hexameter
verses, apparently of his own composition, of the type characteristic of William de Montibus of Lincoln; Grosseteste does
not use such verses. A pervasive feature of the *Moralia* is its
author's uncritical acceptance of the traditional lore of the
bestiaries and lapidaries, and his use of it, equally tra-
ditionally, for Christian allegory and moral teaching; there is
little of this in Grosseteste, who, when he has similitudes
from birds and animals, sticks generally to their more commonplace and observable characteristics or to etymological
speculation.[2] In the *Moralia* there is a greater use of 'interpretations' of Biblical names, and a smaller use of etymologies
(of the fanciful medieval type), than in Grosseteste's sermons
and *Dicta*. The range of authorities cited in the *Moralia*
(chiefly Augustine, Gregory, Bede, Anselm, and Bernard of
Clairvaux) is far narrower than we know Grosseteste's reading to have been.[3] In *Moralia* IV. 10 and IV. 39 there are two
similitudes from which it appears that the author held that
in the rainbow the colours were 'almost' (*fere*) reducible to
two, or were 'especially' (*precipue*) two, the 'fiery' red and the
'watery' blue, and that it was somehow an image (*ymago*) of
the sun by reason of the association of fire and water;[4] this

---

[1] See Thomson, op. cit., pp. 13–17, and R. W. Hunt in *Robert Grosseteste*, pp. 138–40.

[2] So *Dicta* 83 (sparrow), 121 (bear), and 122 (lion); but *Dictum* 88
has the asp stopping its ears against the voice of the enchanter.

[3] See R. W. Hunt, 'The Library of Robert Grosseteste', in *Robert
Grosseteste*, pp. 121–45.

[4] 'Item libet contemplari igneum colorem et aquaticum fere sibi as-
sociatos esse in yri . . . Yris igitur mistice est quecumque fidelis anima
in qua [qua L, in aqua T] resultat ymago ueri solis iusticie, in qua ignis
aque associabitur' (IV. 10). 'Sed quomodo potest arcus esse signum
misericordie . . . cum precipue habet arcus duos colores in quibus osten-
dit iudicia: in ceruleo iudicium aque, in rubeo iudicium ignis?' (IV. 39).

shows a very limited understanding of the spectrum, and none at all of the refraction of light. I do not believe that Grosseteste, whose discussion of the rainbow was an important contribution to the theory of optics and who did understand spectra and refraction,[1] could possibly have written in such loose and ignorant terms; great scholars of scientific bent do not deny their own conceptions even in the illustrations of lectures on divinity. Miss Hudson, who agrees in thinking the *Moralia* unlike Grosseteste's undoubted work, informs me that though Wyclif and his followers admired Grosseteste and though it is easy to show the influence on their writings of his sermons and *Dicta*, she could find no evidence that the *Moralia* had influenced them;[2] and it is odd also that there is no evidence that the Franciscans of Oxford, to whom Grosseteste bequeathed his library,[3] ever possessed a copy of the *Moralia*, especially if it represented lectures that he had delivered in their house. Miss Smalley had already in 1955 expressed surprise that there is so little sign of the influence of the *Moralia* on Grosseteste's successors (especially William of Nottingham, an Oxford Franciscan of about 1312 who might have been expected to use the work) and had also remarked on Wyclif's use of the *Dicta* but not of the *Moralia*;[4] I suspect that she may have felt some doubt, though she did not explicitly ask, whether 'a long period of neglect' would really have befallen the published text of an important series of lectures by a famous Oxford scholar who was also revered as a saint.

It seems, therefore, legitimate to reconsider the authority

[1] See A. C. Crombie in *Robert Grosseteste*, pp. 103–6.

[2] Miss Hudson also observes that though manuscripts of Grosseteste's sermons and *Dicta* survive in Bohemia (owing to the link between the Wycliffites and the Hussites), there is no known Bohemian manuscript of the *Moralia*.

[3] R. W. Hunt, art. cit., p. 130.

[4] *Robert Grosseteste*, pp. 73–4.

of the ascriptions given in the surviving manuscripts of the *Moralia* and by Alexander Carpenter, and this in turn involves an examination, which I think has not previously been attempted, of the textual tradition—which, as it turns out, is significant also for *Ancrene Wisse*.

III

THE TEXTUAL TRADITION
OF THE *MORALIA*

THERE are four extant manuscripts of the *Moralia*, two of the thirteenth and two of the fifteenth century; the earlier require detailed description and analysis, the later are treated more summarily.

(1) MS. Lincoln College Oxford Latin 79 (L); leaves about 26·2 by 18 cm. The manuscript may be described in five sections.

(*a*) ff. 1–10 are a separate quire of 10 originally part of another manuscript; the hand is earlier than any of those in the rest of the present manuscript, and the parchment is of different quality. In the lost manuscript this quire must have been at the end; though the worm-holes in the early leaves have obviously penetrated from the front (i.e. after the quire was in its present position) and grow progressively fewer and smaller (the most persistent only just penetrates f. 9 to mark faintly the recto of f. 10), f. 10 has, well away from the edges, half a dozen holes, two fairly large, that do not affect either the preceding or the following leaves and must have been made by worms working in through a back cover or wrapper. Moreover, on the verso of f. 10, on the upper half of the page, there is a large stain near the inner margin which penetrates the leaf to the recto and faintly affects the verso of f. 9, but which does not affect at all the recto of f. 11, though the latter is now in contact with it; the stain must have been caused by the spilling of some liquid when f. 10 was at the end of a manuscript (or when the quire had been separated from the original manuscript but not yet bound up in its present position).

ff. 1–9^v contain a classified subject-index to the *Moralia* (Index A): two columns of 40 lines each; writing 'above top line'; writing-area about 16·6 by 11·7 cm. Main entries, normally a single word, in red; subordinate entries, with chapter-references, in black. f. 10 was originally blank; on its verso there has been pasted a slip of parchment bearing the note, in a hand of the later fifteenth century,

> Moralia Magistri Alexandri Necham | super euangelia cum tabula cum | aliis contentis Ex dono Magistri Roberti | Flemmyng Decani Lincol*n*ii.

Robert Flemmyng was dean of Lincoln from 21 January 1452 until his death before August 1483.[1]

(*b*) ff. 11^r–248^v: text of the *Moralia*, in a single hand; writing 'above top line'. Single column, writing-area within margin-lines 16·8 by 8·4 cm; wide margins; chapter-headings in red within text-space, subheadings (of which some of those intended are omitted) in black in margins. On f. 11, in left margin against the first two lines of the brief introduction to the text, in red in hand of text-scribe,

Moralia ma*gist*ri Alexandri | de Ba super ewangelia.

Throughout manuscript, notes in plummet in margins by text-scribe for corrections to text, almost invariably carried out in ink and/or by erasure in text. Some textual corrections, obviously conjectural, by a later hand or hands, e.g. in first line of f. 11.

There are many notes to the text. Those (mostly short) at the feet of the pages are in the hand of the text-scribe and undoubtedly copied from his exemplar; many occur also in T. Those in the margins, which are usually longer (some very long), are in other hands. (1) Notes written in the hand of the rubricator of Index B (who is not the same man as the rubricator of the text). There are three subdivisions. (i) ff. 15 and 192$^{r–v}$, two complementary notes, fully rubricated and ending with rubricated cross-references to the text of other chapters of the *Moralia*; probably originally authorial (see pp. 25–6 above). (ii) ff. 11^v, 14^v, 15^v–16, 27, 43^v, 54^v,

[1] A. B. Emden, *Biographical Register of the University of Oxford* (Oxford, 1957–9), ii. 699.

58, 58^v, 107^v, 116^v, 148, 148^v, 193, 244: notes (some cropped by binder) in black ink, with provision normally made for intended rubricated initial capital which in fact was added only on f. 14^v. (iii) ff. 137^v, 138: notes in red ink, same hand. (2) Short notes, perhaps in same hand though different in size, ink, and quality of penmanship: ff. 63^v, 64, 89 (the last intended to be begun by a rubricated capital: small guide-letter *a* written to left of beginning of note). (3) Notes on ff. 11 and 12 in a different hand, found nowhere else in the manuscript. Those listed under (1) and perhaps (2) were evidently added before the manuscript was completed and were probably copied from the exemplar, though the text-scribe had chosen to omit them; the same scribe supplies one or two index-headings (ff. 31, 32^v) that the text-scribe had left out. Those under (3), on the rectos of the first two leaves of the text, were almost certainly added later and were not copied from the exemplar.[1]

(*c*) ff. 249–57^v (of which ff. 249–50 are part of the same quire of 10 as the last 8 leaves (ff. 241–8) of the text, the rest part of a quire of 8): classified subject-index to the *Moralia* (Index B), a direct copy of Index A (see below). Main entries in red, in a single hand throughout. Subordinate entries in black, in three other hands: (i) text-scribe, to left column of f. 252; (ii) second hand, only for right column of f. 252 (last line exceptionally left blank); (iii) third hand, f. 252^v to end of index. The third rules the page differently and less suitably and observes the layout of the tabular index less well. In the parts written by the first two scribes the rubricator retains the single-word main entries, in that written by the third he normally replaces them by more elaborate forms derived usually from the first or only subordinate entry,

---

[1] The reference to these notes by Callus in *Oxoniensia*, x. 60, is very incomplete and inexact, and I can see no justification for Miss Smalley's reported opinion that they 'appear like extracts from a complete commentary' (on the Gospels?), even though they may include '*distinctiones, quaestiones*, and references to *claustrales*'. When Callus proceeds to say that 'it is tempting to ascribe it [the hypothetical commentary] to Grosseteste himself, or to one of his school', he has gone on to the merest conjecture, based on the supposed connection of the *Moralia* with Grosseteste.

thus destroying the intended distinction between main and subordinate entry (but he reverts to the simpler main entries towards the end). He must in the third section have been following drafts written by the third of the black-ink scribes. All the scribes of Index B were obviously contemporary, despite some differences in style and letter-forms, and write 'above top line'.

(*d*) f. 258: originally blank; pricked as preceding leaves of same quire but left unruled. Later ruled differently and filled (recto and most of verso) by a table of *distinctiones* on various topics, with Biblical citations. Hand of about 1250, writing 'above top line'.

(*e*) ff. 259–70ᵛ: Johannis de Abbatis Villa, *Liber Sermonum*. Originally separate manuscript, in hand of late thirteenth or early fourteenth century; two columns, 50 lines each (except on f. 269ʳ⁻ᵛ, where there are 48); writing-area about 18·1 by 13 cm; writing 'below top line'. At top of f. 259, in a later cursive hand, the note 'Joanis de abbatis villa vixit anno domini 1230', which is substantially correct.[1] This, with the table of *distinctiones*, must be the 'other contents' noted in the fifteenth-century nscription on f. 10ᵛ.

Harrison Thomson[2] dates L to the middle of the thirteenth century. Mrs. Sonia Patterson kindly informs me that in her view the decoration of the initials is to be dated about 1250, but to others whom I have consulted the text-hand, and those of the two continuators of Index B, seem earlier than this, and all the scribes of the main part of the manuscript write 'above top line'. Dr. R. W. Hunt has suggested, and Mr. M. B. Parkes agrees, that the text of the *Moralia* (and necessarily Index B) should, taking all the evidence together, be dated 'second quarter of s. xiii, towards the middle of the century'; it was therefore written, in all probability, during

[1] See J. B. Schneyer, *Repertorium der lateinischen Sermones des Mittelalters*, vol. I–J, p. 510: Johannes Halgrinus de Abbatisvilla, until 1216 a master of theology at Paris, was created cardinal in 1227, preached the cross in Spain between 1228 and 1231, and died in 1239.

[2] Op. cit., p. 135.

Grosseteste's episcopacy (1235–53). But Index A is obviously older; the layout of the table is less sophisticated than that of Index B, and the hand, in Mr. Parkes's opinion and mine, is to be dated to the first quarter of the century. This palaeographical dating is consistent with the method of arrangement of the index.[1]

---

[1] The first part of the index consists of major entries in non-alphabetical order, but it is followed by a longer section in which the headings are arranged by the alphabetical order of their initial letters only. This is a primitive method of alphabetical ordering that had been largely superseded by the second quarter of the thirteenth century.

Medieval methods of alphabetical arrangement are well illustrated by the lists of *Interpretationes nominum hebraicorum*, which, though they cannot be dated absolutely (the dates of the manuscripts in which they survive do not correspond to their dates of compilation), can nevertheless be arranged in a sequence of development by considering the names that they include and the details of the interpretations given for individual names. The starting-point is Jerome's *Liber de nominibus hebraicis*, in which they are arranged under the books of the Bible (excluding the Apocrypha) and then according to the alphabetical order of the first letter of each name (with some subordinate distinctions, e.g. of long vowels and short). Its medieval descendants give a single consolidated list for the whole Bible, begin to introduce names from the Apocrypha, and elaborate, multiply, and alter the 'interpretations', probably by use of another source indicated by references to the 'interpretationes Remigii' (which is not simply a name for the standard thirteenth-century list, though often applied to it in the manuscripts). The earlier twelfth- or thirteenth-century lists begin with the name *Aaron*, and the earliest (still mostly dependent on Jerome) already arranges the names in the order of the first two or three letters; the same arrangement, but better carried out, is followed by several later 'Aaron' lists that diverge from Jerome and introduce more names and 'interpretations' (it is this type that *Ancrene Wisse* and the *Moralia* probably used, and certainly not Jerome or lists merely dependent on him); and the latest 'Aaron' lists and the 'Aaz' lists that follow (more particularly the standard list beginning 'Aaz apprehendens') have a fully alphabetical arrangement, though with differences from modern conventions and some mistakes. Now the standard list is intimately associated, in numberless manuscripts, with the standard Parisian text of the Vulgate, is evidently due to the same desire for uniformity, and was certainly subjected to the same efficient system of control to prevent the development of unauthorized variants; and the Parisian Vulgate text is believed to have been decided on about 1226 (Smalley, *The Study of the Bible*, p. 334). As L's index to the *Moralia*

(2) MS. Trinity College Oxford 50 (T): leaves about 32 by
23 cm (originally still larger; the binder has trimmed away
most of the catch-words at the foot of the last page of the
quires). At top of f. 2, the signature of Sir Thomas Pope,
the founder in 1555–6 of Trinity College. At either end of the
book many leaves have been damaged, apparently by damp,
especially at the foot, and the ink of the letters has peeled off
wholly or partly; this, and the transparent paper that has
been pasted on many of the leaves to protect them from
further damage, make the text sometimes difficult to read,
though it is admirably clear where undamaged. The book
may be divided, for description, into three sections.

(*a*) ff. 1–6: introductory material. Leaves bound in wrong order;
it should be 1, 2, 3, 5, 4, 6. ff. 1–3 and 5 in book-hand of text-
scribe; the intended coloured initials, on title-page and in table
of contents for Parts I–III, were never supplied. ff. 4, 6 in cursive
hand of about 1300, supplying table of contents for Part IV. Obviously this introductory section was written after the text, in
which the rubrication is complete; something had happened to
prevent the text-scribe from finishing his work. There are three
subdivisions of this section:

(i) ff. 1: title-page, as follows:

[A]uctor huius libri est magister [R]obertus | [G]rosseteste
[E]piscopus [L]incolniensis. | [T]homas de [L]ondoniis [P]recen-
tor [T]heouk' | hunc librum perquisiuit & de labore suo scri-|
bere fecit assignando eum claustro theouk'.' | ad necessitatem
claustralium ibidem studentium.[1]

uses a system of alphabetical arrangement more primitive even than that
of the type of list of *interpretationes* that its author seems to have used,
and certainly far more primitive than that of the standard 'Aaz apprehendens' list, it is unlikely to have been compiled later than 1225, and is
probably earlier (and even so made by an old-fashioned man).

[1] Thomson, op. cit., p. 134, reads (in both places) *Theolet*, an impossible
suspension for (or form of) *Tewkesbury*, though he accepts the identification with the latter. He has misread *k* with a stroke (as a mark of suspen-

The rest of f. 1ʳ and f. 1ᵛ were originally blank, but are now occupied by later medieval notes.

(ii) ff. 2, 3, 5: table of contents for Parts I–III, with the heading (f. 2)

> [I]ncipiu*n*t cap*itu*la *i*n om*ili*is mag*ist*ri rob' grosse teste sup*er* hystoriam euuang*e*lica*m*. Cap*itu*la prime partis

Chapter-numbers on extreme left, in roman numerals; chapter-headings, taken from rubrics in text, in left-hand column; gospel texts, as given at beginning of chapters, in right-hand column.

(iii) ff. 4, 6: table of contents for Part IV. Chapter-numbers in arabic throughout, sometimes also in roman (regularly from ch. 56 onwards). For chapters 1–5 the scribe maintains the previous arrangement (chapter-number at left, heading in left column, text in right column); thereafter he writes both text and heading in the same column, the text usually above or before the heading. On lower two-thirds of f. 4ʳ, chapters 6–15 in left column, 16–29 in right; on f. 4ᵛ, chapters 30–45 in left column, 46–61 in right; on f. 6ʳ, chapters 62–4 at top of left column, followed by *Expliciunt capitula*. Rest of f. 6 originally blank.

(*b*) ff. 7–407ʳ: text of the *Moralia*, with the heading (f. 7)

> Moralis tractatus secun|dum ordinem quatuor | euangelistarum

in red within the text-space above the author's introduction, which begins 'Intentioni quatuor euangelistarum...' Two columns, in large book-hand; writing area about 22 by 14·2 cm; writing 'below top line'. Chapter-headings in red within text-space; subheadings also in red, often in margin though mostly

---

sion) through its right-hand extremity as *l* plus the mark of suspension for *et*, as is possible in the first instance but hardly in the second. *Theouk*- is an abnormal form of the first syllable of the name, but is a blend of *Theok*- and *Theuk*-, both of which are found in *The Register of Walter Reynolds Bishop of Worcester 1308–1313* (ed. R. A. Wilson, Dugdale Society, 1928); for *Theokesbury* (-*byri*) see p. 32, etc. (nine instances) and for *Theukesbyri*, p. 136. The suspension *Theok'* occurs in *The Register of Bishop Godfrey Giffard, 1268–1301* (ed. J. W. Willis Bund, Worc. Hist. Soc., ii, 1902), pp. 285, 296, 343, and 427 (between 1286 and 1292).

introduced into text-space, sometimes in mid-sentence or break-ing up groups of verses or otherwise inappropriately.[1] Two leaves are misplaced. Between f. 12 (which contains most of I. 5) and f. 13 (which begins with the latter part of I. 7) two conjugate leaves, originally central in a quire of 12, have dropped out. They are now bound as ff. 383–4, interrupting the text of IV. 49, but the binder has folded them wrongly: f. 384, containing the end of I. 5 and most of I. 6, should precede f. 383, containing the end of I. 6 and the beginning of I. 7. As the damage from damp to these two leaves matches that to their neighbours, they would seem to have long been bound in their false position. There are many notes to the text, some in later hands, most in that of the text-scribe; his numerous brief notes are at the foot of the pages, sometimes in red, his longer notes mostly also at the foot, sometimes in two columns (so ff. 90^v, 91, 208, 208^v); on f. 43 exceptionally long notes occupy the left and right margins and the foot. On f. 208^v an index-heading *Vinea i*, properly one of two (the other being *Ecclesia ii*) which belong to the text at this point (as the Indexes of L show), is written in black immediately above a footnote, as if it belonged to the footnote and not to the text; this must show that T's exemplar had the subheadings (as in L) in black in the margins, and that the second subheading was written in the ex-emplar immediately above the note to the text. T, like L, omits some intended subheadings of the 'indexing' type (*Caritas v*, etc.), but most are kept, despite the absence of the index from T. The scribe makes many corrections of his own text, the longer omissions (of which there are many) being supplied, when he notices them, in the margins.

(c) ff. 407^v, 408–9: originally blank; now occupied by later medieval notes, mostly references to the text of the *Moralia* with some comments on the merits of its discussions.

Harrison Thomson[2] dates the manuscript to the first half of the thirteenth century, though necessarily after 1235, since it refers to Grosseteste as bishop; but Mr. N. R. Ker dates

[1] Their original place was obviously in the margins, as regularly in L.
[2] Op. cit., pp. 134–5.

it 's. xiii ex.',[1] and his view is shared by all those whom I have
consulted. Mr. Parkes suggests that Thomson may have been
misled by the monastic scribe's use of old-fashioned features,
in letter-forms and abbreviations, beside others that are more
modern, including a form of *a* hardly used before 1280. On
ff. 381 and 398ᵛ footnotes, undoubtedly copied by the text-
scribe (it is his ink, and the same or similar footnotes occur
at these points in L, so that they must come from the exemplar), are not in his book-hand, but in a cursive script
which is unmistakably of the late thirteenth or early fourteenth century.[2] The words of the title-page, as they stand,
leave doubtful the part played by Thomas of London in the
production of the manuscript; *scribere fecit* ought to mean
that he 'had [it] copied', whereas *de labore suo* suggests
that he did it himself. Probably the scribe has copied the
phrases in a wrong order (a recurrent fault in T), and the
sentence should read:

Thomas de Londoniis . . . hunc librum perquisiuit & scribere
fecit de labore suo,

with *de labore suo* qualifying both verbs; we could then understand it as meaning that Thomas, by his own exertions,
had obtained[3] the book and had it copied. I have been no
more successful than Thomson in identifying this Thomas
of London; the name occurs frequently in thirteenth- and
early-fourteenth-century records, but none of its bearers is
identifiable with the precentor of Tewkesbury.[4]

[1] *Medieval Libraries of Great Britain* (2nd edition, 1964), p. 188.
[2] Other notes in this cursive script, some of moderate length, occur on
ff. 265ᵛ–6, 295, 322ᵛ, 323ᵛ, 327ᵛ, and 377ᵛ, but cannot be proved to come
from the exemplar because they are not in L.
[3] Thomson, op. cit., p. 134, renders *perquisiuit* as 'sought out . . .
diligently', following Lewis and Short's glosses s.v. *perquiro*. But Ker,
Medieval Libraries, p. 330, records that the word is common in *ex libris*
inscriptions and treats it as a synonym of *acquirere*.
[4] Only one that I have discovered was a monk: in August 1311 brother

(3) MS. Balliol College Oxford 35B (B).

Described by R. A. B. Mynors, *Catalogue of the Manuscripts of Balliol College Oxford* (Oxford, 1963), pp. 25–6. Text of the *Moralia*, ff. 2–165ᵛ; begins imperfectly in I. 2 with *quid fecerunt*, the first leaf of the text having been cut out and with it any title written above the text by the scribe. But on f. 1ᵛ there is the note

> Moralitas Roberti Grosseteste super 4 Evangelia | Liber Domus de Balliolo in Oxon. | ex dono Williami Gray Eliensis Episcopus.

On ff. 166–70ʳ there is a table of contents, with the heading (as in T)

> Incipiunt capitula in omiliis[1] magistri Roberti | grosseteste super hystoriam euangelicam. | Capitula prime partis.

No subject-index. A note at the end of the table of contents, on f. 170, says that the scribe finished his work on 3 April 1443. On the scribe (Tielman Reynerszoon) and his employer (William Gray, formerly Chancellor of Oxford University), see Mynors, pp. xxiv–xxvii.

(4) MS. Cambridge University Library Kk. ii. 1 (C).

Described briefly in *Catalogue of the Manuscripts Preserved in the Library of the University of Cambridge*, iii (Cambridge, 1858), 598–9, which follows an older ink numbering of the folios, now superseded by a pencil numbering. The manuscript contains five theological works, of which the third is the *Moralia*, and the fourth and fifth two other works attributed to Grosseteste, *De Penis Purgatorii* and *Exameron*. ff. 190–231ᵛ and 238–303ᵛ (pencil numbering), the text of the *Moralia*, with the heading (f. 190ʳ)

> Compendium moralitatum domini lincolniensis super evangelia continens 4ᵒʳ partes.

Thomas of London was at Lenton, a Cluniac house near Nottingham (*Cal. Pat. R. 1307–13*, p. 419).

[1] The abbreviation *oml'* is transcribed 'omelias' by Mynors, but *-ias* seems a mistake; the mark used is the normal abbreviation, in these manuscripts, for *-is* but is here used for *-iis*, and the sense is 'the chapters in Robert Grosseteste's *Homilies on the Gospels*', which requires the ablative.

At the foot of col. b of f. 231ᵛ, at the end of Part II, is the note

> Hec tabula e*st* supe*r* morale*m* tractatum lincolnie*nsis* se*cundum* ordine*m* 4ᵒʳ euu*a*ngeli*starum*.

The following leaf (f. 232) is blank, and on ff. 233–7ᵛ there is an alphabetical index to all four parts of the *Moralia*, beginning *Aduentus*, *Adulacio*, *Adulterium* and ending *Ypocrita*, *Ymago*, *Yris*, with the note

> Explicit tabula s*uper* morale*m* tractatu*m* lincolnie*nsis* supe*r* 4ᵒʳ euu*a*ngelistas.

ff. 232–7 are not a separate quire, wrongly bound, but part of the same quire as the ending of Part II of the text. Part III begins at the head of f. 238, and Part IV ends on f. 303ᵛ, followed immediately by a table of contents (ff. 303ᵛ–7ʳ), with the heading (in red), as in T and B,

> Incipiu*nt* capitula i*n* omi*liis* ma*gist*ri Robe*rti* gros|seteste s*uper* hystoriam euu*a*ngeli*c*am. Capitula p*ri*me p*a*rtis.

The manuscript is a much cheaper production than B; in the text, even the chapter-headings are not rubricated, but are written in black in heavier lettering; nevertheless there are obvious resemblances to the script and conventions of B. Dated by Harrison Thomson (op. cit., p. 135) 's. xv m.'

Harrison Thomson says that T is 'probably a copy of the archetype' (which, as the sequel shows, he uses inaccurately to mean the autograph), but this is another romantic guess based on the assumption that the book which Thomas of London 'sought so diligently—*perquisiuit*—refers, in all likelihood, to Grosseteste's own copy'.[1] Enthusiasm is all very well, but Thomson can never have collated the texts nor considered them critically.[2] L and T are independent of each

---

[1] Op. cit., p. 134.

[2] It is not surprising, in view of the range and complexity of the material with which Thomson was dealing, that he did not have time to analyse nice textual details. But without such analysis one can make no

other; in the whole text there must be many hundreds of substantive variations, and one can hardly collate ten lines without finding examples, even if only the variation of word-order. They begin in the first line of the author's introduction (where L f. 11 omits *eque* from the sentence 'Intentioni quatuor ewangelistarum nichil eque uitio superbie aduersatur', though a later corrector has intelligently supplied *magis* before *aduersatur*) and continue to the last chapter and the last leaf of L (where L f. 248 has correctly *mane* but T f. 406 has *magne*, and L f. 248ᵛ has wrongly *detestabile* for T's *delectabile* (f. 406ᵛ) in the phrase 'dulce est et delectabile'). As these three examples show, neither text is reliable, though in general L is the better; to produce an intelligible text of any passage one has to begin by choosing between their variants. But this is not enough; emendation is often required, which can only mean that they descend from a common ancestor which already had many errors. There may, in the whole text, be several hundred instances, for in the passages which I have considered closely,[1] though they amount only to a small proportion of the whole, I have noted over thirty cases in which, though L and T agree, their reading cannot stand, and a further six in which, though they vary slightly, neither is acceptable. In IV. 11 (L f. 194, T f. 324), in the sentence

Octauus est achates qui nigri coloris [est] et ramos habet candidos,

both manuscripts omit *est*. In III. 82 (L f. 171, T f. 284ᵛ),

pronouncements on textual relationships; one cannot tell that a manu-script is copied from the autograph from its appearance or from what its scribe chooses to say on its title-page. Even if the scribe of T had said (as he did not) that he had worked from the autograph, one would still have to analyse the readings of the texts to check his statement; he might be honestly mistaken, or he might be deliberately lying.

[1] These are mostly passages relevant to *Ancrene Wisse* or to the question of authorship, or those quoted by Alexander Carpenter in the *Destructorium Viciorum*. The majority are in Parts III and IV.

Struccio speciem uolandi habet sed uim uolandi non habet, [quasi] ypocrisis cunctis uidentibus ymaginem sanctitatis de se insinuat, sed uitam tamen sanctitatis non seruat . . . ,

both read *quia* (abbreviated) for *quasi*, 'just as';[1] there has been a miscopying of an abbreviation. In IV. 51 (L f. 234, T f. 387) both read *eterne hereditatis*, which does not fit the syntax, where a parallel sentence in I. 39 has *ratione hereditatis*, which does; an abbreviation for *ratione* has been mis-read as one for *eterne*. In III. 92 (L f. 180, T f. 300), both manuscripts omit *in* from the phrase [*in*] *integritate anime et corporis* and in the next sentence,

Status etiam uirginalis statui [matrimoniali] precellet,

they both have the abbreviation for *matrimonium* instead of that for *matrimoniali*; later in the same passage on virginity (which I believe influenced the author of *Hali Meiðhad*) they both omit a word, probably *lucem*, from the phrase *preter* [*lucem*] *auream est corona aureola* (L f. 180ᵛ, T f. 300ᵛ). Another instance which seems to involve the misreading of an abbreviated form is in IV. 10 (L. f. 193ᵛ, T f. 323), in the phrase for which I would conjecturally read

. . . consolatio seculi, que inuitat hominem ad delectacionem [secularem ac] dulcedinem.

Here there is a succession of difficulties: for *inuitat* L reads *mutat* and T has *mutat* altered to *inuitat* (apparently a correct scribal emendation); for L's *delectacionem* (which must be right) T has *dilectionem*; and for my *secularem ac* both have *seculi non ad*. But *non* must be wrong and *seculi* is suspect, for its mere repetition would be unstylish and uncharacteristic of the author. 'To worldly (*or* transitory) pleasure and

---

[1] The abbreviation, in each manuscript, is unmistakably one regularly used by the scribe for *quia*.

sweetness' is the sort of sense that the context requires.[1] In IV. 42 (L f. 223ᵛ, T f. 370), in the phrase

Item si matrone cuiuis, prepotenti et [nobili uiro] copulate, constaret quod . . . ,

both have the evidently wrong word-order *prepotenti et uiro nobili*, as if *prepotenti* were a noun parallel to *uiro*. In two places a reader of T has corrected an error which T, as originally written, in fact shares with L: these are IV. 14 (L f. 196ᵛ, T f. 328ᵛ),

Si tantum caritas potuit in deum, quantum, homo, [debet] posse in te ipsum,

where LT have *debes* but the corrector of T inserts *o* before *homo* (to show that it is vocative) and changes *debes* to *debet*, and in IV. 34 (L f. 216, T f. 360), in the verses

Assit amor; noris, si desit [funis] amoris,
Numquam tractus eris, numquam super astra fereris,

where both LT have *finis* but the corrector alters to *funis* (though he was unable to emend T's other corruption, *fateris* for L's *fereris*). In IV. 51 (L f. 234, T f. 387ᵛ), in the passage

Item ad memoriam Cristum reuocant sol et signata per uersum subscriptum:

[Soluit] et [ex]siccat, teres est et circuit orbem,

both L and T have *sol luit* for *soluit* and *siccat* for *exsiccat* (thus preserving metre), but *sol luit* does not make acceptable sense. Moreover T has interlined notes on the verse-line, which must be derived from the exemplar; they are exactly similar to the interlinear explanations that in both manuscripts are often given for the verses copied in footnotes. In these,

---

[1] The *non* (abbreviated *ñ*) of the two manuscripts may be a misreading of *-rem* (abbreviated *rē*) at the end of *secularem*, and their *ad* a consequential misreading of *ac*.

the word written above a verb is commonly not a gloss but a supplied object (as here in T, where *lutum* is written above *siccat*); and above the false *luit* T writes *tenebras*, which presupposes *soluit* ('disperses the shadows'). Evidently the scribe of the common ancestor, though he altered *soluit*, nevertheless uncritically kept the interlined note which accompanied it.

In some of the instances already cited an inherited error has been corrected in one or other manuscript either by the scribe or by a later corrector; others were noticed by Alexander Carpenter when citing from the *Moralia* in his *Destructorium Viciorum*, though his usual reaction is to rewrite the sentence, not to attempt conservative emendation. In I. 69 (L f. 59, T f. 83), in the sentence

Ita, sicut adamas ferrum, et [Cristus attrahit] nos, qui sumus ferei, id est ad bonum duri et ad malum acuti,

both manuscripts omit *Cristus attrahit*;[1] Carpenter (*Destructorium* III. 9) rewrote the sentence as

sicut adamas ferrum *sibi naturaliter attrahit*, ita . . . *Christus* nos qui *ad modum ferri* ad bonum *sumus* duri et ad malum acuti,

in the course of which he correctly supplies the two omitted words, but not as they must originally have stood. In the next sentence, where LT read *quia non est tam durus* for an intended rhetorical question *quis non est tam durus*, Carpenter emends to *non est aliquis tam durus*, which gives an 'easier' but less suitable construction and sense. In III. 17 (L f. 121ᵛ, T f. 188), in a passage which throughout deals with a *malus*

---

[1] In L a later reader has attempted to emend the corrupt text, by erasing *Ita* at the beginning and by altering the ampersand after *ferrum* by erasure to *i*, above which he writes *a* to give an abbreviation for *ita*. As altered, L now reads *sicut adamas ferrum, ita nos qui sumus . . .*, but it still lacks a main verb and a second subject parallel to *adamas*.

prelatus in the singular, both manuscripts end with the clause

quia auferet eis contemplationem eternorum non temporalium,

where the context requires the singular *ei* for *eis*; Carpenter (D V. 2) emends *eis* to *eius*, but again this is unlikely to have been the original reading, for though singular it spoils the syntax. In II. 46 (L f. 99, T f. 149ᵛ), in the passage

Ille [*sc.* Oza] tamen ex debito officio, quia de Leui erat et sacerdos, accessit ad subleuandam arcam, sed indigne: tradunt enim Hebrei quod nocte precedenti concuberat cum uxore. Quanto magis nostri sacerdotes ad corpus Cristi accedentes?

it is evident that before or after *ad corpus Cristi* something has dropped out, such as *de meretricum corporibus*, for the argument is incomplete.[1] Carpenter (D III. 9) evidently thought so, for he rewrote the final phrase as

. . . nostri uoluptuosi sacerdotes cum meretricibus in nocte concumbentes et in die manibus pollutis corpus Christi irreuerenter tractantes.

In III. 73 (L f. 164ᵛ, T f. 273ʳ⁻ᵛ) both manuscripts have a reference to Ecclesiasticus 28 which should in fact, by the standard chapter-numbering, be to chapter 27 (verse 17),[2] both have *siquidem confitendo* where the context requires *siquidem confidendo* 'at least with confidence', and both have *cogitationes imitando* where *cogitationes immittendo* 'by implanting thoughts' is needed;[3] the last of these errors is correctly emended in L, in the margin, by a later thirteenth-century hand, and also by Carpenter (D V. 13), who has *cogitationes malas immittendo*, but the other two are uncorrected both in the manuscripts and by Carpenter. In III. 28

---

[1] Cf., in a parallel passage in Giraldus Cambrensis, *Speculum Ecclesiæ* (ed. Brewer, Rolls Series, 1873), p. 316, 'accedentes ad corpus Christi concubinarum vel meretricum . . . concubitores'.

[2] But this may be an error of the author's; see p. 105 n. 2 below.

[3] For the text of the latter part of this passage, see below, p. 82.

(L f. 129, T f. 204) both L and T have simply *regnum* where *regnum celorum*, as in the next sentence but one, seems necessary, and in III. 96 (L f. 184, T f. 306ᵛ), in the sentence

Usurarius . . . tempus ergo [pendendo] uendit,

'a usurer sells time in which to pay', they both have *uendendo uendit*, which is impossible; but Carpenter corrects neither of these faults, though he quotes the passages in D IV. 62 and D IV. 20 respectively.

Of the instances in which L and T differ but neither is right a simple example is in II. 51 (L f. 102ᵛ, T f. 155ᵛ), where L reads 'Multi . . . interficiuntur et intercipiuntur', T omits *interficiuntur et* (perhaps deliberately), but sense requires a transposition of the verbs, *intercipiuntur et interficiuntur*. Another is in IV. 18 (L f. 199ᵛ, T f. 334), in the sentence

Non enim particulariter remittit deus, [atqui] simul aut omnia peccata mortalia aut nulla,

where for *atqui* T has *qui*, evidently reproducing the corruption of the common ancestor, but L, perceiving that a conjunction of some sort was required, 'emends' to *quia*. At II. 54 (L f. 105, T f. 159ᵛ), in an attack on pluralists who

multiplicant altaria, scilicet ecclesias parochiales et prebendas, ad [pacandum], quia non curant de salute animarum sibi commissarum, sed de pecunia congreganda,

ad pacandum 'for payment' is evidently required, but T has *ad paccandum*, a minor spelling-error which must come from the common ancestor, and L has *ad peccandum*. In III. 71, in the phrase *diei natalis . . . festiuitate*, T has *die* and L *in die* though both scribes retain *natalis*. A more complex and perhaps doubtful example is in III. 85 (L f. 174, T f. 290), in a sentence which I would emend to read:

Caritas enim omnem scientiam plenificat et sufficientem facit ad

promerendum regnum dei; quantumlibet enim [exilis est], et
exilis scientia sufficit cum caritate.

Here T repeats *ad promerendum regnum dei* at the end, after
cum caritate, which I cannot believe the author intended,
fond though he is of repetition; but the phrase must have been
repeated in the common ancestor, for L omits the second half
of the sentence, from *quantumlibet* onwards, either by 'eye-
skip' or (less probably) in deliberate avoidance of a difficulty.[1]

The shared errors that I have noted are usually widely
separated from each other, but in IV. 10 (cited above) there
are two in one sentence and in III. 73 (also cited above) there
are three in a couple of sentences,[2] and a passage in IV. 49
(L f. 231ᵛ, T f. 382) has no less than four in a few lines. In it
the author quotes a group of hexameters and goes on to
expound them. He begins:

O quam commendabiles lacrime, que et uisionem angelorum et
Cristi pepererunt!

> Lacrima munit, [alit], salis instar uermibus obstat,
> Conciliat, facit ingenuos, et mitigat iram.

Munit ab insultibus demonum ut aqua castrum; [*alit*], id est
fecundat, terram corporis nostri bonis operibus . . .

Here both L and T misplace *lacrima* before *salis*, where it
will not scan; it must come either first (preferably) or second
in the line. For *alit* T in both places has *huic*, which is non-
sense; L has *huic* altered to *huit* in the verse-line and *huit*
without alteration in the exposition. Obviously when the

---

[1] In consequence T is the only independent witness to the latter part
of the sentence, but its text does not make grammar or sense and is
obviously corrupt. I assume the omission of the words supplied in
brackets, and that the following *et* was intended in the sense 'even'.

[2] Cf. also the passage from IV. 22 quoted in entry no. 56 in the
Appendix (p. 161 below), in which there are three shared errors in a
single sentence—two in verse-lines, to the detriment of metre.

scribe of L saw the gloss *fecundat* he realized that a verbal
form in *-it* was required, but his powers of emendation went
no further than to change *huic* into *huit*; what he thought it
meant I cannot imagine.[1] A little later two more hexameters
are introduced, but before their exposition begins there are
a couple of extra notes on the first pair; these notes are obvious afterthoughts which the author must have written in
the margin of his autograph, whence a copyist has taken them
into the text immediately after, when they should have been
inserted immediately before, the second pair of hexameters.
Then, in the exposition of the first phrase of the second pair
of verses, we have (with allusion to the Vulgate text of Tobit
3 : 11, though without explicit citation):

Exulat hac Belial: [lacrime] a Sara demonium fugauerunt,

but both L and T omit *lacrime*, leaving *fugauerunt* without a
subject; fortunately it is obvious, from the following two
sentences (which run parallel), that *lacrime* was intended.
Most of the shared errors of L and T, it will be seen, are
very simple and can be explained satisfactorily from a single
process of copying, but this does not apply to the corruption
of *alit* to *huic*; we must assume in this instance that the common ancestor of L and T was itself separated from the autograph by at least one (but probably only one) intervening
copy. In this, I would suppose, *alit* was replaced by *luit*,
which, though it neither scans nor fits the gloss *fecundat*,
makes more 'obvious' sense in the verse-line itself; it is easy

---

[1] The conditions for emendation, if *lacrima* is moved to the beginning
of the line (as it should be), are very precisely defined. The word before
salis must be a verb which (i) ends in *-it* to account for the *-ic* of the corruption *huic*, (ii) has a short first syllable, (iii) begins with a vowel or *h*
so as not to give length 'by position' to the *-it* of *munit*, (iv) fits the gloss
fecundat. The only word that I can think of is *alit*, which is part of the
author's vocabulary. If *lacrima* is put second, after *munit*, *alit* still fits.

to see how, if the final -*t* was indistinguishable from *c*, *luit* could be misread as *huic*.[1]

Of special significance are instances in which a shared error of L and T is avoided by *Ancrene Wisse* in a parallel passage. There are four clear examples.

(*a*) In III. 68 (L f. 160, T f. 264^v) there is a passage which runs:

> Ut dicit Ysaias, Cristus fuit 'uir dolorum', nam 'in agonia factus est sudor membrorum quasi gutte sanguinis decurrentis in terram'. Super quem locum dicit [Bernardus], 'Non solum oculis sed omnibus membris Cristus fleuisse uidetur, ut totum corpus eius, quod est ecclesia, tocius corporis lacrimis rigaretur'.

The citation is from Bernard's *In Dominica Palmarum Sermo III*,[2] but both L and T read *Beda*[3] for *Bernardus*, and again in IV. 24 (L f. 205, T f. 343) they attribute the same citation, once more after the quotation of Luke 22: 44, to *Beda*. It seems that the common abbreviation *B'.* for *Bernardus* had been wrongly expanded in their common ancestor, for there can be little reason to attribute the error to the author, who was obviously learned.[4] In any case *Ancrene Wisse* (f. 30b/2–9)

[1] Especially if it had been written with a capital *L*, as it might well have been. Compare also the corruption *sol luit* for *soluit* in IV. 51, only two chapters later, which shows that the scribe of a manuscript antecedent to L and T knew the verb *luit* and was prepared to introduce it into his copy.

[2] Migne, *P.L.* clxxxiii. 262.

[3] Bede's comment on Luke 22: 44 ('Et factus est sudor eius sicut guttae sanguinis decurrentis in terram') in his *In Lucae Evangelium Expositio* (Migne, *P.L.* xcii. 603–4) has nothing in common with Bernard's.

[4] There are other instances of the ascription to Bede of quotations which I suspect may be from Bernard, but which I have not checked. In *Moralia* IV. 50 (L f. 233^v, T f. 386^v), the quotation 'Breuis est uoluptas fornicationis, sed perpetua pena fornicatoris' is attributed to Bede (and is immediately followed by a sentence of similar import cited from Gregory); in I. 72 (L f. 61, T f. 86) it is attributed to Gregory; and in II. 23 (L f. 82^v, T f. 121^v) it is cited without attribution. The instance may show that the author was not always sure of the source of his quota-

has a parallel passage, citing Luke 22: 44 immediately *after* a paraphrase and partial quotation of Bernard's comment, which is correctly ascribed to 'sein Beornard'.

(*b*) In III. 71 (L f. 163, T f. 270ᵛ) there is a similitude comparing the human body to a castle:

Ad bene muniendum carnem nostram ipse [*sc.* Cristus] idem, nisi eum eiciamus, positus est 'murus et antemurale' . . . Et quod titulus domini positus sit in carne nostra habemus in Ysaia xix, 'Erit altare in medio terre Egypte, et titulus domini iuxta turrim eius' . . . In carne est titulus: maceratio et proprie carnis afflictio. Certe, titulo domini cognito, non audet diabolus insultare; sed ubi proprium carnis titulum inuenit (scilicet delicias, luxum, pruritum), arma sua cognoscit et gentem suam, et [it] intra securus.

Here L has *iter intra*, which makes impossible grammar with *securus*, and T has *iter intrat*, which in the context is not satisfactory sense (since the devil is to enter a castle, not a road); a later corrector has altered L, in the margin, to *intra intrat*, which gives sense but is clumsy and cannot be original. L as first written must preserve the transmitted reading, which T and L's corrector are conjecturally altering; but the required emendation is *it intra*.[1] This is confirmed by *Ancrene Wisse* f. 98b/2–9:

Eise ant flesches este beoð þes deofles mearken. Hwen he suð þeos mearken i mon oðer i wummon, he wat þe castel is his, ant geað baldeliche in þer he suð iriht up swucche baneres as me deð i castel. I þet totore folc he misseð his merken, ant suð in ham iriht up Godes banere, þet is, heardschipe of lif, ant heaueð muche dred þrof, as Ysaie witneð.

tions; nevertheless I think that in III. 68 and IV. 24 the false attribution to Bede must be due to scribal error.

[1] I assume that a *t* with a turned-back stroke above the cross-bar, such as often occurs in L and T themselves, has been misread as the abbreviation for *ter*.

Plainly *geað baldeliche in* is a direct translation of *it intra securus*.[1]

(*c*) Both in *Ancrene Wisse* and in the *Moralia* there are more passages than one in which the crucifixion is compared to a blood-letting, and these are certainly parallel. In particular, *Moralia* IV. 38 (L f. 220[v], T f. 366[v]) has a set of verses on the theme:

> Iuncta quies tenebris est grata cruore minuto;
> [Solem] deuitat, baculum tenet, utitur idem
> Deliciis. Posito secus accidit in cruce Cristo:
> Expositus uentis et soli fleubotomatur.
> In cruce plus aliis premitur caro uiuida Cristi.
> Cur? Quia peccatum numquam corrupit eandem.
> Hanc etiam [querit] de uirgine, cui caro queuis
> Mollicie minor est. Tumulo dormitat ad horam.
> Nec crux sed claui, [baculi] uice, sustinet ipsum;
> In cruce cum felle mixto potatur aceto.

In these lines there are two errors shared by L and T; in l. 2 they have *sompnum deuitat* 'avoids sleep', which is obviously not the intended sense and fails to give the necessary antithesis to *Expositus . . . soli* in l. 4, and in l. 7 they both have the meaningless *que arit* for *querit*, 'derives'. But *Ancrene Wisse*, in a brief parallel passage (f. 70b/4–6), has

Oþre habbeð reste, fleoð liht i chambre, hudeð ham hwen ha beoð ilete blod on an earm eðre; ant he o Munt Caluaire steah ȝet o rode herre . . .

---

[1] *Ancrene Wisse* in this passage, and in the lines preceding it from f. 98a/18 onwards, is also influenced by a passage in *Moralia* IV. 33 (L f. 214[v], T ff. 357[v]–8) concerning the 'vestimentum dilaceratum' of poverty (equated with Christ's 'caro . . . dilacerata et perforata') which our Lord left 'amicis suis et beatis pauperibus, quia diuites non induunt uestimenta dilacerata undique perforata'; this is the germ of the idea of 'þet totore folc'.

in which *fleoð liht* renders the emended text *solem deuitat*;[1] and in another (f. 30b/17–19) it has

Euch monnes flesch is dead flesch aȝein þet wes Godes flesch, as þet te wes inumen of þe tendre meiden, ant na þing neauer nes þrin þet hit adeadede,

in which *wes inumen of* corresponds to *querit de* in the Latin verses.[2]

(*d*) *Moralia* IV. 53 (on the text *Pax uobis*) has a chapter-heading which in both L (f. 236) and T (f. 389ᵛ) reads:

De multiplici pacis reformatione, inter deum et hominem, angelum et hominem, *carnem et spiritum*; et de triplici pace in triplici uita necessaria; et de tribus perturbantibus pacem, disseritur.

But though the latter part of this, from *et de triplici pace* onwards, corresponds to the content of the chapter, the first part does not; the text, after dealing with the restoration of peace between God and man and between angel and man, proceeds immediately to the restoration of peace between Jew and Gentile because of the bringing of the new law by Christ. This, and the run of the phrases, shows that for *inter . . . carnem et spiritum* the text intended by the author was *inter . . . hominem et hominem*. This is confirmed by a much

---

[1] It might equally translate *lucem deuitat*, which would scan as well; but the corruption *sompnum* points to *solem* as the original.

[2] *Ancrene Wisse*, in the second passage, is also influenced by *Moralia* I. 69 (L f. 59ʳ⁻ᵛ, T f. 83):

'. . . caro mortua, lesa et percussa, non sentit penam tam acerbam sicut et caro uiua. Sic caro nostra, per peccatum mortificata, passionem sibi illatam non sentit sicut et caro Cristi, que uiua fuit et, immunis a peccato, preciosa fuit et attrahens, unde "Cum exaltatus fuero a terra, etc."'

But this, though it explains what *Ancrene Wisse* means by 'na þing . . . þet hit adeadede' (i.e. no sin), lacks the other reason given by the verses for the tenderness of Christ's flesh, that it was derived from the Virgin's.

earlier chapter, I. 18 (L f. 23, T f. 24), which has the heading
De triplici pace reformata per Cristum and begins

. . . Salomon interpretatur 'pacificus' et significat Cristum, qui
uenit reformare pacem inter deum et hominem, inter angelum et
hominem, inter hominem et hominem (id est inter iudeum et
gentilem uel inter carnem et spiritum).

This shows why the heading of IV. 53 has gone wrong, and
suggests indeed that there has been a major omission; perhaps it originally ran

De multiplici pacis reformatione, inter deum et hominem, angelum et hominem, [hominem et hominem, id est inter iudeum et
gentilem uel inter] carnem et spiritum . . .

Now *Ancrene Wisse* f. 67b/4–9 is based on the first part of
the heading of IV. 53 and the following gospel text:[1]

Hwa halt wreaððe þe bihalt þet Godd lihte on eorðe to makien
þr[e]ofald sahte: bitweone mon ant mon, bitweone Godd ant
mon, bitweone mon ant engel; ant efter his ariste, þa he com ant
schawde him, þis wes his gretunge to his deore deciples, *Pax
uobis*, 'Sahtnesse beo bitweonen ow'.

The English writer has altered the order, and spoiled the
parallelism, of the phrases, being characteristically less neat
than the Latin author; but unless he has corrected the text of
the heading by cross-reference to I. 18, which seems unlikely,
he must have had in front of him the reading *inter . . .
hominem et hominem*. The series of instances can leave no
doubt that he used a copy of the *Moralia* which was independent of, and (at least at these points) more correct
than, the line of descent that resulted in L and T.

---

[1] The passage in *Ancrene Wisse* cannot be based on I. 18, which nowhere cites or refers to the text *Pax uobis*; primarily at least, and I think
entirely, it depends on IV. 53.

At another point, however, *Ancrene Wisse* represents the intended text of the *Moralia* less accurately than L and T. In III. 83 (L f. 172, T f. 286) the *Moralia* recounts the legend that the eagle, to protect its young from noxious things, places in its nest a precious stone, which is named as the *echites*, or 'adder-stone'. This is certainly what the author meant; both L and T give various inflected forms of *echites* four times (thrice in the text, once in the accompanying subheading), and both copies of the index in L have *echites* both in the main and the subordinate entry. But in this legend (which derives from Pliny) the stone is usually said to be the *aetites* or 'eagle-stone', though in some later versions it is the *gagates* or jet;[1] in the source used by the author of the *Moralia* the *aetites* must have been replaced by the *echites*.[2] But in *Ancrene Wisse* (f. 37a/8–22), whose account follows the *Moralia*, the stone is said to be called *achate*, i.e. 'agate';[3] there has been confusion between *echites* and *achates*, and the former has been wrongly taken as a variant or erroneous form of the latter. The substitution may have been made either by the author of *Ancrene Wisse* himself or by the scribe of the copy of the *Moralia* which he used; the first alternative is much the more likely.

I have written hitherto of the 'common ancestor' of L and T, but I am strongly of the opinion that this was in fact the direct exemplar of both manuscripts. Such a judgement is

[1] I owe this information to my pupil, Mrs. Carol Mills, who first drew my attention to the singularity of *Ancrene Wisse* in this matter. Carpenter, *Destructorium*, IV. 66, in a passage independent of the *Moralia*, says that the stone is 'nomine gagates'.

[2] Cf. *OED*, s.v. *echites*, which cites from T. Maplet's *Green Forest* (1567) 'Echites is a stone . . . without the which the Eagle cannot bring forth her young'.

[3] This has led both *OED* and *MED*, s.v. *achate*, to suppose that in the passage from *Ancrene Wisse* there is confusion between *achates* and *gagates*, but the explanation is more complex; proximately *achate* is a substitute for *echites*.

impossible to prove beyond doubt by the methods of textual criticism, since in theory one can, if one wishes, always postulate intervening copies. But the variations between L and T are never complex;[1] at most points one or other text is obviously right, though sometimes both diverge from the original, and it is always evident, from the text accepted or reconstructed, how and why the error has occurred. The differences between the two never require the assumption of more than a single stage of copying. There is also more positive evidence that L and T are copied from the same manuscript. They agree very closely in their headings and subheadings, and especially in their preservation of the footnotes, which, not being an integral part of the text, were liable to be dropped (and were dropped in the fifteenth-century manuscripts). It is remarkable how often they agree in their use of abbreviations, even when the word concerned could have been abbreviated in other ways, and this despite their great differences in format and style—T a copy on a grand scale, with large pages and large lettering, produced regardless of expense, L much more economical and by comparison cramped. The clearest indication of all, however, is that there is a significant number of places where one scribe goes wrong and the other gets the text right only after hesitation. Some instances may be explicable as emendations, by one or other of the two scribes, of an uncorrected error in his exemplar,[2] but more often I think that both were

[1] They are simple misreadings of abbreviations, letters, or words; simple omissions, of small or abbreviated words or at the turn of a page or by 'eye-skip' (homoeoteleuton), for which the author's fondness for repetition gave much occasion; the substitution of synonyms, usually for connectives, or the omission of connectives that seemed (and often were) otiose; alterations of word-order; errors in grammar, especially the inflexions of verbs; and occasionally an attempt to emend a transmitted reading that was, or was thought to be, unsatisfactory.

[2] As in the instance cited from IV. 10 on p. 47 above, in which T alters *mutat* to *inuitat*.

dealing with a point of difficulty in a common exemplar; possibly errors in the exemplar had been corrected by faint plummet markings[1] (either marks of transposition, or interlined or marginal corrections) which one of the successor scribes failed to notice, the other noticed only belatedly. In I. 24 (L f. 27, T f. 31ᵛ), in the sentence

Seniores quos condempnauit Daniel species muliebris decepit, et de Iudith et de Holoferne legitur . . .

T omits *decepit* and L interlines it. In I. 25 (L f. 29, T f. 34), where *cuiuis* is required, T has *cuius* and L *cuiuis* by alteration (perhaps from *siuis*), and where *sibi in* is required, L has *in sibi*, T *sibi in* in smaller lettering (but by the original scribe) over an erasure, almost certainly of *in sibi*. In I. 61 (L f. 53, T f. 73), in the chapter-heading, T has *singillationem* for *sug(g)ilationem* and L has *suggillacionem* by alteration from *siggillacionem*. In III. 56 (L f. 150ᵛ, T f. 247), where *etsi non* is required, L has *et non si* and T has *et ⟨si⟩ non* with *si* interlined (i.e. T began to write the words in the same order as L but corrected himself immediately). In IV. 10 (L f. 193ᵛ, T f. 323), for *subiecto* T has the abbreviation *subîto*, L has *subito*. In IV. 30 (L f. 211ᵛ, T f. 353) both are in slight trouble expanding an abbreviation for *misericorditer*; L has *misercordit*er, T has *miscdit*er. Also in IV. 30, on the same pages, in the sentence

De quibus in Iob, '[Vir] uanus in superbia erigitur',

T has *in iob Ubi* and L has *iob v*; the exemplar evidently had *in iob V.* meaning *in Iob Vir*, but T took *V.* as a suspension for *Ubi* and L as a numeral (the correct reference in fact being Job 11 : 12). In IV. 42 (L f. 223ᵛ, T f. 370), in the phrase *ad locum sibi assignatum*, L interlines *assignatum* (originally

---

[1] Cf. the plummet notes for corrections in L itself.

omitted) in accordance with a plummet note made by the
scribe himself in the margin, T for the whole phrase has *ad
dolum sibi*. In IV. 44 (L f. 226^v, T f. 374^v) L has *notandum*
altered from *notum*, T has *notum*. Also in IV. 44 (L f. 227,
T f. 375), for the accusative of *aloes*, L has *aloen* altered from
aloem by erasure, T has *aleon*, though a little earlier both have
aloem. In IV. 46 (L f. 229, T f. 378^v), in the phrase *et reputare
semper se peregrinum* 'and always to account oneself a pilgrim',
L has *se semper* marked for transposition, T has *se semper*
uncorrected. In IV. 49 (L f. 232^v, T f. 385) L has *enim* by
correction from an abbreviation for *autem*, T has this abbreviation. My impression that the two manuscripts are direct
copies of the same exemplar is so strong that I shall assume
it in my further argument; but even if the assumption were
incorrect, though the form of my arguments would be different, their substance would be unaffected.[1]

The presence in L of two copies, A and B, of a subject-
index to the *Moralia* is of considerable significance for the
history of the text. As was pointed out above in the description of L, Index A is contained in a separate quire which was
originally part of another (lost) manuscript and was its final
quire; Index B was from the start an integral part of L,
written after its text and begun though not completed by the
text-scribe. Undoubtedly Index B was a direct copy of
Index A; its first scribe, though he successfully attempted to
improve in detail on the layout of Index A, obviously modelled
himself on it and ruled his page with the same number of
lines (40), with the clear intention of following its paging
exactly. In practice discrepancies developed from the second
page of Index B (f. 249^v), for various reasons (chiefly omis-

---

[1] Thus statements about 'the exemplar' would have to be understood
as applying to 'the common ancestor' of L and T, and its features would
have to be considered as having been transmitted by any intervening copy
that separated either L or T from it.

sions, in Index B, of main or subordinate entries), and B got ahead of A by a varying number of entries. The third scribe therefore decided to reduce the number of lines per page (to 38) on f. 253ᵛ, and by the end of that page he was all square, but he continued with the reduced number of lines for three more pages and so fell twelve entries behind, and this, with one temporary variation, remains the position to the end. Nevertheless, despite the discrepancies, the desire to follow the paging of Index A is clear, and the content of Index B confirms its dependence: it reproduces the errors of Index A except for two obvious corrections,[1] and has additional errors of its own.[2] The third scribe of Index B, however, obscures its derivation from Index A by his misguided editorial activities. He disliked the single-word main entries, though they are certainly what the compiler intended, and replaced them whenever possible by longer main entries which as a rule are derived from the first (or only) subordinate entry; even when he could not do this he altered (for example) *Echites* to *De Echite*, and similarly *Articulus* to *De vij. Articulis fidei*. A more confusing divergence is at the foot of col. *b* of f. 252ᵛ, the first page on which he worked.

---

[1] On f. 8ᵛ the scribe of Index A omitted a main entry (properly *Sambucus*, though what he writes is *Sambuco*) and, noticing his error, was obliged to squeeze it in (but in red ink) in mid-column, between the two parts of the subordinate entry; Index B restores it to its proper position on a separate line. On f. 3ᵛ, under *Crux Cristi*, Index A has the subheading 'Crux Cristi iiii' against two successive chapter-references; it is obvious that there has been a mistake and even that the subheading belongs with the second reference, not the first, but the scribe of Index B, if in doubt, had only to look up the references to discover that it belonged to the second, which is where he puts it.

[2] On f. 251 (col. *b*) it omits the main entry *Contritio* (supplied in black ink in the margin); on f. 252ᵛ (col. *a*) it omits the main entries *Prelatus* and *Arma* and the first subordinate entry under the latter, and adds the second subordinate entry at the end of those under *De vij. Articulis fidei*; on f. 253ᵛ (top of col. *a*) it omits the main entry *Capra*, and on f. 257 one of the four subordinate entries under *Vestis*.

Here, where he should either have left a line blank or put the main entry *Aqua*, he has a new and unauthorized entry which is written in red as if it were a main entry but which in form is a subordinate entry ('De duplici Sapore carnis Cristi et carnis Asse') without its chapter-reference; and it is in fact taken from the first subordinate entry under *Sapor* (Index A, f. 8ᵛ, col. *b*). What he seems to have been trying to do was to introduce a new main entry (effectively for *Assa*) between *Anulus* and *Aqua*, but he so confused himself that he gave no chapter-reference and, at the top of col. *a* of f. 253, omitted the main entry *Aqua*, though he gave correctly its subordinate entries. Fortunately he did not repeat the experiment, or he might have made the derivation of Index B from Index A much harder to discern.[1]

Index A itself has copying errors, as already remarked. Thus the heading *Accidia* is omitted (f. 1ᵛ), its place being taken by a red line drawn across the column;[2] under *Eucaristia* (f. 4) the first reference, to II. 66 (a non-existent chapter), is an error for II. 46 (*lxvi* for *xlvi*); under *Lac* (f. 7) the reference should be to III. 73 not III. 77; under *Mater* (f. 7) the last reference should be to II. 32 not II. 22; and under *Fons* (f. 6) the second reference, which should be to IV. 27, is given as III. 62, identical with and obviously picked up from the immediately following reference under *Faber*. More significant for the textual history, because more complex, are the errors under *Caritas*, where the proper entry

---

[1] Strictly speaking all the main headings, and the entry in red at the foot of col. *b* of f. 252ᵛ, were written by a single rubricator, but he must have been following drafts written by the other scribes; the responsibility for the changes of plan in the third section of Index B must rest with the third of the black-ink scribes.

[2] This may, however, have been deliberately planned, for the form of the entry is abnormal. Index B at this point omits both the heading and the line, so that the *Accidia* entry follows immediately, without intervening space, that for *Pax*; but the scribe allowed for a rubricated capital (which was not supplied) to begin the *Accidia* entry.

for 'Caritas iii', which should refer to I. 28,[1] is omitted, and all the following entries have in consequence been renumbered, thus 'Caritas iii' where we should have 'Caritas iiii' and so on to 'Caritas xv' for 'Caritas xvi'.[2] This situation must arise from two successive stages of corruption, one in which the entry for 'Caritas iii' was simply omitted, and a second in which the remaining entries were renumbered because it was wrongly assumed that there had been a mistake only in the numbering.[3] It follows that Index A is not merely itself an erroneous copy, but is separated from the original by an intervening copy which already had its own errors; and the same deduction, as we have seen, has to be made concerning the text of the common exemplar (or ancestor) of L and T. In all the circumstances it is clear that the manuscript to which Index A originally belonged was the exemplar from which L was directly copied; for some reason its index had been detached from the exemplar[4] and was never restored to it, but instead was bound in at the beginning of the copy, the surviving manuscript.

T lacks the subject-index and has in substitution a table of contents, prefixed to the text (at least as it is now bound) but made after the text had been copied, since the original

[1] Cf. the text of L, f. 31ᵛ, where the subheading 'Caritas iii' is given half-way through I. 28. At the corresponding point T (f. 38ᵛ) has 'Caritas ii', but this is a mere copying slip, since T itself has already had 'Caritas s*ecu*ndo' at f. 23, the proper point.

[2] That the subheadings are wrongly numbered in the Index is shown by comparison with the subheadings in the text; I. 76 (L f. 63ᵛ) has the subheading 'Caritas iiii', not 'Caritas iii' as the Index states, and so on.

[3] A scribe attentive enough to notice that there was a jump in numbering from ii to iiii would certainly have checked his exemplar to make sure that he had not himself omitted entry number iii. The scribe who renumbered cannot have been the scribe who was guilty of the omission.

[4] Probably for the convenience of the scribes who were making the copy, Index B; thus the first scribe may have been checking his text against that of the exemplar while the second and third scribes were continuing the index.

scribe finished the text but not the table of contents; it is compiled from the chapter-headings and the gospel texts at the beginning of each chapter. Though of some use, it is far inferior, as a guide to the text, to L's classified index. To make the contents-list must have cost the original scribe and his successor who completed it (with some change of plan) a good deal of time, and it is unlikely that they would have taken the trouble if their exemplar had included a more useful index which they had only to copy. The simple explanation is that the exemplar had already lost its index (now bound in at the beginning of L) before it came into their hands, and this gives us a textual argument to confirm the palaeographical evidence that T is later than L.

The Balliol MS. (B) and the Cambridge MS. (C) are obviously descended from T. It is almost a sufficient indication that they both include a table of contents, listing chapter-headings and gospel texts, with exactly the same *incipit* as T's, but the proof is in their detailed readings. I have collated over 100 test passages (some of only a sentence or two, but many extensive), mostly in Parts III and IV, containing over 250 substantive variations between L and T, and the story is always the same: B and C follow T not only when it is certainly or possibly right, but also when it is certainly, even absurdly, wrong. In the test passages TBC share twenty undoubted omissions, five of phrases or longish parts of sentences omitted by homoeoteleuton and the rest of one or two words essential to the sense,[1] and seventy-nine readings

---

[1] As homoeoteleuton is an obvious cause of error, omissions due to it may occur independently in unrelated manuscripts; nevertheless it is unlikely that any considerable group of such omissions will occur independently. The case is different with omissions of single words for no apparent reason except mere carelessness; to these the traditional doctrine that shared omissions are good evidence of a genetic relationship applies with full force, and most of the omissions shared by TBC are of this sort. Particularly significant is the omission in IV. 27 of *in quibus*, which in T occurs for an obvious reason, at the turn of a page (f. 348^{r-v}), but in

which are plainly false or inferior.[1] Two types of error, of
which instances are not counted in these figures, are especially
significant of the genetic descent of BC from T. The first
is that T, in moving subheadings from the margin into the
text-space, sometimes introduced them in mid-sentence or
so as to break up a group of verses. In four of the instances
checked, BC follow T exactly (III. 84, IV. 14, IV. 16 twice)
and in two (IV. 51 and IV. 55) they make matters still worse
by appending to the subheading an 'index-heading' which T
itself had left in the margin; only in one instance (IV. 31)
do they move the subheading to the beginning of the sentence
which in T it interrupts. The second type is readings in BC
that are due to failure to understand, or to follow correctly,
alterations to T's text made either by the original scribe or
by some later reader.[2] In III. 47, where L has *reseratus*, T
wrote *reseratur* but altered it to *reseratus*; BC have *reseratur*.
In III. 90, for L's *sancti*, T wrote *sīt* (for *sint*) but clumsily
altered it to *scī*; BC read *sint*. In IV. 10, for L's *gusta*, T
wrote *gustu* but it has been unclearly altered to *gusta* (the

B (f. 143ᵛ) and C (f. 288) in mid-page; the omission clearly originated in
T, since L has the correct text.

[1] Examples are: *Absit* L *Ac sic* TC *Ac si* B (III. 1); *saciatur* L *saciatur
se communicanti* TBC (interlined gloss introduced into verses, to ruin of
metre), *sursumque* L *sensumque* TBC (III. 30); *ut qui uiuus* L *utque unius*
TBC (III. 47); *noluit* L *nouit* TBC (III. 56); *specie* L *spe* TBC (III. 82);
fine L *fide* TBC (III. 83); *mundus cura* L *munda* TBC (III. 84); cross-
reference to rubric of chapter 55 of the same part L (correctly), of
chapter 65 (in words, *sexagesimi quinti*) TBC (III. 88); *sitit deus* L *sint
deo* TBC (also III. 88); *fons* L *foris* TBC (IV. 7); *peccata mortalia* L
peccata peccata TB *peccata* C, *in te extolli* L *in textolli* TB *in extolli* C,
cur L *crux* TBC (IV. 18); *fereris* L *fateris* TBC (IV. 34); *salutaris* L
saturans TBC (IV. 35); *quies* L *qui es* TBC, *queuis* L *quis* TBC (IV. 38);
i. (= *id est*) L *hel* TBC (IV. 40); *tria* L *circa* TBC (IV. 46). In each case
L is obviously right.

[2] I do not find the two cases always easy to distinguish; T's hand in
interlinear alterations can be very different from his text-hand. Most of
the alterations I think are his own, but probably not all. The point is not
material to the argument.

resulting *a* being uncharacteristic in shape); BC read *gustu*.
In III. 83, for L's *acutius uel limpidius*, T wrote only *acutius*
but interlined *i. limpidius* above; BC have only *acutius*. In
IV. 22 T omitted *habita gracia* but interlined it, and also
omitted *offendit* (so L, correctly) but interlined *diffendit*; BC
omit both interlinings.[1] In IV. 14, in the passage discussed on
p. 48 above, they follow the corrector's unessential alteration of *homo* to *o homo* but not his essential correction of
debes to *debet*; the former is more obvious to the eye, the
latter unobtrusive. But the commonest cause of trouble was
a failure to understand T's use of deleting points beneath
letters. In IV. 46, for L's *temporali*, T wrote *temporalibus* but
subpuncted the abbreviation for *-bus*; BC read *temporalibus*.
In IV. 63, for L's *nudans*, T wrote *nudatis* but altered it by
writing *n* (quite clearly) above the line and deleting the *ti* by
a single point which in fact is under the *i*; BC read *nudatus*, i.e.
the point has been taken as applying only to the *i* and the
interlined *n* has been misread as *u*. The nicest case is in III.
74, where L has *cilia* 'eyebrows' four times (as the context
plainly requires); T, however, wrote *cilicia* each time, but
attempted to correct the first two instances by subpunction.
Unfortunately he again used only a single point, and BC
consequently read *cilica* in all four instances; the point has
been taken as deleting only the final *i* (though in the first case
it is much nearer the *c*) and the 'correction' has been carried
on to the two instances which in T remained unaltered. In
IV. 10, where T as first written has *angulline* as a poor spelling
for **anguilline* 'of eel-flesh', the T scribe himself interlined
i after the *u* and subpuncted the *-in-*, intending to make
anguille 'of an eel'; but the point under the *n* is in fact
placed directly under its first minim. B reads *anguillie*, i.e.
the point has been taken as deleting only the first minim of

---

[1] This is characteristic; they regularly fail to copy the interlined comments on verses given in T.

the *n*, leaving the second to be read as *i*. But C has *anguille*, which must be its scribe's own correction of the form. He also makes corrections in three other such cases. In III. 83, where L has *in*, T has *ut* altered to *in*, B has *ut*, but C has *in*; and in IV. 18, where L has *tradit* (obviously required), T has *trahit* altered to *tradit*, B has *trahit*, but C has *tradit*. In both these cases C probably had the text as given by B in his exemplar, for there is ample evidence (cited below) that they had a proximate common ancestor other than T, but he emended it correctly; it would be easy to do in both places.[1] In III. 71, in the phrase *pro innocentia collata* (so L), T has the abbreviation for *per* altered to that for *pro*, B reads *per innocentiam collatam*, but C has the correct reading; I assume that their proximate common ancestor had *per innocentia collata* (as T before it was corrected), which B altered in the wrong direction and C in the right.

Neither B nor C is a copy of the other; each has, peculiar to itself, both a few corrections and many new errors (by which I mean false readings which are not descended from T and other readings, not evidently false in themselves, which are shown to be innovations by the evidence of T supported, usually, by L). In the test passages there are, by my count, thirty-four new errors[2] in B which are not in C and nine corrections;[3] but C, obviously copied more hastily (as the

---

[1] Alternatively, the common ancestor may have given both T's readings, corrected and uncorrected, and B chose wrongly, C rightly.

[2] Examples are: *intelligebatur* LTC *intelligitur* B (II. 54); *uiuida* TC *inuida* L *munda* B (III. 47); *et ipsam* LTC *ut ipsum* B, *sua* LTC om. B (III. 71); *tamen sanctitatis* LTC *cum sanctitate* B (III. 82); *uirus* LTC *intus* B (III. 83); *uanus* LTC *manus* B (IV. 30); *spoliauit eam* LTC *spoliatus* B (IV. 63). The reading given first is in each case obviously correct.

[3] Most are very minor, indeed several are probably chance agreements with L resulting from purposeless variation in B at points where I accept L only because it is the best manuscript. Of the rest, one is a correction of a dittography in T and C (III. 83), another of a grammatical fault (*habent* LBD rightly, *habet* TC wrongly, in I. 69; see p. 79 and n. 2 there),

handwriting and the free use of abbreviations shows) but also rather more intelligently, has fifty-five new errors[1] not in B and fifteen corrections of inherited errors.[2] But B and C, though neither is dependent on the other, are not independently descended from T, as indeed is shown by the evidence already cited of their identical treatment, in the test passages, of subheadings wrongly placed in T and of most of the alterations made in T of its text as first copied. In addition B and C share, in these passages, thirty-one new errors[3] and

a third of an obvious error (*mane* LB *magne* TC where the latter is absurd, in IV. 64). What seems a perceptive change, but is perhaps the mere result of unthinkingly reversing the misreading of *u* as *n*, is in IV. 31, where for L's *leuigauit et lenigauit* T has *lenigauit et lenigauit*, C has only *lenigauit* ('correcting' an apparent dittography), but B reverts to L's reading.

[1] Examples are: *cuiuis* L (by alteration, but rightly) *cuius* TB *tuus* C (I. 25); *erigit in presumptionem timor uero sine amore* L (so TB but with *enim* for *uero*) om. C by eye-skip, *opera mala* L *mala opera* TBD *mala vestra* C (I. 69); *memoriales* LT *memorales* B om. C (III. 30); *lecto* LTB *loco* C (III. 35); *Vnde Ambrosius* LTB om. C, *Munera . . . hostes* (first line of verses cited on p. 7 above) LTB om. C (III. 47); *fixuras* LTB *figuras* C (III. 66); *passionis sue* LTB *proauis sue* C (III. 83); *uentis* LTB *mentis* C, *uiuida* LTB (in T corrected from *in uida*) *inuida* C (IV. 83, in the verses cited on p. 56 above, ll. 4–5); *ex mirra et aloe ad unguendum* L (TC with variants), om. C by eye-skip (IV. 44).

[2] The errors corrected do not all descend from T. On C's correction (or avoidance), in four instances, of errors due to misunderstanding of alterations in T see above. Of the other instances, most are very minor and easy; for example *readiecto* LC for *re adiecto* TB (III. 85), *qua* LC for *que* TB (in a citation from Zech. 14: 18, which has *qua*) and *instat* LC for *instar* TB (both IV. 46). C's best emendation is in IV. 30, in the passage cited on p. 61 above, where he succeeds in recovering the intended reading, *in Job Vir*, where both L and T are corrupt; but to make the correction he only needed to recognize the Biblical citation.

[3] Examples are: *manus quinque* LT *manusque* BC (III. 1); *dares unum* LT *unum dares* BC (III. 29); *leuatur* LT *lauatur* BC (III. 30); *sufficere deberet* LT *sufficeret* BC, *luxurie* L *luxurio* T om. BC (III. 66); *titulus domini iuxta turrim eius* LT om. BC by eye-skip (III. 71); subheading *De efficacia lapidis qui echites dicitur*, marginal in LT, introduced into text before *Uersus de echite* BC (III. 83); *sinum* LT *signum* BC (III. 84); index-heading *Gladius iiii*, marginal in LT, introduced into text-space after

eighteen corrections[1] (apart from their regular correction of chapter-numbers wrongly given in T and instances of the clear division of a preposition from the noun that it governs). They must therefore derive from a lost descendant of T which I shall denote ϵ. This can in fact be demonstrated from the table of contents alone. In T it is at the front of the manu-script, before the text; in both B and C it is at the end. In T the original scribe wrote the chapter-headings and the gospel texts in separate columns with the headings on the left, but the continuator, quickly abandoning this system, wrote them in the same column, the text usually above or before the corresponding chapter-heading and with the chapter-number necessarily against the text. B and C follow the continuator in putting both in the same column, but the heading regularly precedes the gospel text for the same chapter;[2] nevertheless, like the continuator of T, they put the chapter-number against the text (with the exception that for I. 1, which has no text, the number is of course against the chapter-heading). Despite this, the heading which belongs with the numbered

---

signatur BC (III. 86); *exprimimus* LT *exprimemus* BC (III. 91); subhead-ing *De triplici effusione aque facta a Cristo*, marginal in LT, introduced into text-space in mid sentence BC (IV. 2); *iminutione* (for *in minutione*) T *ininucione* BC, *potamur* LT *potamus* BC (IV. 17); *corrupit* LT *corripit* BC, *caro* LT om. BC (IV. 38); *conciliat* LT *consiliat* BC (IV. 49).

[1] Of these, seven are mere corrections of spelling or little more, and two are corrections of obvious dittographies in T. Some were probably automatic or unthinking, the result of reading what might have been expected in T when in fact T did not have it: so *uiuunt* LBC for *iniunt* T (III. 48); *Maris Rubri* LBC for *Maris Rubi* T (IV. 5); *separabitur* LBC where T in fact has *sepabitur*, having omitted the stroke through the de-scender of *p* (IV. 10); *fui* LBC for *sui* T (IV. 18). Slightly more significant are *ipso strato* LBC for *in ipso strato* T (III. 35), *sed* LBC for *si* T (III. 82), *uersatilem* LC *uersatilem* altered from *uersabilem* B for *uersabilem* T (III. 85), and two other instances shared with D (see pp. 79–80 below); but in each case the correction is obvious from the context.

[2] Doubtless because in T, in the contents-list of Parts I–III, the chapter-heading is in the left-hand column.

text is the one *before* it, not the one after. This is reasonably
clear in B, whose contents-list is more carefully written; each
heading and text is begun on a separate line with a coloured
initial capital (alternately red and blue), and the chapter-
number is written in the margin against the text. In C the
texts are written in red and the chapter-headings in black,
with a separate line (or lines) normally allowed for the latter;
but at the beginning of the contents-list for Part I, and
occasionally elsewhere, the scribe writes the heading (or
begins it) on the same line as the text, and in such cases
it is clear that, confused by the arrangement, he believed
that the heading following each text belonged with it. In such
combinations of text plus heading, therefore, the number
prefixed is right for the text but one too many for the heading. In the contents-list for Part IV he gets into worse trouble
still.[1] The obvious cause of his confusion was that he was
following an exemplar, direct or indirect, which used the
system more accurately reproduced by B.[2]

There is no reason to suppose that the scribe of either B or
C had any knowledge of L. When B and C, either jointly
or independently, correctly emend T's errors, they necessarily agree with L unless L itself is also corrupt at the same
point; but all the emendations are very minor and are obvious in the context, and there is no need at all to assume
consultation of a manuscript independent of T, whether L
or any other. In the test passages I have noticed only two
instances in which either B or C agrees in *error* with L against

[1] Here he puts the number 1 against his note 'Incipit quarta pars',
which is followed by the heading of chapter 1, and the number 2 against
the text 'Ante diem festum pasche . . .', which in fact is that of chapter 1;
and so on, the number prefixed to each text being one too many, though
right for the chapter-heading below the text.

[2] I think it possible, indeed probable (in view of the closeness of B and
C in date and the similarity of their texts), that each was a *direct* copy of
ε, but the point is not significant.

T. In II. 54, in the passage cited on p. 51 above, where for
*pacandum T has *paccandum* and L *peccandum*, BC also have
peccandum, but this must be a coincidence; ε has made the
same false 'emendation' of T's form as occurs in L. In III. 85,
in another passage discussed above (pp. 51–2), C omits the
half-sentence which T and B give (corruptly) as

quantumlibet enim et exilis scientia sufficit cum caritate ad promerendum regnum dei.

In C's case the omission, unless deliberate, was observably
due to homoeoteleuton, for we can see from T and B what the
C scribe had before him in his exemplar; the same omission
occurs in L, but there is no difficulty in assuming that it
happened independently in the two manuscripts. In I. 25, in
the passage mentioned on p. 61 above and quoted on p. 101
below, for *sibi, in necessariis* TB (in T by alteration), L has
in sibi necessariis and C has *in similibus necessariis*; but the
latter, though it resembles L in the placing of *in*, is not based
on L but is an independent attempt at an 'emendation' that
in fact was unnecessary. (The scribe of C had clearly lost the
run of the sentence, for he goes on with *subuenire pauperes* for
subueniret. Pauperes . . . LTB.) The only matter for serious
consideration is the presence in C of a subject-index (as in L)
as well as a table of contents (as in T). In C the index is
copied between Parts II and III, and is placed where the
scribe intended, as is shown by the quiring and his note at
the foot of f. 231^v. But no scribe would break off his job of
copying, between two parts of a work, to compile a subject-
index to the whole of it; C's index cannot have been compiled by the scribe himself, but must be a copy, as indeed
its whole appearance suggests. Presumably the C scribe
found it in his exemplar somewhere near the end of Part II
and decided to copy it between Parts II and III (especially as

Part II ended conveniently at the foot of a page).[1] But it is
not a copy, or even a recasting, of L's index, from which it
differs in arrangement,[2] layout, and content; it is an entirely new index, largely based on and probably suggested
by the 'index-headings' preserved in T, usually in the
margins, and obviously transmitted to T's descendants
(since they turn up in B and C themselves). The compiler
had little more to do than to copy out these 'index-headings'
and arrange them in alphabetical order. It is perhaps surprising that he took the trouble, but there is no reason to
believe that he was in any way influenced by L and its two
copies of a different index; indeed the fact that C's index is
both preceded and followed by notes calling it a 'tabula
super moralem tractatum . . . secundum ordinem quatuor
euuangelistarum' (or '. . . super quatuor euuangelistas') is
proof that it was made from T or a copy of T, for these
phrases come from T's heading (f. 7) to the text of the
Moralia,[3] which in C itself is replaced by a different heading
(as it probably also was in B, if the note on f. 1ᵛ of B essentially reproduces the heading of the lost first leaf of the
text).[4]

There remains the question of the type of manuscript used
in the 1420s by Alexander Carpenter,[5] who in his *Destruc-*

---

[1] The index must originally have been on a separate quire, which in
C's exemplar (or some earlier copy) had either been misplaced by the
binder or slipped in loose near the point where C copied it. Its absence
from B does not necessarily mean that it was absent from B's exemplar;
the scribe (Tielman Reynerszoon) may have decided or been instructed
to omit it, or may have intended to move it to the end of the book and have
forgotten it.

[2] L's index, even in its latter part, is not fully alphabetical in arrangement, since it takes account only of the initial letter of each main entry.
But C's index is in intention fully alphabetical, though there are many
errors (e.g. *Ypocrita* precedes *Ymago*).

[3] See the description of T, p. 41 above.

[4] See the descriptions of B and C, p. 44 above.

[5] On Carpenter, see G. R. Owst, *The* Destructorium Viciorum *of*

torium Viciorum[1] (which I denote D) repeatedly cites the *Moralia* as 'Linconiensis super Evangelia', usually with precise references to part and chapter.[2] I have searched to the end of Carpenter's Part V (i.e. somewhat less than three-fifths of the *Destructorium*) and have found twenty-two such references, involving the quotation of nineteen passages from the *Moralia* distributed, though unevenly, over all four of its parts;[3] and it is clear that the reason for Carpenter's interest

Alexander Carpenter (London, SPCK, 1952) and Emden, *BRUO*, i. 360. The surname 'Carpenter' is deduced from the colophon of the *Destructorium*, which says (in the version of MS. Balliol College 81, f. 391ᵛ) that he was 'fabri lignarii filius', but it has been impossible hitherto to identify an Alexander Carpenter in the records. MS. Peterhouse 41 (flyleaf, facing f. 1) calls him 'Filius Fabri de Oxon.' If the Latin phrases are translations of an English surname, it may have been Wrightson (or Woodwrightson, if such a name existed) rather than Carpenter; but this does not seem to help.

[1] I have used, primarily, the Cologne edition of 1485 (the second), but have compared it with the Balliol MS. (written in 1475). The differences between the two, in the passages quoted from the *Moralia*, are not great, and are seldom significant for the question of the type of text of the *Moralia* used by Carpenter. But in D IV. 62, in the quotation from *Moralia* II. 47, the Balliol MS. has the forms *adquisite*, *adquiruntur*, as in TB, where the 1485 edition normalizes to *acquisite*, *acquiruntur*, as in LC; and also in D IV. 62, in the quotation from *Moralia* III. 28, the 1485 edition has the corruption *nummum*, as in BC, where the Balliol MS. has *minimum*, as in LT (see further below). In D IV. 62, where the Balliol MS. has correctly *delectabiles* (as in the *Moralia*), the 1485 edition has *delectabile*. There is another (incomplete) text in MS. Peterhouse Cambridge 41.

[2] But a couple of the references are wrong, both in the Balliol MS. and the 1485 edition.

[3] These are, in the order of the text of the *Moralia*, as follows: (1) *Moralia* I. 37 quoted in D IV. 28 and (a little more fully) in D IV. 62; (2) I. 39, quoted in D IV. 62 (with a wrong reference to I. 37); (3) I. 59, quoted in D IV. 25; (4) I. 64, quoted in D IV. 11; (5) I. 69, quoted in D IV. 65, with a brief summary in D IV. 2 and a cross-reference in D VII. 11, in each case without chapter-reference to the *Moralia*; (6) a second passage from I. 69, quoted in D IV. 26; (7) a sentence from II. 34, quoted in D IV. 21; (8) II. 46, quoted in D V. 12; (9) a second, longer, passage from II. 46, quoted in D III. 9; (10) II. 47, quoted in D IV. 62;

is the attribution to Grosseteste, from whose other works,
undoubted or doubtful, he also often quotes.[1] The collation
of Carpenter's texts with the manuscripts of the *Moralia* is
complicated by his inability or unwillingness to quote accurately. In D IV. 62, despite a bland (and accurate) biblio-
graphical reference, he rearranges sentences culled from two
successive chapters of the *Moralia* (III. 28 and 29) into a
continuous passage with a line of argument which, though
it does not misrepresent the original author, he certainly did
not use in this form. In D IV. 2, retelling an *exemplum* from
Moralia III. 35, he diverges into a free paraphrase in which
the details of the story, as well as the words, are altered. Even
when he is quoting with comparative fidelity he frequently
alters the word-order or the grammar (commonly for the
worse), or substitutes synonyms, or omits or adds or alters
sentence-connectives; and he is always ready to rewrite a

(11) III. 17, quoted in D V. 2; (12) III. 22, quoted in D IV. 59; (13) and
(14), sentences from III. 28 and III. 29, quoted in rearranged order in D
IV. 62; (15) III. 35 (the passage pointed out by Miss Smalley), quoted or
paraphrased in D IV. 2, with a cross-reference in D IV. 57; (16) III. 73,
quoted in D V. 13; (17) III. 96, quoted in D IV. 20 (with wrong though
different chapter-references both in the Balliol MS. and in the 1485
edition); (18) IV. 7, quoted in D IV. 38; (19) two brief sentences from
IV. 28, quoted in D V. 2. The quotations vary greatly in length.

In D IV. 15 there is a brief quotation from 'Linconiensis', without
further reference, which I think may be from the *Moralia* but have failed
to identify.

[1] Up to the end of Part V of the *Destructorium*, there are quotations
from (1) the *Dicta*, in III. 10, IV. 2, 5, 8, 10, 22, 35, 62, V. 2, 10 (twice),
12, 21 (some of these quotations are very extensive); (2) *De Mandatis*,
in I. 3, III. 5, IV. 2; (3) *Sermons*, in IV. 2, 22 (twice), 59, 62 (twice); (4)
Epistolae, in IV. 9, 14 (twice), 21 (twice); (5) *Commentarius in Psalmos*, in
IV. 31; (6) 'In diuinis' (*De Divinis Nominibus*), IV. 57. Carpenter also
attributes to Grosseteste the *De Oculo Morali* (on which see Harrison
Thomson, op. cit., p. 256), from which he quotes in II. 7, IV. 2, 13
(twice), 51, V. 2 (thrice), 22 (twice), and the *De Venenis* (Thomson, pp.
268–70), quoted in II. 8, III. 5, 10, V. 2. Thomson allows neither of these
to Grosseteste.

sentence which he finds difficult (sometimes because it really was corrupt) or not to his taste.[1]

Nevertheless, it is clear that the manuscript which he used gave a text derived from T and closely related to the proximate common ancestor ϵ of B and C. There are, in the nineteen passages cited from the *Moralia* in Parts I–V of D, thirty-one instances in which D exactly follows T against L: thirteen when T is right, thirteen when it may be considered doubtful whether L or T preserves the original reading (though I should follow L in an edition), and five when T is in my judgement wrong. In addition there are eight instances in which, though D does not exactly agree with either L or T, its reading is plainly based on T's—thrice when T is right, five times when it is wrong. Some of the instances are minor variants (including variations of word-order) of no particular significance in themselves, but collectively the evidence is clear that there is a genetic relationship between D and T. Thus in *Moralia* III. 22, where L has *ualde molesta erat ei*, D agrees with T in reading *ualde erat ei grauis*; in III. 23, where L has *manifestatus*, TBCD have *manifestus*; and in I. 69, where L has *caro*, TBCD omit it (as is possible in the context). These are instances where either text may be right. But in III. 28, where L has the subjunctive *accipiat* in two successive and parallel sentences, T, followed by BCD, has *accipiat* in the first but the future *accipiet* in the second; in II. 46, where L has *tamen* (which is much more appropriate in the context), TBCD have *enim*; and in II. 47, where L has the correct spelling *spargi*, TBD have *spergi*, and C uses the

[1] In D IV. 62, trying to compress a sentence from *Moralia* III. 29, he produces a version (as given in both manuscripts and the 1485 edition) which lacks a principal clause. The fault cannot have been in his manuscript of the *Moralia*; BC give the sentence with only a variation of word-order, and Carpenter's version itself shows that he must have had the full text before him. The scribe (or a reader) of MS. Peterhouse 41 (f. 77ᵛ) marks with a caret the place where the omitted clause ought to be.

abbreviation which can be read as either -*per*- or -*par*-. The
most striking instances, however, are those in a passage from
III. 17 quoted in D V. 2. L's text of this passage is perfect,
and T''s mostly agrees, with two major exceptions. (i) For
L's *gregem sibi commissum* T has *gregem suum commissum*, but
an abbreviation for *sibi* has been written (certainly in a later
hand) above *suum* without deletion of the latter; D has *gregem
suum sibi commissum*, combining T's error with the correction. (ii) In the sentence which runs, in L's correct text,

Gladius autem, id est uindicta dei, extenditur . . . super oculum
eius *dextrum, non super oculum eius* sinistrum,

T omits, by eye-skip, the words italicized, and is exactly
followed by B and C. But Carpenter, who had cited the text
from Zacharias 11, 'Gladius domini . . . super oculum tuum
dextrum', immediately before his quotation from the
Moralia, recognized that the sentence as it had been left by
T's omission ('gladius . . . super oculum eius sinistrum') was
impossible, and to remove the discrepancy simply omitted
sinistrum.[1]

The evidence for D's relationship with BC is less plentiful.[2]
When all three follow T exactly they necessarily agree. BC, as
we have seen, share certain new errors and variations from T,

[1] It is fortunate that he did not replace it by *dextrum*, which would
have obscured his dependence on T's text.

[2] In the nineteen passages quoted by Carpenter in Parts I–V, there are
only nine certainly new errors or variations shared exactly by B and C,
plus two in B which must have stood in C's exemplar (see p. 80 n. 3
below), and a third where the difference is merely that C uses a suspension (*lu.*) where B has the full word (*luceat*); and there are only four correct
emendations shared by B and C of T's errors. The possibilities of D's
agreeing with them in a new variant or an emendation are therefore
limited, especially in view of Carpenter's propensity for rewriting (which
in fact removes one of the shared BC errors and two of the emendations).
I have not counted the instance discussed in p. 82 n. 1, since I am uncertain whether the error in BC is to be regarded as a new one or descended from T.

but only two occur also in D. One is not very significant: in III. 96, where LT write *lux perpetua etc.*, BD replace *etc.* by *luceat eis* and C by *lu. eis*. But in III. 28, for LT's correct *minimum*, BC have *nummum*, and so has D in the text of MS. Peterhouse 41 (f. 77ᵛ) and of the 1485 edition, which must represent Carpenter's intention.[1] The lack of further evidence of a BCD grouping by new errors is almost certainly due to emendation or chance variation by one or other of the three texts. Thus in I. 37, for LT's *uos*, BD have *nos* but C has *uos*, probably by emendation (unless the error is independent in B and D); in II. 46, for the name given by LT as *Oza*, BD have the spelling *Osa* but C reverts to *Oza*; in III. 22, for LT's *amodo* BD have *ammodo* but C again reverts to *amodo*. In III. 35, where LT have *cum domina colloquium*, D has *colloquium cum domina* and B *colloquium cum domino*, but C has the word-order of LT; probably C has changed back, but D and B may independently have varied from T. There are even cases in which two of the three fifteenth-century texts seem independently to emend: in I. 69, for L's correct *habent*,[2] TC have *habet* but both B and D have *habent*, and in II. 46, for L's correct *incarcerare*, TB have *in carcere* but both C and D have *incarcerare*. Chance variation accounts for the groupings *huiusmodi* LBD and *huiuscemodi* TC in III. 17. But there are two places in which BCD agree in an emendation of T's reading which brings them back into

---

[1] MS. Balliol 81 (f. 167) has *minimum*, with a hair-stroke over the first *i*. This is evidently a scribal emendation, based on the contrasting *maximum* of the next sentence. But Carpenter's copy of the *Moralia* must have had the false reading *nummum*, for his rearrangement of the order of the sentences taken from *Moralia* III. 27 and 28 depends on it.

[2] The subject of the verb, in the original text, is *huiusmodi* used as an equivalent of *tales*; T's *habet* is probably due to misunderstanding of the syntax. D, in addition to emending to *habent*, also rewrites to bring in *tales* as its subject and to change the function of *huiusmodi* ('ut qui rapit ... uel superbit et huiusmodi sed tales non habent ...', in which *sed tales* is an addition not found in B and C).

conformity with L: in I. 39 they supply a necessary *sunt* after *peiores* where T had omitted it, and in IV. 48, where T has *accensus*, BCD have *accessus* as in L. These two shared emendations, though obvious enough, may be added to the two shared variations from T (one an error) as evidence, however slight, that Carpenter's text of the *Moralia* was not independently descended from T (which in any case would be improbable) but was related to the common ancestor ϵ of B and C.[1] It was, however, not identical with ϵ nor dependent on it, but was either a slightly earlier manuscript δ from which ϵ descended or a copy of δ independent of ϵ; for there are eight places where D avoids an error or innovation introduced by ϵ, six where B and C share the reading,[2] and two others where the exemplar used by C must have had the same false reading as is given by B, though the C scribe at the last moment corrected it.[3] A further example of a difference between D and ϵ is in III. 17, where D, as we have seen, has *gregem suum sibi commissum*, combining T's original *suum* with the correction *sibi*, but BC have T's original reading, *gregem suum commissum*; either the scribe of ϵ jibbed at the tautologous *suum sibi* and copied only the first word, or δ had exactly reproduced the appearance of T as corrected, with *sibi* above *suum*, leaving D free to combine the alternatives and ϵ to ignore the correction.

[1] D agrees with BC in two of the eleven new variants, and in both the correct emendations, that remain as possibilities after Carpenter's rewriting is taken into account; see p. 78 n. 2 above. Though the numbers are small, the proportion is high.

[2] In I. 39, *saltem* BC for *salutem* LTD; in II. 34, *commedit* BC for *comedit* LTD and *uel* BC for *nec* LT, *nec tamen* D; in III. 22, *erat ualde ei grauis* BC for *ualde erat ei grauis* TD (*ualde molesta erat ei* L); in III. 29, *pauperum id est spiritu humilium* BC for *pauperum spiritu id est humilium* LTD; and in III. 35, BC omit *matrone deueniens ad hostium* LTD.

[3] In III. 35, for *domina* (ablative) LTD, B has *domino* and C *domina* by alteration (perhaps from *domino*), and for *domine* (dative) LTD, in the next sentence, B has *domino* and C *domine* by alteration (certainly from *domino*).

The conclusion that Carpenter's text was descended from T is unaffected by the fact that occasionally he agrees with L against T. Five of these agreements, in the passages examined, are the coincidental result of his alterations to word-order or wording or sentence-connectives; when L and T agree, these alterations are shown up as Carpenter's innovations, but when they differ it is not surprising that he should occasionally, in varying from T, hit upon L's reading, for the possibilities of variation are limited.[1] More frequent (nine instances in the passages examined) are cases in which D emends an obviously faulty reading derived from T and recovers exactly the true reading as given by L. Most of these emendations are very simple and are clearly required by the context.[2] In *Moralia* III. 28, where there are two parallel sentences including (in L's text) the phrase *qui tecum accepturus est* in the first and *qui tecum recepturus est* in the second, TBC omit *tecum* in the latter; D restores it, obviously because of the parallelism, for he also alters *recepturus* (on which LTBC agree) to *accepturus*. In IV. 7, where for L's *Quo inspecto* TBC have *Quo inscripto*, D restores *Quo inspecto*, a perceptive emendation but one essential to the immediate context; moreover, the previous sentence includes the verb *inspiceretur*. A characteristic instance is in III. 96, in the phrase (as given by L) *Credibile est dominum sic responsurum*, where for *sic* TC have *sic et* and B *et sic* (attempting to

---

[1] The instances are: (*a*) variations of word-order: *hunc locum* LD *locum hunc* TBC (I. 39), *dicit tibi* LD *tibi dicit* TBC (III. 29); (*b*) substitution of synonyms: *totis uisceribus* LD *cunctis uisceribus* TBC (III. 35), *sibi prepararet* LD *ipsi prepararet* TBC (also III. 35); (*c*) omission or insertion of connective: *sanctificatus ... inuitatus* LD, *sanctificatus et ... inuitatus* TBC (II. 46); *cum enim dies breues* LD *cum dies breues* TBC. It is in each case immaterial whether L or T represents the original.

[2] So *spiritualis* (gen. sg.) LD *spirituali* TBC (I. 37); *incarcerare* LCD *in carcere* TB (II. 46); *aqua* LD *qua* TBC, *sic uana gloria* LD *sic ut uana gloria* TB (*sic et ... C*), *per deum* LD (required by the sense) *ad deum* TBC, *longe ... dies* (plural) LD *longi ... dies* TBC (all II. 47).

emend?), but Carpenter, simply dropping the *et*, gets back
to L's reading.[1] Against these places where Carpenter successfully emends his text must be set others in which he fails
to detect an error derived from T or else, detecting one, he
fails to recover the original text as given by L. An instance
is that already cited from *Moralia* III. 17 where, to mitigate
the consequences of a damaging omission in TBC, he makes
a further omission, of the word *sinistrum*. In IV. 7, where L
has the noun-clause *quod ydolis sacrificare non possum* but
TBC omit the conjunction *quod*, he supplies *vt*. In III. 73,
in a passage which should run

Factus enim amicus diaboli per peccatum, si reuelaueris tibi ab eo
latenter suggestum, reuelaueris qui, siquidem [confidendo], de
cetero tibi secretum suum non communicabit cogitationes [im-
mittendo]

(i.e. '. . . you will have revealed one who thereafter will not
—at least with confidence—make known his secret to you
by implanting thoughts [in your mind]'), both L and T have
confitendo for *confidendo* and *imitando* for *immittendo*, and T
(followed by BC) further inserts *si* before the second *reuelaueris* and omits *qui* after it. Carpenter cuts through the
difficulty by reading

. . . si reuelaueris tibi ab eo latenter suggestum *veraciter confitendo*,
de cetero tibi secretum suum non communicabit cogitationes
malas immittendo,

[1] To these instances should probably be added another, in III. 73,
where the *Moralia* quotes Jerome. The name is abbreviated in all the
manuscripts. L has *ier* plus the abbreviation for *-us*; this may be taken
as an abbreviation for *ieronymus*. T has *ier* with an ambiguous mark of
suspension over the *r*, and may perhaps be given the benefit of the doubt,
though I think the scribe meant *ieremias*. But C has *Ie* with a mark of
suspension, which is properly an abbreviation for *Ieremias*, and B has
Ierem', which is undoubtedly for *Ieremias*. D, however, has *iherom'*; he
has certainly avoided the BC error, and has probably emended one
descended from or caused by T.

but the first phrase italicized is rewriting not emendation and involves the acceptance of the false *confitendo*. Carpenter does not in fact limit his attempts at emendation to corruptions originating in T; he also notices errors shared by L and T and derived from their common exemplar, but in only one instance (*immittendo* for *imitando* LTBC in the sentence last cited) does he achieve a fully satisfactory emendation (also made by a corrector of L, without Carpenter's addition of *malas*) and in three he is reduced to rewriting the sentence concerned to recover the general sense intended.[1] Moreover, there are shared errors of L and T which he does not notice,[2] and in another place he makes a 'correction' that is both unnecessary and false.[3] My conclusion is that he did not have access to L or any manuscript derived from L, still less to a superior manuscript independent of both L and T; his emendations, successful or unsuccessful, are purely conjectural. He was not a mere copyist, laboriously transcribing a long and sometimes difficult text, but a learned and well-trained independent author, quoting selectively, able to scrutinize carefully the text of the passages chosen, and always willing to alter or rewrite anything which seemed to him unsatisfactory.

Apart from the emendations in the fifteenth-century texts, the evidence is unusually clear and uncomplicated—much more so than would be expected in a vernacular text whose history had extended over more than two centuries. There is no real suggestion of any contamination of the tradition, even in the fifteenth century, since the cross-agreements of B, C, and D may all be satisfactorily explained as the results either of emendation or of independent variation. The relations of

---

[1] See pp. 49–50 above.   [2] See pp. 50–1 above.

[3] In III. 96 LTBC have *ista* neuter plural referring back (as is legitimate) to two feminine nouns denoting inanimate objects, *lucem et requiem*. Carpenter 'emends' to *iste* (i.e. *istae*), but the accusative is required.

the copies, as revealed by the internal textual evidence alone, may be expressed by the *stemma codicum* given below, in which X represents the archetype (in this case presumably identifiable with the author's holograph), α an early copy used by the author of *Ancrene Wisse*, β another early copy which introduced errors and must in particular be assumed to explain the complex corruption of **alit* into *huic*,[1] γ a copy of β of which only the index (Index A in L) by chance survives, δ a copy or descendant of T, either itself used by Carpenter or the direct antecedent of his manuscript, and ε a copy or descendant of δ from which B and C derive.

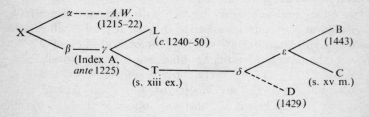

The textual relations thus depicted agree well with the probabilities to be deduced from the dates. *Ancrene Wisse* in my view is to be dated between 1215 and 1222 and Index A of L (and therefore γ) to the first quarter of the thirteenth century; L belongs to the end of the second quarter, and T to the end of the last. By 1300 there were at least five copies of the *Moralia* besides the holograph, of which two and the index of a third survive; nevertheless, the work does not seem to have been widely known, and in the fourteenth century, from which no copies survive and in which there is no indication of any copying, it had obviously lapsed into obscurity.[2] But

---

[1] See pp. 52–4 above.

[2] As assumed by Miss Smalley, *Robert Grosseteste*, p. 74, who says that 'The lack of both quotations and manuscripts from the fourteenth century suggests a long period of neglect' before 'a post-Wyclif cult of

at the end of the century or, more probably, during the first twenty years of the fifteenth, when the Wycliffite movement had led to a renewed interest in Grosseteste's writings, a copy or descendant of the Tewkesbury manuscript T, which attributed the *Moralia* to him, was brought to Oxford, where it (or a copy made from it) was used by Alexander Carpenter in writing his *Destructorium Viciorum*, between *c.* 1425 and 1429.[1] About the same time there was also made from it the lost copy ε, to become in turn the exemplar, direct or indirect, of the surviving manuscripts B (finished in April 1443) and C (written about the mid century). B's Oxford connections are clear, since it was commissioned by a former chancellor of the university and given by him to Balliol College; and though C has long been a Cambridge manuscript, it too probably originated in Oxford. But there is no sign that any of this group of Oxford scholars and scribes had any knowledge of L; it was not given to Lincoln College until after 1452.

Grosseteste, which led to a revival of interest in his lesser-known commentaries'.

[1] See Owst, op. cit., p. 6. The note at the end of the *Destructorium*, properly construed, means that it was finished (not started, as stated by R. Lane Poole in *DNB*, ix. 153) in 1429. In D V. 12, about half-way through, there is a reference to the date of the current year as 1426 (so MS. Balliol 81, f. 201ᵛ) or 1428 (so MS. Peterhouse 41, f. 97), though both are later; the difference between the two must be due to copying-error, not to deliberate revision in the Peterhouse MS., as Owst seems to assume. If the Balliol MS. is right, the latter half of the *Destructorium* took three years to write, and at this rate it may be calculated that it was begun about 1423; if the Peterhouse MS. is right, it may have been begun about 1427, though it is doubtful whether so enormous a book could have been written in two years. Splitting the difference, one might estimate that it was begun 'about 1425'. The first quotation from the *Moralia* is in D III. 9.

That Carpenter was an Oxford man rests only on the statement of the Peterhouse MS. that he was 'de Oxon.', but it is very probable. G. Powell, *Disputationum de Antichristo Libri ii* (1605), says that he was a fellow of Balliol, but there is no confirmation of this.

IV

ALEXANDER OF BATH

IT follows, from the preceding discussion, that there are only two independent witnesses to the text of the *Moralia*, the thirteenth-century manuscripts L and T; an editor, having established the dependence of B, C, and Carpenter's lost manuscript on T, would bother no further with their readings and would know that his text must be constructed from the evidence of L and T alone. But equally B, C, and Carpenter are not admissible witnesses to the authorship; they say that the *Moralia* was by Grosseteste only because T told them so. There are only two surviving independent witnesses to the authorship and the original title: L, which says that the work is *Moralia magistri Alexandri de Ba super ewangelia*, and T, which calls it *Omili[e] . . . super hystoriam euuangelicam* and *Moralis tractatus secundum ordinem quatuor euangelistarum* and says it is by Robert Grosseteste bishop of Lincoln. There is every reason why L's evidence should be preferred. It is the earlier manuscript by about half a century, written during Grosseteste's life and probably after he had become bishop, and it is based on an exemplar belonging, if Index A is rightly dated, to the first quarter of the century; T, though based on the same exemplar, was written at least a generation after Grosseteste's death. L's rubric giving the ascription is in the hand of the text-scribe and there is nothing to suggest that he did not write it as he began to make his copy; the only thing to distinguish it from L's other headings and subheadings, which were certainly derived from its exemplar (as they agree with T's), is that it is the only marginal entry written by the text-scribe in red—but its exceptional nature would account for that. In its place T has, within the text-space above the introduction, the heading *Moralis tractatus . . . euangelistarum* cited above, which has the appearance of a scribal substitute for L's rubric; it is partly suggested by the opening words of the introduction, 'Intentioni quatuor euangelistarum', and if it is intended to mean that the *Moralia* follows the order of the four gospels it is wrong, for in fact it follows a gospel harmony which conflates them and its division into four parts does not correspond to texts taken from Matthew, Mark, Luke, and John respectively. It may be significant that this heading, written when the scribe was beginning his work, says nothing about the authorship; the ascription to Grosseteste comes (twice) in the prefixed quire of introductory matter, which was written last and never completed by the original scribe and which contains material (title-page and table of contents) not derived from the exemplar but made up presumably by Thomas of London himself. It is almost as if his willingness to assert that the work which he had acquired was by Grosseteste had become stronger after he had finished with, and presumably returned, the exemplar, which, if it is faithfully copied by L, contained a rubric which conflicted with his claim. But even if L's rubric did not come from the exemplar but was added by the scribe of L himself, he was still writing in Grosseteste's lifetime; he was in a much better position to know than Thomas of London at the end of the century.

There is in any case one overriding reason for preferring L's ascription. Harrison Thomson, in his text,[1] says that L is 'unasc[ribed]', by which, rather oddly, he must here mean 'not ascribed to Grosseteste', and in his footnote deals very offhandedly with the original scribe's rubric, saying that he

[1] Op. cit., p. 135.

'adds to our confusion' and that Alexander de Ba 'remains unidentified'. But this is just why he should have taken the ascription seriously. Every textual critic knows the doctrine that the more difficult reading is to be preferred (or, as some would rather put it, the more obvious reading is to be distrusted); and the same applies even more clearly to ascriptions. No scribe in his right mind is going to substitute an ascription to an 'unidentifiable' author for one to a famous scholar, especially if he is writing at a time when the famous scholar is one of the leading bishops of England; but at all times, and especially perhaps in the Middle Ages, men have been very willing to attribute works by obscure or anonymous authors to famous writers.[1] *Arden of Feversham* has been ascribed to Shakespeare on no other real ground than that it shows dramatic talent, despite the great differences of style. In literature as in other spheres, to him that hath is given; and it is the business of literary scholarship to see that not too much is given. Thomas of London probably had no more idea than Professor Thomson who 'Alexander de Ba' was, and had as little compunction in dismissing his claim. I prefer to accept the 'difficult' evidence of the earlier and better manuscript, and to try to identify Master Alexander.

Ba must seem an improbable English place-name, and indeed it is not strictly English at all; it is Anglo-Norman, a form of *Bath* developed by purely Anglo-Norman, and not English, phonetic processes. Its starting-point is the late Old English (eleventh-century) pronunciation /baðə/, represented

---

[1] Thomson himself (op. cit., pp. 268–9), discussing the attributions of the *De Venenis*, says that 'any ascription at all to a relatively obscure person, provided that it has intrinsic probability, has great weight', even though in this case the ascriptions to the 'relatively obscure person' (Malachias de Hibernia) are not 'demonstrably older than the oldest ascription to Grosseteste'. The same applies, *a fortiori*, to the *Moralia*, since in its case the ascription to 'Alexander de Ba', though Thomson failed to realize it, is 'demonstrably older' that that to Grosseteste.

by the Doomsday Book spelling *Bade* (with the early Old French and Anglo-Norman use of *d* for /ð/). But during the earlier twelfth century intervocalic /ð/ became silent in Anglo-Norman,[1] which would leave /baə/, and in the later twelfth century final unstressed /ə/, in hiatus with a preceding vowel, was lost,[2] which would leave /ba/, spelt either *Ba* or *Baa* (the latter perhaps to indicate lengthening of the tonic vowel when the /ə/ was absorbed). *Ba* is recorded for the place-name itself in 1200,[3] 1204,[4] and later, and the variant *Baa* in 1210.[5] It was still in use in the later fourteenth century; an example which suggests the Anglo-Norman status of the form is the reference to an ancient chantry in the church of St. Mary de Stalles in Bath called 'la comune chanterie de Baa'.[6] In personal names *Ba* is found a little earlier than as an explicit place-name: *Thomas de Ba* in 1195 (varying with *Tomas de Bath'* and *Tomas de Bada*);[7] *Reginaldus de Ba* in 1194–5,[8] apparently the same man as *Reginaldus de Bathon'*, who occurs in 1203;[9] and Gilbert and Henry *de Ba* (otherwise *Baa* and *Bad*) about 1200.[10] Among later instances is *Galfridus de Ba*, otherwise *Galfridus de Bathon'*, in 1237.[11] As in the cases of Gilbert and Henry, *Baa* occurs as a variant to *Ba* in personal names; the *Geruasius de Ba* of 1208[12] is *Geruasius de Baa* (or *Bâa*) in 1209 and 1210.[13] But *Ba* (*Baa*)

---

[1] M. K. Pope, *From Latin to Modern French* (Manchester, 1934), §§ 1175–6.   [2] Ibid., § 1133.   [3] *Pipe R. 2 John*, p. 93.

[4] *Pipe R. 6 John*, p. 177.   [5] *Pipe R. 12 John*, p. 71.

[6] *Cal. Pat. R. 1354–8*, p. 208 (1 May 1355).

[7] *Pipe R. 7 Ric. I*, p. 78; cf. *Pipe R. 8 Ric. I*, p. 136, *9 Ric. I*, pp. 236, 244, *10 Ric. I*, pp. 84, 90, *1 John*, p. 268.

[8] *Rot. Cur. R.* in Pipe Roll Soc. xiv, p. 120.

[9] *Pipe R. 5 John*, p. 96.

[10] *Registrum Antiquissimum of the Cathedral Church of Lincoln* (Lincoln Record Soc. xxvii, etc., 1931–68), iv. 3–5, 193 (four documents, three dated 'c. 1200', the fourth 1192–1205).

[11] *Cartae Antiquae* in Pipe Roll Soc. N.S. xvii, no. 31 (pp. 15–16).

[12] *Pipe R. 10 John*, p. 110.

[13] *Pipe R. 11 John*, p. 100; *12 John*, p. 72.

never occurs in the numerous extant Pipe Rolls of Henry II, which suggests that the form, though well established after 1195 and probably known before that date,[1] was of comparatively recent development, as one would expect from the chronology of the sound-changes involved.

When, therefore, the original scribe of L, towards the middle of the thirteenth century, wrote 'Alexander de Ba', he must certainly have meant Alexander of Bath, and so would the scribe of any earlier thirteenth-century manuscript from which the rubric was derived. But on the blank page (f. 10^v) facing the rubric in L there is pasted the slip of parchment which, before recording that the manuscript was the gift of Robert Flemmyng, dean of Lincoln from 1452 to 1483, gives the title of its first item as 'Moralia Magistri Alexandri Necham super euangelia'. This note, being so late, lacks evident authority, but as it might perhaps depend on some independent tradition its ascription, which chronologically is possible, must be tested. As names were evidently abbreviated in the original of the *Moralia*,[2] it is conceivable, though unlikely, that *de Ba* in L might be a copying error for *de B.A.*, meaning *de Beato Albano* 'of St. Albans' (especially as the *Moralia* much more often uses *beatus* than *sanctus* for 'Saint'); but the recorded form of the place-name is *de Sancto Albano*, as in the colophons of the *De Naturis Rerum* themselves.[3] It is possible to see some points of resemblance between the style, both in prose and verse, of the author of the *Moralia* and of Nequam (in particular, their liking, in prose, for exclamations, especially *Proch dolor*, and in verse, for running on the sense after a strong caesura near the end of the line);

---

[1] *Walterius (Galterius) de Ba* is mentioned in letters dated February 1188 and October 1189 (*Epistolae Cantuarienses*, ed. W. Stubbs (Rolls Series, London, 1865), pp. 169, 312), but the collection is believed to have been assembled between 1201 and 1205 (p. xi) and the form might be due to the copyist.

[2] See p. 54 above.   [3] See Wright's edition, p. 1, n. 1.

and the author of the *Moralia* had an evident talent for
Latin verse-composition, as Nequam certainly had. But
Nequam's Latin style, both in prose and verse, is altogether
more accomplished. Moreover, though Nequam has frequent
citations of verse in his prose works, they are mostly from
classical authors, and he does not cite verses of his own composition,[1] whereas most of the verses in the *Moralia* seem
to be its author's own; and the *Moralia* does not begin to
display Nequam's remarkable knowledge of classical poets—
indeed the only classical author that I have noticed it quoting
is Seneca (II. 11 and III. 69). Both authors make frequent
use of the absurd medieval 'etymologies' of Latin and other
words, but in this they are only reflecting the scholastic
method of their time; equally conventional is the discussion
of the rivers of Paradise in *Moralia* III. 58, which has resemblances not only to *De Naturis Rerum* II. 2 but also to the
preface of Nequam's commentary on the Psalter, especially
to the 'interpretations' of the names in the latter. In general,
however, the *Moralia* makes very much more use of *interpretationes nominum hebraicorum* than Nequam does. But the
most obvious resemblance is the interest of both authors
in birds, beasts, and precious stones and their real or legen-
dary characteristics and qualities—with this difference, that
Nequam often merely describes them, and that the author
of the *Moralia*, truer to the medieval tradition, regularly gives
them a 'spiritual' interpretation. There are many resemblances, but also some differences: thus both authors tell
how the eagle, to counteract its own excessive heat, places
the jet (*gagates*) among its eggs,[2] but only the *Moralia* also

---

[1] Admittedly two chapters (I. 11–12, pp. 48–9 in Wright's edition) of
the *De Naturis Rerum* are in verse, and it also includes rare examples
of unascribed verse-citations; but even these do not seem to be his own.
In any case his chosen metre is the elegiac, not the pure hexameters used in
the *Moralia*.

[2] *De Nat. R.* I. 23 (p. 71); *Moralia* I. 77.

tells how it puts in its nest the *echites* to keep off noxious creatures.[1] The material in the two books is derived from a common tradition, the medieval bestiaries and lapidaries, and many of the parallels between them may be sufficiently so explained; nevertheless they are sometimes so alike[2] that it is hard to avoid the conclusion that the author of the *Moralia* had read, and was paraphrasing and 'moralizing', the *De Naturis Rerum*. But it is in this feature, where they come closest, that they also differ most significantly. Dr. R. W. Hunt has pointed out to me that Nequam, when in one of his works he makes use of material that he has already used in another, does so succinctly and with a cross-reference;[3] but though the use in the *Moralia* of matter which also occurs in the *De Naturis Rerum* gave ample and repeated occasion for such cross-references, there is never a single one.[4] One must conclude that though the author of the *Moralia* had probably read, and been influenced by, the *De Naturis Rerum*, he was certainly not Nequam himself. The fifteenth-century ascription of the pasted-in slip in L is a mere guess,

[1] See p. 59 above.

[2] Both compare the *struthio* (ostrich) to a hypocrite (*De Nat. R.* I. 50 (p. 101), *Moralia* III. 82 (cited on p. 47 above)), and both say that bitumen can be dissolved by menstrual blood (*De Nat. R.* II. 156 (p. 252), *Moralia* III. 84). But the most obvious parallel, it seems to me, is in their discussion of the barnacle-goose. The *Moralia* (IV. 9) says:

'Primo incarnationi scilicet attestantur aues quedam que gallice bernaches dicuntur. Aues enim proposite sine seminali materia que ex coitu eliciatur [eiciatur T] ab arboribus ortum contrahunt.'

This is very similar to *De Nat. R.* I. 48 (pp. 99–100), with its reference, in the chapter-heading and the first sentence, to the 'avis quæ vulgo dicitur bernekke'; but Nequam does not draw a parallel, as the *Moralia* explicitly does, with the conception of Christ 'sine semine uirili'.

[3] So *De Nat. R.* I. 2 (p. 16), with references to Nequam's *Solatium Fidelis Animæ* and *Corrogationes Promethei*, and II. 2 (p. 128), with a vaguer reference to 'alibi in opusculis nostris'.

[4] The *Moralia* has cross-reference to other chapters within itself, but none to distinct works by the same author.

possibly due in part to a recognition of some affinity in thought and method between the *Moralia* and Nequam's undoubted works, but probably based primarily, or even entirely, on the Christian name alone.

Two others of the literary connections of the *Moralia* require discussion and also illustration (since the texts are unprinted). There is much in its author's methods—especially his similitudes and *exempla*, his use of verses to summarize or illustrate a discussion, and his practice of explaining these verses by interlined or appended notes—to suggest the influence of William de Montibus (or de Monte) of Lincoln.[1] William was a well-known theologian whose pupils included Alexander Nequam[2] and Gerald of Wales. Born in a suburb of Lincoln (it is guessed about 1140), he studied and taught in Paris, but was brought back to Lincoln by St. Hugh shortly after 1186; he was a canon there by 1189, and chancellor from about 1191 until his death in Scotland in 1213, about Easter. Under him, in Gerald's opinion, the school of Lincoln became the best in England for theology. His *Versarius*, written 'not later than the early years of the thirteenth century', is a didactic work in which the verses (hexameters, like the *Moralia*'s), though sometimes themselves the vehicle for instruction, are commonly for mnemonic purposes but are 'generously glossed', the glosses then serving to impart the teaching;[3] his *Similitudinarius* is

[1] On William, see J. C. Russell, *A Dictionary of Writers in Thirteenth-Century England* (London, 1936), pp. 196–7, and (better) H. MacKinnon, 'William de Montibus: a medieval teacher', in *Essays in Medieval History presented to B. Wilkinson*, ed. T. A. Sandquist and M. R. Powicke (Toronto, 1969), pp. 32–45. MacKinnon's article is based on his unpublished Oxford dissertation, 'The Life and Works of William de Montibus' (1959), which I have also consulted.

[2] So Russell, op. cit., p. 196, who cites as evidence Nequam's encomium of William in *De Laudibus Divinæ Sapientiæ*, ll. 835–48 (ed. Wright, Rolls Series, p. 460).

[3] MacKinnon, art. cit., pp. 39–40.

a collection of similitudes and *exempla* under headings which, in the earlier part of the work, are arranged alphabetically. Now the later (alphabetical) part of the subject-index in the Lincoln College manuscript of the *Moralia* largely consists of entries listing material objects, animals, birds, etc. used in the course of the work as the basis of similitudes, and its headings often bear a remarkable resemblance to those of the *Similitudinarius*, which (or William's general liking for alphabetical arrangement) may well have provided a model for the index of the *Moralia*. This is the more likely because the two works have material in common. In the earlier (alphabetically arranged) part of the *Similitudinarius*, under 'Beneficium',[1] there is the brief similitude

Qui autem uerbis diligunt et non factis, sambuco similes sunt, que florem profert elegantem sed fructum degenerem,

and in the later (non-alphabetical) part, under 'Perseuerancia',[2] a slightly longer version:

Nolite similes esse sambuco que florem elegantem et uenustum et sapidum emittit, sed postea in fructu degenerat. Sic quidam sunt qui felicia habent inicia sed in fine degenerant, dulciter preponunt sed amara est ipsorum conclusio.

The *Moralia* (III. 10) applies the same material differently:

Unde mundana prosperitas congrue comparatur sambuco, que flores germinat speciosos, suauis odoris et ualentes ad cibum, fructus autem eius uilis est et immundus. Sic mundus florem habet speciosum et germinat messem infelicem et sordidam.

In the earlier part, under 'Tribulacio',[3] the *Similitudinarius* gives the passage

Nec miles equum odio habet quem calcaribus urget, nec faber

---

[1] MS. Peterhouse Cambridge 255, f. 85; cf. MS. Bodley Add. C. 263, f. 98.   [2] Peterhouse MS., f. 104.
[3] Peterhouse MS., f. 97ᵛ; cf. Bodleian MS., f. 109.

ferrum quod malleo contundit, nec uinitor uuam uel fullo pannum quem pedibus conculcat,[1] nec pelliparius pellem quam uirga percutit. Ita nec deus odit quem flagello corripit, sed proficere facit.

The *Moralia* (III. 36) has a version only slightly different:

Miles equum quem pungit, faber ferrum quod tundit, fullo pannum quem calcat, permentarius pellem quam percutit, vinitor uuam quam calcat, non odit. Sic nec Cristus quos cruciatibus exponit odio habet.

In these two instances it may be doubtful which of the works has priority (though in the second it is my impression that the *Moralia* is altering the text of the *Similitudinarius*, to the detriment of the sentence-construction), but in a third there can be no doubt. In the earlier part, under 'Peccata', the *Similitudinarius* has a passage which in the Peterhouse MS. (f. 94^v) reads:

Qui plurima peccata habet, si omnia dimittat preter unum, similis est illi qui, ligatus multis cathenis, omnes preter unum rumpit et tamen illa sola ad ligandum sufficit. Similis est nauiganti qui habet multa foramina in naui et omnia obturat preter unum; per istud aqua subintrat et ad ima deducit. Similis est etiam illi qui habet multas sagittas in corpore; si, aliis extractis, una sola remaneat, illa sola est causa mortis.

The third of these similitudes involves the ridiculous supposition that, though all the other arrows were removed, one might be left sticking in the poor man at the cost of his life.[2] This is avoided in a parallel passage in the *Moralia* (I. 43):

Qui enim omnia [*sc.* peccata sua] uno excepto confitetur, homini

[1] So Peterhouse MS., but *calcat* Bodleian MS.
[2] The version in the Bodleian MS. (f. 107^v) is briefer and seems to be a summary, but is identical in substance. The last sentence, however, is even more absurd in the Bodleian version: 'Item similis est uulnerato multis sagittis qui omnes *extrahit* et un[a]m tantum reliqui[t], que ipsum ad mortem deducit.' Here the man himself leaves one arrow sticking in.

assimulandus est, multis cathenis astricto, cui omnia uincula soluuntur preter unum, quod ad ipsum sufficit retinendum. Similis est naui in pluribus locis perforate, quorum singula obstruuntur, uno foramine superstite, per quod nauis periclitari potest. Similis etiam est homini pluribus uulneribus sauciato, quorum, singulis curatis, unum restat incuratum, quod ad hominis sufficit interemptionem.

No one who had seen this credible version would turn it into the other, and it is this which *Ancrene Wisse* follows (though it puts the blame on the wounded man, appropriately in view of the parallel with the sinner who fails to confess, by saying that he shows the physician all his wounds except one).[1] Though William de Montibus is known to have included extracts from other men's works in his compilations, we must I think acquit him of having excerpted the *Moralia*; the debt, if direct, is the other way round. Unfortunately the *Similitudinarius* is not exactly dated, and was probably compiled over a period;[2] but it must belong to the time after William's

---

[1] *Ancrene Wisse* f. 85b/19–22. Its further improvement on the *Moralia* is due to an influence from one of Langton's sermons; see p. 4, n. 3 above.

It is a matter for investigation whether the author of *Ancrene Wisse* may have had direct knowledge of the *Similitudinarius*, for there are possible parallels. So *Similitudinarius*, under 'Prelatus' (Peterhouse MS., f. 92),

'Quanto maior honor, tanto maiora pericula. Alta arbor a uento forcius agitatur, et rami eius cicius in ruinam constringuntur; excelse turres grauiori casu procumbunt, altissimi montes crebro fulguribus feriuntur',

which resembles *Ancrene Wisse* f. 47b/21 ff. (the beginning of Part IV) and f. 58b/21–3; and *Similitudinarius*, under 'Protectio dei' (Peterhouse MS., f. 103ᵛ),

'Scutum est protectio dei, in temporalibus angustum, in superioribus (id est, in celestibus) dilatatum',

which involves the same basis of comparison (a shield's width at the top and narrowness at the bottom) as *Ancrene Wisse* f. 106a/1–3, though very differently applied.

[2] The second, non-alphabetical, part is believed to consist of material added later.

return to Lincoln, for the manuscripts are English, it includes extracts from Nequam's sermons,[1] and it has now also been shown that extracts from Stephen Langton's sermons are included in the latter part,[2] so that it is probably later than 1190 and may be later than 1200.

The *Moralia* is also indebted to Langton's sermons. One parallel has already been noticed—the use made by Langton and the *Moralia* of the saying that a bounteous man has holes in his hands (*manus perforatas*).[3] The French setting of Langton's sermons is revealed by his use of *exempla* and similitudes beginning with such formulae as 'Si rex Francie';[4] the *Moralia* seems almost deliberately to counter this by *exempla* based on English customs and beginning 'Si rex Anglie'.[5] The *Moralia*'s view that the rainbow's colours are 'principally' or 'almost' two[6] corresponds to an unqualified statement in Langton:

... ex repercussione solis a nuba aquosa provenit yris, et notandum quia in arcu duo sunt colores, igneus et aquosus,[7]

though the application of the similitude is different in Langton from either of those in the *Moralia* (II. 23 and II. 57). Langton compares the life of man to a ship, narrow at the prow (*prora*) and the stern (*puppa*), wide in the hold (*carina*);[8] this is paralleled in *Moralia* II. 40,

Navis igitur uita hominis est que, naui materiali conformis, principium et finem angusta habet et ardua ... Carina, que

---

[1] MacKinnon, art. cit., pp. 36–7. [2] Roberts, *Studies*, pp. 92–4.
[3] See above, pp. 3–4. [4] Roberts, pp. 71–2.
[5] See below, p. 101. [6] See above, p. 32.
[7] Quoted more fully by Roberts, p. 106.
[8] Roberts, p. 116 and n. 38, who translates *carina*, following the classical sense, as 'keel'; but the keel of a ship is not wide. See *OED*, s.v. *holl*, sense 2, for fifteenth-century glosses of *carina* as *holl*, i.e. 'hold'. The continuation shows that Langton means the middle of the ship where the cargo is carried. Cf. also the entry '*Carina* medium navis' in Papias, *Vocabularium* (completed in or shortly after 1053).

spaciosa est et lata, medium tempus hominis significat quo homo
ad libitum se habet . . . ,

and by verses at the end of the chapter, which include the
lines

> Sit tibi sentina puppis pars ultima uite,
> Prora prior, medium tempus spaciosa carina.

The last line of this verse-passage,

> Sermo dei regimen, Hel[1] rector, stella Maria,

may perhaps owe something to another of Langton's similitudes, in which those navigating the perilous sea of this
world are said to need as their guiding star Maria, whose
name signifies 'maris stella'.[2] More striking is an extended
exemplum in Langton's 'Sermon 17a' comparing Christ to
a champion:[3]

Si aliquis amitteret hereditatem suam nec auderet pugnare pro
ea recuperanda nec haberet pecuniam qua conduceret pugilem,
si aliquis pugil diceret ei, 'Pro te pugnabo sine precio', et pugnaret et obtineret victoriam et vulneraretur in prelio et suscipere-
tur in hospicio illius pro quo pugnaret, turpe esset ei si eiceret
eum a domo, scilicet antequam curarentur vulnera eius.

---

[1] *Hel* 'God' (from Hebrew), as in Jerome; cf. the gloss *el* 'deus' in
Moralia I. 59. Both L and T have *el* in this verse-line, but *hel* in verses
in IV. 40. The form with *h* is metrically preferable here; Roman gram-
marians, and consequently Christian poets, held that a following *h* might
or even ought to contribute to 'length by position' (W. R. Hardy, *Res
Metrica* (London, 1920), p. 34). But in IV. 40 the preceding syllable (the
-it of *erigit*, which scans as a dactyl) is not lengthened 'by position';
perhaps there the form *El* would be better.

[2] Roberts, p. 110 and n. 7. The word for 'signifies' is *sonat*, which
Mrs. Roberts, p. 117, renders 'sound[s] like'; but in expounding 'interpretations' of Biblical names *sonat* is often used as a synonym of *significat*
(so in the *Moralia* itself), and 'stella maris' is one of the regular 'interpretations' of *Maria*.

[3] Roberts, p. 114 n. 1.

This corresponds to a more succinct version in *Moralia* IV. 17:

Quis autem homo tam crudelis esset ut, si aliquis athleta pugnasset pro hereditate illius et multis uulneribus sauciatus esset, eum expelleret ab hospicio suo quousque saltem illius uulnera sanarentur?

But the most significant instance, as showing the dependence of the author of the *Moralia* on Langton, concerns a passage in which Langton, in 'Sermon 97c',[1] compares the Church to a vine for three reasons principally (*maxime propter tria*): that it is dry (*arida*) in winter but flourishes (*floret*) in summer, requires great labour yet perishes very easily, and is good for nothing except to bear fruit or to feed a fire. This is expanded in *Moralia* III. 31, which to begin with agrees closely enough:

Item uinea ecclesia est . . . Hec est uinea in qua pauperes spiritu in hyeme presentis uite laborant, ut in ea uita gracie et in futuro uiuant uita glorie. Notum quod *propter tria* que in uinea reperiuntur fideles in ecclesia uinee comparantur. Primum est quod uinea in hyeme arida apparet et despecta ualde, sed florens in estate. Ita uerum est quod omnes pauperes et amici dei ualde contemptibiles habentur in uita presenti, sed proculdubio ualde erunt honorificati cum fulgebunt sicut sol eorum corpora in regno dei . . . Valde contemptibiles sumus in presenti, sed in futuro erimus gloriosi . . .

In this Langton's phrases keep reappearing; but the author of the *Moralia* then goes on to elaborate so ingeniously, and at such length, the winter–summer antithesis that he entirely forgets the second and third reasons; he has given us either a single reason in multiple subdivisions, or more reasons than the three which he promised. There can be no doubt that he

---

[1] Roberts, pp. 117–18, with citations from the Latin text (rather fuller than the translation) in n. 45. I differ from her in thinking that by *vinea* is meant throughout a vine, not a vineyard; but there is an essential ambiguity.

was following and attempting to improve on Langton; he announced three reasons because Langton had done so, and in the same phrase, but lost his way in his elaborations. Now these examples are all based on Mrs. Roberts's citations from Langton's sermons, and though she is not ungenerous with quotations to illustrate his use of similitudes and *exempla* and his view of society, it is clear that they are only a small part of the material scattered through the numerous manuscripts that she has examined; there are 122 sermons (with variants) in her strictest category and 107 others 'extant in one named copy only'.[1] As her quotations are chosen for her own purposes, they are, from the point of view of comparison with the *Moralia* (and with *Ancrene Wisse*), in the strictest sense a random selection; it can hardly be doubted that if the whole *corpus* of the sermons were available for study (as is greatly to be desired) in a modern edition, there would prove to be many more parallels with the *Moralia*. Its author must have used some collection, though probably far from complete, of Langton's sermons. Mrs. Roberts has shown (pp. 67–73) that the sermons she has studied belong to Langton's time in Paris, i.e. between *c.* 1180 and 1206, but it is clear from the way in which they are distributed among the manuscripts (mostly French) that there was never a single authorized and collected edition; they were made available piecemeal, in *reportationes*, and mixed up with sermons by other men. Many of them may therefore have been in circulation before 1200; and they were widely known in England as well as in France.

The *Moralia* is written in an impersonal and anonymous style, but there are clues to the sort of man that the author was and to the date at which he wrote. Obviously he was academically trained and taught in some school where divinity was studied; this follows from the nature of his book, but

---

[1] Roberts, p. 31.

there are more particular indications. His example of the sort of thing that a man might pawn to help his friend is a book (III. 47); he is concerned with the duty of a 'uir theologus litteratus et prudens' to teach and to reprove sin (III. 94); and in II. 51 he warns those 'qui requiescere deberent . . . in claustro uel in scolis' of the dangers that result from failing to do so and becoming *uagabundi*. In IV. 17 we get a glimpse of a grammar- or choir-school in a similitude drawn from boys who before Christmas go about crying 'Noel, Noel' but once the dinner is over forget 'Noel' completely. He was an English subject, probably Anglo-Norman,[1] and addressing an English audience, for in a number of his similitudes, where 'Si rex quidam . . .' would have served, he writes 'Si rex Anglie . . .'[2] So in I. 25:

Si rex Anglie cuiuis destinasset litteras in hec uerba, 'Quod isti feceris, mihi factum reputabo', proculdubio eidem, si facultas adesset sibi, in necessariis subueniret.

Again, in III. 71:

Si rex Anglie uel aliquis prepotens robam preciosam tibi conferret ad hoc, ut [diei] natalis ipsius interesses festiuitate, et ipsam amitteres, multum super hoc esset dolendum.

This shows acquaintance, whether at first or second hand, with the custom whereby English kings rewarded their servants by the gift of robes on special occasions. In III. 22 he tells a story of 'Ricardus rex Anglie' and a knight who had long served him: when the knight fell ill he was visited by the king, who asked if there was anything he wanted and received the reply 'Only my health', which the king was obliged to say he could not give; whereupon the knight declared that he would henceforth serve the king of heaven, who

[1] See p. 17 n. 1, above.
[2] Probably in imitation of Langton; see above, p. 97.

gives health of body and soul, and entered a monastery. A marked feature of the *Moralia* is its frequent discussions of prelates and their duties, with attacks on worldly prelates; and when once (in III. 94) he gives a definition of 'prelates', it is not, as one might have expected, bishops and abbots:

Per Leuitas episcopi et *decani* signantur, prelati qui debent pronuntiare, id est predicare.

The addition of 'et decani' seems a personal touch. He appears to count himself among prelates: in IV. 35, in one of the sections 'de prelatis', he writes

Immo uereor ne cadat super *nos* iudicium sine misericordia,

but the force of the instance is somewhat weakened by the fact that the vice to which, immediately before, he had alluded was the keeping of mistresses, which was not confined to prelates, so that it is possible that he had diverged from his announced subject to the clergy generally. He was a member of a body of clergy accustomed regularly to perform the canonical hours, as is shown by the verb-forms that he uses when writing of the nocturns of Matins in III. 91:

In prime uigilie principio miseriam nostram exprimimus, ibi ploremus 'Coram domino etc.'

In IV. 23 he again uses the first person plural (*radimur*) in speaking of what are obviously communal *rasurae* before the solemn festivals of the Church, and in this chapter and IV. 61 (on ecclesiastical processions) he addresses his audience as *fratres* and *fratres karissimi*. In III. 92 he says that 'obedientia ... religionem consolidat' and that 'castigatio discipline ... necessaria est omni collegio'. Though *collegium* can be used to mean simply 'a community', one would have expected a monk, or a regular canon of one of the Augustinian 'independent congregations', more naturally to say 'omni monasterio', and the choice of word suggests that the author was a member of a college of secular canons. The evidence, slight and scattered though it is, is that he was a member, and apparently the dean, of a collegiate church in which the divine office was regularly performed, which had a school attached, and where divinity lectures were given.[1]

There is nothing that I have observed in the *Moralia* to indicate where its author was born or where he taught, unless very obliquely he shows knowledge of Bath in his discussion of springs in IV. 27. Describing the characteristics of springs in general, he says that they rise in valleys in stony places, emit sand as they burst forth, and are cold in summer but warm in winter. The last feature (which is generally true, since any spring from a deep source is relatively cool in summer and warmer than its surroundings in frosty weather) shows that he is not explicitly thinking of the springs of Bath, whose distinguishing characteristic is their consistent heat. But most springs do not rise in valleys, but on slopes; and springs do not necessarily rise in rocky places or emit sand. The springs of Bath, however, do rise in the valley, 'in the level space within the fold of the river', are bordered by rocks which they 'tinge with a red colour', and 'often bring up sand'.[2] It is possible, then (one cannot put it higher), that the author's views on the properties of springs have been affected by a knowledge of the characteristics of the springs of Bath, and that, suppressing their obviously peculiar feature (their heat), he has nevertheless generalized other features which in fact are by no means universal.

The clearest indication of date in the *Moralia* is the

[1] Much of this would of course fit Grosseteste, especially after he had become a canon of Lincoln. But he was never a dean, and did not become a prelate until his election as bishop in 1235, after the *Moralia* was in circulation.

[2] *The Victoria County History of Somerset* (London, 1906–11), i. 9, 219.

reference in III. 22 to Richard I, which must be later than his
accession in 1189. It is probably also later than his death in
1199; it is not likely that the anecdote (which may well be
apocryphal, since versions of it occur elsewhere) would have
been attached to him during his lifetime, and the form of title
used (*Ricardus rex Anglie*) is one more naturally applied to
a dead king than to a living (who would ordinarily be referred to more simply as *Ricardus rex* or *dominus rex*). If, as
I think, the *Moralia* is influenced by Nequam's *De Naturis
Rerum*, it is likely to be later than 1200, for the *De Naturis* is
now thought to have been 'written between *c*. 1197 and
c. 1204';[1] and the use of material found also in William de
Montibus and in Langton's Paris sermons is consistent with
this. The reference to Greek fire in III. 18 is unlikely to have
been made before 1194[2] and is probably later than 1200,
since Nequam's very similar reference[3] comes in the *De
Laudibus Divinæ Sapientiæ*, a late work thought to have been
written 'in or after 1213'.[4] A more definite pointer in the
same direction is the twice-repeated statement (in III. 61 and
III. 66) that in the crucifixion Christ's feet were placed one
above the other and fastened by a single nail. The similar
(but qualified) statement in *Ancrene Wisse* (f. 106a/2–3) has
been discussed by English medievalists since Miss Beatrice
White first drew attention to it in 1945,[5] arguing that it
reflected a new form of iconography not known before the

[1] Emden, *BRUO*, ii. 1343. Dr. Emden's account of Nequam is
acknowledged to be based largely on Dr. R. W. Hunt's unpublished dissertation. As we have seen in p. 92 n. 3 above, the *De Nat. R.* has a cross-
reference to the *Corrogationes Promethei*, which were 'based on lectures
given at Oxford' and 'written after he became a canon' (loc. cit.), which
was between 1197 and 1201 (p. 1342).
[2] See Shepherd, op. cit., p. 65, and A. L. Poole, *From Doomsday Book
to Magna Carta* (Oxford, 1951), p. 373 n. 2. Greek fire was used at the
siege of Nottingham in 1194.
[3] See p. 11 n. 1 above.   [4] Emden, ii. 1343.
[5] 'The Date of the *Ancrene Riwle*', *MLR* xl. 206–7.

thirteenth century; the earliest reference hitherto discovered
to this disposition of the feet is in a text of which the earliest
known manuscript is dated to the beginning of the thirteenth
or possibly the end of the twelfth century.[1] Again there is
the form of the Biblical references in the *Moralia*. Most give
simply the name of the book, but in a significant minority
of instances there is a reference by book and chapter-number;
such references are shared by L and T and must come from
their common exemplar, and in some cases they are so
worked into the structure of the sentence as to leave little
doubt that they are authorial, and not added by an editing scribe. Though there are minor discrepancies, they certainly depend on the 'modern' system of chapter-division.[2]

[1] Shepherd, op. cit., p. 57. For further discussion see A. Zettersten,
Studies in the Dialect and Vocabulary of the Ancrene Riwle (Lund, 1965),
pp. 16–18.

[2] Significant instances are the references in IV. 50 to Luke 13 'in
principio' (in fact to verse 4) and in IV. 63 to Ecclus. 22 (in fact to verse
33, the last of the chapter). I have noticed only two divergences from the
modern chapter-divisions, both of which might be due to miscopying of
the roman numerals in the common exemplar of L and T but are probably
to be explained otherwise. (1) In III. 71 there is a reference to Isa. 25
when the words quoted in fact come from 26: 1. Thirteenth-century
copies of the Bible in the Bodleian (including especially MS. Rawlinson
G. 7, which in the *Summary Catalogue*, no. 14742, is dated '*c.* 1200' but
is probably a little later) divide chapters 25 and 26 of Isaiah as in modern
Bibles. But scribes sometimes made mistakes (or deliberately used different divisions): thus Bodleian MS. Auct. D. 5. 21 (s. xiii m.), ff. 210^{r-v},
begins Isa. 26 and 28 at wrong points (25: 9 and 27: 13), though red lines
have been drawn in to transfer the chapter-numbers to the right points.
A minor discrepancy of this sort in the copy used by the author of the
Moralia could have added Isa. 26: 1 to the end of chapter 25. (2) In III. 73
there is a reference to Ecclus. 28 which should be to chapter 27 (verse 17).
Thirteenth-century Bodleian copies divide Ecclus. 26, 27, and 28 as now
(though MS. Auct. D. 5. 21, f. 198, again makes a mistake, corrected by
a red line, at chapter 28); so in particular the early thirteenth-century
MS. Rawlinson G. 7. But in this copy Ecclus. 27: 17, the verse quoted
in *Moralia* III. 73, begins with a blue capital of the same size as those
used for the beginnings of chapters, and the reason is apparent from MS.
Rawlinson Q. b. 15 (s. xii²). In the latter, Ecclesiasticus is divided into

Medieval tradition ascribed this system to Stephen Langton, but if it was his, 'he introduced it towards the end of his teaching period'; it is found in a copy dated 1203 of his gloss on the minor prophets, 'although he did not use it in his lectures'.[1] Its occasional use in the *Moralia* is therefore another indication of a date after 1200.

There is no definite *terminus ante quem* for the composition of the *Moralia*. It must of course be earlier than Index A of L, which Mr. Parkes and I would date to the first quarter of the thirteenth century, and earlier than the composition of *Ancrene Wisse*, which I would put between 1215 and 1222. In Gerald of Wales's *Speculum Ecclesiæ*, written between 1215 and 1218,[2] there is, in IV. 24,[3] a passage closely parallel to that concerning Oza in *Moralia* II. 46 (cited in part on p. 50 above), as if Gerald knew the *Moralia*; but perhaps there is a common source. It is dangerous to argue from negative evidence, but I have detected no sign in the *Moralia* of the influence of the Lateran Council of 1215, and no allusion to the Interdict of 1208–14. On this evidence the probability is that the *Moralia*, as published, was compiled between, at the outside, 1200 and 1215.

Alexander was a surprisingly common name in the late twelfth and early thirteenth centuries, and several of its

numbered chapters or sections shorter than the modern ones (though a later scribe has added the modern chapter-numbers in the margins); in this older system, Ecclus. 27: 17 is the first verse of a separate section (numbered 72). If the author of the *Moralia* had used a Bible like MS. Rawlinson G. 7, with the 'modern' chapter-numbers but with rubrication influenced by the older system, he might have been misled into thinking that 27: 17 was the first verse of a new chapter and have wrongly deduced, if his eye caught the number 27 higher on the page, that it was the beginning of chapter 28, the reference given in L and T.

[1] Smalley, *The Study of the Bible*, pp. 221–4.
[2] J. de Ghellinck, *L'Essor de la littérature latine au XIIe siècle* (2nd edition, 1954), pp. 143–4.
[3] Ed. J. S. Brewer (Rolls Series, 1873), p. 316.

recorded bearers, beside Alexander Nequam (otherwise Alexander of St. Albans), were entitled to the designation *magister*. In the diocese of Lincoln alone there were at least three: (1) Magister Alexander (without territorial designation), who was a canon of Lincoln from 1186[1] and who is perhaps to be identified with the Magister Alexander (again without territorial designation) who was archdeacon of the West Riding of Lindsey just before 1200;[2] (2) Magister Alexander of Bedford, who was also a canon of Lincoln before 1200;[3] (3) Magister Alexander of Elstow or *de Aunest'*, who was archdeacon of Bedford.[4] In 1199 there is a Magister Alexander (yet again without territorial designation) who occurs in the records of the Curia Regis in connection with a case in the diocese of London.[5] But there is nothing to connect any of these with the city or diocese of Bath.

Serious consideration must, however, be given to the Magister Alexander who was dean of Wells at the end of the twelfth and the beginning of the thirteenth century. The

[1] *Final Concords* (Lincoln Record Soc. xvii, 1920), ii. 309; *Registrum Antiquissimum* (Lincoln Record Soc.), viii. 77–8 (and note on p. 78); *Chancellor's Roll 8 Ric. I* (1196), p. 245, continuing to *Pipe Roll 1 John* (1199), p. 140. This is probably the same man as the Magister Alexander who in 1191 acted as one of two sureties for Reginald dean of Covenham, Lincs. (*Pipe R. 3 Ric. I* (1191), p. 19, continuing to *Pipe R. 1 John* (1199), p. 141), and in 1200 was named as one of two alternative attorneys in a suit of darrein presentment concerning the church at Melton, Lincs. (*Cur. R. Rolls*, i. 278, 282–3, 290).

[2] *Registrum Antiquissimum*, iv. 14, v. 157–8, vii. 49, 103 (and Appendix I, p. 201), ix. 64, 105 (and the discussion on p. 260, where Miss K. Major points out that he had been replaced as archdeacon by 1201); *Charters of Gilbertine Houses* (Lincoln Rec. Soc. xviii, 1922), p. 84.

[3] Emden, *BRUO*, i. 146; *Registrum Antiquissimum*, i. 255 (1203–5), ii. 274 (1196–9).

[4] *Registrum Antiquissimum*, ii. 27 (1192–1200), 288 (12 June 1218). Cf. also the index to the volume.

[5] He was named as defendant in a suit of darrein presentment concerning a church in Barstable Hundred, Essex (*Rot. Cur. R.* i. 332), presumably as attorney for the bishop of London, who appears as the successful defendant in two later records of the case (*Rot. Cur. R.* ii. 7, 104),

clergy of the church of Wells had been reorganized as a
collegiate chapter of secular canons by Robert of Lewes,
bishop of Bath (1136–66), and further developed by bishop
Reginald of Bath (1174–91); by the end of the century it was
a numerous, flourishing, and well-endowed community.[1]
By this time, too, there was an active cathedral school,[2] still
directly under the chancellor of Wells, who is styled *magister
scolarum* in a document of between 1174 and 1185;[3] and the
instruction included lectures in theology. Magister Alexander
is usually said to have become dean of Wells in 1180,[4] but
this is plainly mistaken;[5] his predecessor Richard is named
(as 'R. dean of Wells') in the report of an inquiry ordered by
Pope Urban III (1185–7),[6] and was the principal witness to
a confirmation by bishop Reginald (of a grant by Henry II
to Buckland Priory) which is precisely dated 'the sixth of the
Ides of November' (i.e. 8 November) 1186, at Taunton;
'Magister Alexander' was also a witness, much lower on the
list.[7] To about this period belongs another confirmation (un-

[1] Cf. *VCH Somerset*, ii. 162–8.

[2] Ibid., pp. 435–40.   [3] Ibid., p. 436.

[4] J. Le Neve, *Fasti Ecclesiae Anglicanae*, 'corrected and continued' by
T. Duffus Hardy (Oxford, 1854), i. 149; Somerset Record Society, xv
(1899), p. 9; *VCH Somerset*, ii. 168. A footnote in the *Fasti* cites as
evidence 'Cartular. Glaston. MS. p. 15'. But all the documents in the
chartulary of Glastonbury Abbey attested by 'Magister Alexander decanus Wellensis' are undated; see *The Great Chartulary of Glastonbury*,
ed. A. Watkin (Somerset Rec. Soc. lix, lxiii–iv, 1947–56), pp. 2, 64, and
69 (nos. 1, 92, and 114, issued by bishop Reginald) and pp. 67 and 710
(nos. 103 and 1315, issued by bishop Savaric). The date 1180 must have
been an approximate guess.

[5] As was pointed out by J. Armitage Robinson, *Somerset Historical
Essays* (London, 1921), pp. 64–5. Robinson observes that the date of
Pope Urban's bull must have been 21 August of either 1186 or 1187.

[6] Historical Manuscripts Commission, *Calendar of the Manuscripts of
the Dean and Chapter of Wells*, i (1907), p. 40. The editor (J. A. Bennett)
appends a note suggesting that 'R.' is a mistake, since dean Alexander
'seems to have been contemporary with Pope Urban III', but this is to
prefer secondary authorities (Le Neve) to primary; the record is accurate.

[7] Som. Rec. Soc. xxv (1909), pp. 7–8.

dated) of bishop Reginald with a similar though shorter list
of witnesses, again including 'Magister Alexander',[1] and further references to him simply as 'Magister Alexander' come
in undated documents in the Wells Cathedral archives.[2] But
other documents that must belong to this period show him as
a canon of Wells, holding the prebend of Henstridge, part
of the proceeds of which he bound himself to contribute to
the expenses of the church of Wells,[3] and describe him as
subdean.[4] He must have become dean well before the death,
on 26 December 1191, of bishop Reginald, for he is given
this title in many documents issued by or naming Reginald
and presumably belonging to the last years of his episcopate;
in these, as in later documents, Alexander is still often styled
'magister' as well as 'decanus'.[5] He continued as dean
throughout the episcopate of Savaric, bishop of Bath and

[1] Som. Rec. Soc. viii (1894), p. 58.
[2] *Cal. MSS. Wells*, i. 25, 46.
[3] Ibid., p. 490.
[4] Ibid., p. 38; Robinson, op. cit., p. 65. Robinson argues that as one
of the charters which Alexander attested as subdean was also attested by
Robert fitz Paine as sheriff of Somerset, an office which he held from
Michaelmas 1184 to Michaelmas 1188, Alexander must have become
subdean between November 1186 and Michaelmas 1188; and suggests
that he may have been subdean in 1187–8 and have become dean in 1189
or 1190. But the number of documents in which he is named as dean before the death of bishop Reginald in December 1191 suggests that he had
held the office for more than two or three years.

He is still named simply as 'magister Alexander' in a list of witnesses
appended to the inspeximus and confirmation by Richard bishop of
London of a ratification by his predecessor Gilbert of a grant to Reginald
bishop of Bath (*Cal. MSS. Wells*, i. 56–7). Richard fitz Neal became
bishop of London in 1189; but the witnesses may have been those to the
ratification by Gilbert Foliot, who died in 1187.

[5] *Cal. MSS. Wells*, i. 9 (twice), 22, 24, 25 (second reference), 42, 43,
44, 44–5, 45, 51, 68, 69, 486, 489; Som. Rec. Soc. lvi (1941), pp. 98, 109;
also Som. Rec. Soc. lix (1947), pp. 2, 64, 69 (cited in p. 108 n. 4 above).
Miss D. E. Greenway informs me that there are other references to
Alexander as dean at this time in B.M. MS. Egerton 3316, f. 40[r-v], and
MS. Harley 6968, f. 12, and in Lambeth Palace Library MS. 940, no. 1.

Glastonbury (1192–1205),[1] and was active, as the senior representative of Wells, in the procedures for the election (on 3 February 1206) of his successor Jocelin of Wells, a canon of his own church.[2] There are other documents referring to him as dean which both are undated and include no reference to any bishop.[3] He was still in office under bishop Jocelin, though records become fewer. He signed an ordinance of Jocelin's dated at Wells 'iii. non. Junii' in the fourth year of his episcopate, i.e. 3 June 1209,[4] and is named as dean in a final concord dated 'three weeks after the day of St. John the Baptist', 11 John (i.e. about 15 July 1209).[5] These are the last definite evidences of him, but we can perhaps carry his record a little further, thanks to his sports and not his duties. Sometime before Easter 1208 he had incurred a fine of ten marks because, contrary to the forest laws, his greyhounds had taken a hind.[6] He did not pay, and the Pipe Rolls from Michaelmas 1208 until Michaelmas 1211, in varying phrases, continue to record his debt;[7] but in the roll of Michaelmas 1212 it drops out, without any note that it had been paid. This is not conclusive evidence that he

---

[1] *Cal. MSS. Wells*, i. 10 (6 June 1205; identical with Som. Rec. Soc. vi (1892), p. 24), 26, 47 (twice), 48, 50–1, 57 (twice), 58, 367; Som. Rec. Soc. xiv (1899), p. 51; lvi (1941), pp. 54, 97, 110; also Som. Rec. Soc. lix (1947), p. 67, and lxiv (1956), p. 710 (cited in p. 108 n. 4 above).

[2] *Cal. MSS. Wells*, i. 62, 63, 64, 65.

[3] *Cal. MSS. Wells*, i. 28, 41, 135; Som. Rec. Soc. lvi (1941), p. 93.

[4] *Cal. MSS. Wells*, i. 66.   [5] Som. Rec. Soc. vi (1892), p. 26.

[6] *Memoranda Roll 10 John*, p. 44 (Easter 1208): 'pro leporariis suis qui ceperunt j bisse'. It is interesting, but I would not care to argue that it is significant, that towards the end of the *Moralia*, in IV. 54, there is a far-fetched similitude based on the difference between two types of hunting-dog, the *odorisequus* (variously spelt in the manuscripts), who hunts by the scent of blood, and the *leporarius*, who cannot do so; the poor are compared to the former, the rich to the latter, since they 'uestigia Cristi sequi nesciunt nec eius sanguinem sentire'.

[7] *Pipe R. 10 John*, p. 111 ('pro leporariis habitis contra assisam', under Pleas of the Forest): *Pipe R. 11 John*, pp. 100–1, and *Pipe R. 12 John*, p. 72 ('pro canibus habitis'); *Pipe R. 13 John*, p. 224 ('pro veteri vasto').

was still alive at Michaelmas 1211, for the Pipe Rolls often went on recording debts to the Exchequer for years after the debtor was dead;[1] but in this case we need not perhaps be very sceptical, for the debt was recent and the record was soon dropped. What is certain is that his successor, Magister Ralph of Lechlade, had been given the deanery by bishop Jocelin before June 1212.[2] Dean Alexander must therefore have died[3] between July 1209 and June 1212, and possibly after Michaelmas 1211.

Dean Alexander satisfies all the conditions save one. He was a *magister*, trained in the schools; and as his career in the diocese of Bath must have begun soon after 1180,[4] his student days must have been (roughly) between 1170 and 1180. If he was trained in Paris, as is likely, he would have been a contemporary there of Alexander Nequam and Stephen Langton,

[1] See D. Knowles, C. N. L. Brooke, and V. C. M. London, *Heads of Religious Houses: England and Wales, 940–1216* (Cambridge, 1972), pp. 11–12.

[2] *Book of Fees* (P.R.O. Texts and Calendars, 1920–31), i. 82; see also C. R. Cheney, 'King John and the Papal Interdict', *Bulletin of John Rylands Library*, xxxi (1948), 305 and n. The return of June 1212 says that Ralph was given the deanery 'post interdictum' (i.e. after 23 March 1208) but that it was in the hands of the king. Bishop Jocelin went into exile probably about December 1209 (cf. Robinson, 'Bishop Jocelin and the Interdict', in *Somerset Historical Essays*, pp. 141–56, especially p. 154) and Ralph of Lechlade was dean in exile with him (*Cal. MSS. Wells*, i. 58); he evidently returned with Jocelin in the summer of 1213 (ibid., p. 491), but by 30 September 1213 had been replaced as dean by a man called Leo or Leonius (ibid., p. 53; cf. p. 490 and Som. Rec. Soc. lix (1947), p. 21). I owe most of the references in this note to Miss Greenway.

[3] This is much more likely than that he had resigned, especially in view of the dropping of the record of his debt to the Exchequer from the Pipe Roll of Michaelmas 1212. Miss Greenway, in a private communication, observes that it is impossible to say whether he accompanied bishop Jocelin into exile or had already been succeeded by Ralph of Lechlade by December 1209; she regards the Pipe Roll records as inconclusive.

[4] Only one of the early documents referring to him is dated (that of 8 November 1186), but he was evidently well established in Wells by that time.

and could well have been a pupil of William de Montibus, as his work suggests he was; he would certainly have known all three. He became the dean of a church of quasi-cathedral status and therefore a 'prelate' within the definition of the *Moralia*, the head of a numerous college of secular canons with a flourishing school attached. If he had needed to, he could have learnt about royal writs and the practice of English kings of giving robes to their servants from Jocelin of Wells and his brother Hugh, who were senior clerks of the Chancery[1] while respectively a canon and the archdeacon of Wells; but he himself had served in 1199 as a royal justice, tallaging the abbey of Glastonbury.[2] If by chance the anecdote about Richard I was true, he could have heard it from bishop Savaric on his too rare visits to his diocese, for Savaric was an associate of Richard's, had accompanied him on his crusade, and had negotiated with the emperor for Richard's release from captivity. The condition that is not satisfied is that dean Alexander should be described, in an extant document, as 'of Bath'. But his whole career, from the 1180s onwards, was in the diocese of Bath, and there is some suggestion, in the earliest documents naming him (especially that of November 1186, issued from Taunton), that he was a member of the *familia* of bishop Reginald of Bath. After he had become dean there was no

---

[1] *Memoranda Roll 1 John*, ed. D. M. Stenton (Pipe Roll Soc., N.S. xxi, 1943), introduction, pp. xxxvii–viii. Records mentioning them as king's clerks or as otherwise engaged in the king's service include: for Jocelin, *Rot. Lit. Claus.* i, pp. 1a (1199), 9a (1204), 40b (1205), *Rot. Lit. Pat.*, p. 38b (1204), *Rot. de Liberate*, p. 81 (1204); for Hugh, *Rot. Lit. Pat.*, p. 38a–b (Jan.–Feb. 1204), *Rot. de Liberate*, p. 81 (Feb. 1204). In *Rot. Chartarum* there are various charters issued by King John in 1207 under the hand of Hugh, archdeacon of Wells, including in particular one of 17 September which refers (p. 170) to Alexander dean of Wells, though in reference to a gift made by bishop Reginald, i.e. before 1191. Both Jocelin and Hugh are specifically described as '(dilectus) clericus noster'.

[2] *Mem. R. 1 John*, p. 66.

need to give him a territorial designation, for he was sufficiently identified (as was normal practice) by the designation
'(magister) Alexander decanus Wellensis'; and even before
he became dean, as all the documents that mention him re-
late either to the church of Wells or to the affairs of the
diocese of Bath, it was evidently enough to call him simply
'Magister Alexander', for there is no sign that there was at
that time any other Master Alexander in the diocese from
whom he would need to be distinguished.[1]

If we could accept that dean Alexander of Wells was the
author of the *Moralia*, we could come nearer to dating it,
which is of particular concern to students of *Ancrene Wisse*.
Its numerous discussions of prelates, which I have already
suggested may once have constituted a separate set of discourses, include repeated attacks on worldly prelates, re-
splendent in golden rings and chains ('anulis et monilibus
aureis radiantes', IV. 35), who discourage preaching, are
more concerned with accumulating wealth and exercising
power than with the cure of souls, and who live in luxury
and vice. This is of course a traditional moralist's theme (indeed in IV. 35 the author cites Bernard of Clairvaux in
support), but there may well have been a particular occasion; for Savaric bishop of Bath and Glastonbury was the
greatest worldling among the bishops of his time, a man of
international notoriety.[2] After his death dean Alexander and

[1] Robinson, op. cit., p. 67, records a suggestion that Alexander was,
like bishops Reginald and Savaric, a member of the Bohun family, but
himself shows that there is no valid evidence for it. It seems to me that
in any case it is improbable that *de Ba* in L is a mistake for *de Bo*'; the
scribe would not only have to misread *o* as *a*, but also to ignore a mark of
suspension.

[2] For Savaric's career and character see the article by William Hunt in
DNB xvii. 840–3. He would hardly have relished the citation, in *Moralia*
IV. 13 apropos of prelates, of the text (2 Tim. 2: 4) 'Nemo militans deo
implicat se negotiis secularibus', for this was what he spent much of his
life doing.

the chapter of Wells petitioned Pope Innocent to grant prompt confirmation of Jocelin's election because they had been 'now for several years destitute of a ruler',[1] but this cannot refer to any delay in making the election, for there was none;[2] it is a way of saying that Savaric had neglected his diocese, and the prime responsibility for it must have been Alexander's.[3] The monks of Bath, for their part, set on Savaric's tomb in their abbey the inscription

> Notus eras mundo per mundum semper eundo
> Et necis ista dies est tibi prima quies.[4]

But any cleric of the diocese of Bath would have been wise not to publish the views on prelates that are so prominent in the *Moralia* during Savaric's lifetime, for he was not tolerant of opposition and 'did not sleep'. The most likely period for the discourses 'de prelatis' to be delivered, if they were by dean Alexander, would be after the news of Savaric's death in Italy on 8 August 1205 had reached England and before the election of Jocelin on 3 February 1206, when the clergy of the diocese were considering the qualities required in a bishop. It is also to be remarked that the *Moralia* less obtrusively warns against the dangers of serving at court as a king's clerk. In the final chapter (IV. 64) the author says that

[1] *Cal. MSS. Wells*, i. 63.

[2] Savaric died in Italy in August 1205, Jocelin was elected on 3 February 1206, the temporalities were restored on 3 May, and he was consecrated at Reading by the bishop of London on 28 May, less than ten months after the death of his predecessor.

[3] During Savaric's long conflict with Glastonbury Abbey, which he sought to subordinate to the bishopric, he was supported by the chapter of Wells and especially by dean Alexander, but after his death they changed sides and supported Glastonbury's appeal for the restoration of its independence (Robinson, op. cit., pp. 68–70, 142–3, 145–6). There is no reason to suppose that they approved of Savaric's character and conduct, though they found it expedient to further his schemes.

[4] Cited in *DNB* xvii. 843. Cf. Ralph of Coggeshall, *Chronicon Anglicanum* (ed. J. Stephenson, Rolls Series, 1875), p. 162.

Consilia uero diaboli et mundi sunt in curiis principum, que sunt de terrenis adquirendis et de luxuriis et rapinis perpetrandis, et huiusmodi consilia precipue fiunt cum diuina officia in ecclesia celebrari deberent,

and in III. 82, giving an example of how devils tempt men to evil under the appearance of good, he says that they incite some to attend at court so that they may provide more generously for their kin and the poor.[1] But he is more explicit in IV. 29, when he says of the text 'Egressus Petrus fleuit amare' that it is

In signum quod clerici qui in domibus principum sunt, quod ibidem prunis cupiditatis accensi committunt, ibidem deflere non possunt; sed foras egressi, id est ad propria regressi, quod in curiis turpiter deliquerunt aquis penitencialibus abstergent.

As Jocelin of Wells and his brother Hugh were two of the chief king's clerks during the earlier years of John's reign, this might be a warning to the new bishop (of whose election dean Alexander presumably approved, since he had taken a leading part in it) that he would do well to cut himself off from the court and, returning 'ad propria', devote himself to the affairs of his diocese.[2] But if the discourses on prelates and the warnings to king's clerks belong to late 1205 and early 1206, it does not of course follow that all the materials of

[1] 'Huiuscemodi quosdam ad curiam sectandam inuitant ut parentibus et pauperibus profusius largiantur.' In this, *ad curiam sectandam* is 'to suit of court', i.e. to attendance at the court of a feudal lord, but presumably the king's court is meant. The argument of *Ancrene Wisse* f. 60a/19–60b/13 is the same, though the means of enrichment envisaged is necessarily different.

[2] Jocelin was still dealing with the king's business after John's confirmation of his election at the beginning of May 1206 (Robinson, op. cit., p. 147), and he is even found associated with his brother Hugh in the transaction of royal business in July 1207 (ibid., p. 149). Discreet comments on the dangers of such a course might not have seemed inappropriate to an older man who had been a party to his election to the bishopric.

the *Moralia* are of the same date; it would, however, mean that the compilation and editing of the work as published took place between 1206 and dean Alexander's death in or before 1212. Perhaps it was a task with which he occupied himself after the Interdict came into force in March 1208, when preaching and the ordinary services of his church would have been in abeyance and he would have had time on his hands for literary work.

If Alexander of Bath (whether or not the same man as dean Alexander of Wells) was the author of the *Moralia*, we must nevertheless ask why Thomas of London, the precentor of Tewkesbury who is responsible for the Trinity College manuscript, should have thought that Grosseteste was. Medieval ascriptions of authorship are often unreliable, but he must have had some reason. Part of the answer, I suspect, is in the statement of the title-page that he had taken pains to acquire the book and have it copied; he had probably deduced from Thomas of Eccleston's statement, or from some oral tradition to the same effect, that Grosseteste, while at Oxford, had delivered important *moralitates*, and had set out to discover whether a copy was in existence. The obvious places to look would be Oxford and Lincoln. Now the Lincoln College manuscript was the gift, between 1452 and 1483, of Robert Flemmyng, dean of Lincoln, and though he might have acquired it elsewhere he is most likely to have got it in Lincoln itself. It had been copied from an exemplar of which Index A, as we have seen, is a surviving fragment, and the fact that Index A is bound in with L must show that the exemplar had been held in the same place, i.e. if L originated in Lincoln, the exemplar also was there; and the handwriting of Index A shows that the exemplar must have been made during the episcopate of Grosseteste's predecessor, Hugh of Wells (1209–35). Hugh, whose brother was bishop of Bath, maintained his connections with Wells to the end of his life, and his *familia* included clerks from the diocese of Bath, for example Master Peter of Bath, who was a canon of Lincoln from 1215 and shared a bequest in Hugh's will for his faithful service.[1] That a manuscript of a work by 'Magister Alexander de Ba' should be in Lincoln during bishop Hugh's time would be entirely natural, and perhaps the likeliest owner would be the bishop himself. But as we have seen, the exemplar of L was also the ancestor, and probably the direct exemplar, of T. If Thomas of London, searching for a copy of the *moralitates* which he believed Grosseteste had written, discovered in Lincoln a manuscript of a work of English authorship of exactly the right type and of about the right date, and was told, or learnt from an *ex libris*, that it had formerly *belonged* to the bishop of Lincoln (meaning Hugh of Wells), he might well have been confirmed in a predisposition to believe that it had been *written* by the bishop of Lincoln (meaning Robert Grosseteste); and he would have dismissed as erroneous any initial rubric (if the exemplar had one) that attributed the work to an Alexander of Bath of whom he had probably never heard.[2]

That the exemplar of T (and of L) was a manuscript held in Lincoln may be confirmed by a footnote in T, on f. 208, which, since it is in the hand of the text-scribe, must have been copied from the exemplar. But it is not in L, and though this in itself does not prove that it is not authorial, it differs in form and style, and even in orthography,[3] from the notes which I take to be the author's, either because they are shared

[1] *Registrum Antiquissimum*, ii. 71.

[2] It is more likely than not that L's rubric was copied from the exemplar, but it need not have been; the exemplar may have lacked any attribution of authorship, and Thomas of London may not have been guilty of suppressing an attribution inconsistent with his own belief, though I suspect that he was.

[3] In this note v is regularly used in initial position in a word, though in the text and other notes the T scribe, even more often than the L scribe, normally uses u.

by L and T or for other reasons; moreover it is peppered with errors, as if the T scribe found the hand in which the note was written unfamiliar and difficult. It probably represents a note added to the manuscript by a reader (like two of the long marginal notes in L itself), which T copied but L omitted.[1] It is written within the text-space at the foot of the page, and consists of a passage of prose (in the left column) introducing seven lines of verse (in the right column) on the Seven Gifts of the Holy Spirit (which are referred to in the text of III. 30, the chapter to which the note relates). In the left margin, before the note, is written 'Magister Wl̥ͩ de Monte dicit hoc'. Apart from the reasons already given, it is most unlikely that the author of the *Moralia* wrote this; nowhere else, in his text or his notes, does he refer to a contemporary scholar, and indeed to do so would have been contrary to the normal practice of his time. Lincoln, where William de Montibus had presided over the cathedral school, would be the likeliest place in which an acknowledged quotation from him might be added to a work by another writer.[2]

Concurrent evidence, then, points to Lincoln as the place where the exemplar of L and T was held and where L was copied and itself kept until, over two centuries later, it was given to Lincoln College by Robert Flemmyng. But if L was a copy made in Lincoln of a manuscript written in the lifetime of Hugh of Wells, even greater authority than was claimed above attaches to its ascription of the *Moralia* to Alexander of Bath. As the work is of academic type, the copy (the extant manuscript L) must have been intended for

[1] Perhaps because this note was added to the exemplar after L had been copied from it.
[2] As William de Montibus developed the use of the *distinctiones*, it may perhaps be significant that a set of *distinctiones* was written on an originally blank leaf of L (f. 258) about 1250; see p. 38 above. It is at least a sign of the scholastic provenance of the manuscript.

one of the cathedral chapter or for use in the cathedral school;[1] and the palaeographical evidence is that it was made after bishop Hugh's death and during the episcopate of Grosseteste. But no scribe then working in Lincoln would attribute to Alexander of Bath a book that was really by his own bishop; and if the rubric was not copied from the exemplar but supplied by the scribe of L himself, Lincoln must, even after Hugh's death, have been a place particularly well informed about the diocese of Bath. There, as well as anywhere in England outside that diocese itself, men would have known whether, within the last half-century, there had been a Master Alexander of Bath who had written *moralia*, and whether this book was his. And if in fact the author had been Alexander dean of Wells, they might also know what territorial designation he should be given when, after his death, he could no longer be described as 'Magister Alexander decanus Wellensis'. Hugh of Wells, who as early as the time of bishop Reginald of Bath (i.e. before 1191) had been witnessing the same documents as Master Alexander,[2] had been his colleague for some twenty years before Hugh's own election to the bishopric of Lincoln; there can have been little about the dean of Wells that he did not know, and he must have known his full name. Bishop Hugh is the key figure, whose career explains why the surviving textual

[1] The marginal notes added on the first two leaves (ff. 11 and 12) of the text of L, in a hand different from that of any of the scribes who worked on the text of L and on Index B, are of scholastic type. The other marginal notes in L, presumably derived from the exemplar (since they were added before the manuscript was completed by the rubricator of Index B), and the marginal notes in T (certainly derived from the exemplar, since they were copied by the text-scribe himself) are also of scholastic type, and must show that the exemplar either was used in a school or belonged to someone of scholastic training. But apart from the reference in T to William de Montibus, I can find nothing in these notes to suggest the location of the exemplar or of L.

[2] For example, *Cal. MSS. Wells*, i. 69, 489.

tradition of the *Moralia* stems from a manuscript that was evidently held in Lincoln. But a different, independent manuscript had gone to Herefordshire, to be used by the author of *Ancrene Wisse*, and it is possible that it went there because of the career of Hugh's brother Jocelin; for in February 1204 King John granted the church of Lugwardine, three miles east of Hereford, and the chapel of Archenfield to 'dilecto clerico nostro' Jocelin of Wells, who immediately appointed as perpetual vicar 'Magister Alardus',[1] subsequently subdean[2] and by 1218 chancellor[3] of Wells. From Wells the connections extend in both the required directions, to Lincoln and to Herefordshire.

I conclude that the *Moralia super Evangelia* was not written by Grosseteste and does not represent his lectures given to the Franciscans of Oxford in 1229–30. The author was Alexander of Bath, and though the lectures and other discourses on which the published work was based may in large part have been earlier, it was not compiled in its present form until after the death of bishop Savaric in 1205 had made it safer for clerics of his diocese openly to express strong views about worldly and unworthy prelates. Alexander of Bath is probably to be identified with Alexander dean of Wells, and if so the *Moralia* must be earlier than the date of his death, possibly after Michaelmas 1211 and certainly before June 1212.[4] And if Hugh and Jocelin of Wells were, as I suggest, directly or indirectly responsible for the transference of copies of the *Moralia* to Lincoln and Herefordshire respectively, then it should be added that, as both of them were

---

[1] *Rot. Lit. Pat.*, p. 38b.

[2] *Cal. MSS. Wells*, i. 490 (2 October 1213); see the index, p. 556, for the identification of 'Master A. the subdean' with Master Alard.

[3] Le Neve, *Fasti*, ed. Duffus Hardy, ii. 91; *Cal. MSS. Wells*, i. 42, 135 (April 1239), 201, 320 (October 1234).

[4] Assuming that his replacement as dean was due to death and not resignation.

absent from England from late 1209 to 1213 because of the Interdict, this transference is unlikely to have occurred before their return from exile in July 1213; but possibly Master Alard may have taken a copy to Herefordshire somewhat earlier. The use of the *Moralia* by the author of *Ancrene Wisse* is certainly in favour of dating the English work to the early thirteenth, not to the twelfth, century, and may be in favour of my dating 'after 1215'; but it is no reason for a dating after 1230.

Much wider issues are obviously raised by the dependence of *Ancrene Wisse* on the *Moralia* and by the hints of connections between the latter—and to some extent the former as well—and the writings of William de Montibus, Alexander Nequam, and Stephen Langton. It becomes more and more apparent that about the turn of the twelfth and thirteenth centuries there developed a lively and accomplished English scholastic tradition (or Anglo-Welsh, since Gerald of Wales must be included) which, though it derived from Paris, where its leading exponents had been trained, nevertheless had its own distinctive characteristics and virtues. Its writings are for the most part unprinted and are known only to a few specialists in medieval Anglo-Latin literature; to give even a sketch of its achievements is beyond the scope of this book and the competence of its author. It seems clear, however, that *Ancrene Wisse* may justly be regarded as a vernacular offshoot of the tradition: a book written by a man who was not himself in any true sense a scholar—he lacked academic precision and control and was derivative in his ideas—but who was deeply influenced by scholastic method (sometimes to the point of pedantry), was well-read, energetic, and imaginative, and was quick to adapt to his purpose whatever he found helpful in the books that came into his hands. In one way, indeed, his book was the most notable product of this group of English writers; for the others wrote chiefly for the schools, in a language and using techniques long and carefully adapted to their purpose, but he went outside the schools, revivifying and transforming a native literary tradition which, despite its antiquity, had been rapidly falling into decay. Few still believe that he was solely, or even especially, responsible for the 'continuity of English prose', but to write such a book at that time was a remarkable feat; and he was able to do it because he was well trained not only in the writing of English, but also in academic methods and thought. It is no accident that he made such extensive use of a recent scholastic work of English provenance.

APPENDIX

PASSAGES FROM THE *MORALIA* RELEVANT TO *ANCRENE WISSE*

IN this appendix I print the text of the passages in the *Moralia super Evangelia* which seem relevant to *Ancrene Wisse*; some are extensive, others very brief, most a few sentences long. They are only extracts made for a special purpose and are not intended to illustrate the scope and nature of the *Moralia* itself, though they give some idea of its style and its manner of expounding texts and using similitudes. It is not claimed that all the passages cited are exact parallels to or the direct sources of those in *Ancrene Wisse* to which they are referred, but many of them are. The numbered entries are arranged in the order of the passages in *Ancrene Wisse* to which they are relevant; if a single entry cites more passages than one from the *Moralia* they are normally arranged in the order in which they occur in the latter, though precedence is given in some instances to a close parallel. At the end of these introductory notes I give a list of the chapters of the *Moralia* from which quotations, short or long, are taken, with the number of the entry under which the passage is to be found; if more passages than one are taken from a single chapter, they are listed in the order in which they occur in the *Moralia*.

The texts are critically edited on the basis of the readings of the two independent and early manuscripts L and T, with preference given, in case of doubt, to the readings of L. Substantive emendations lacking the authority of either manuscript are enclosed in square brackets. Substantive variants, and instances of correction in either of the manuscripts, are noted in the *apparatus criticus* at the foot of the page. Capitalization and punctuation are modern, and I do not record departures from the capitalization and pointing of the manuscripts except in a few cases, e.g. when it is apparent that one of the scribes, but not the other, mistook the sentence-division. As regards spelling and word-form I have been eclectic and have normally adopted whichever spelling, at the point in question, was more in accord with classical usage, and very occasionally I have normalized a spelling against the evidence of both manuscripts; but I have accepted a few abnormal spellings because there seemed to me to be indications that they might be the author's. On balance I must have made the spelling more classical than he intended; the earlier manuscript L is, on the whole, the less classical in spelling and is probably closer to the common exemplar. In one exceptional case (entry no. 20), where L's abnormal spelling agrees with that used in *Ancrene Wisse* but T's does not, I have recorded the variation in the text itself. The chief points of difference between the two manuscripts are: (i) variation between *c* and *t* before *i*, where I have adopted *t* (usually from T) unless both agree on *c*; (ii) the frequent doubling, in one or other manuscript, of a consonant which should be single, or more rarely the failure to double a letter which should be doubled; (iii) variation between the letter-shapes *u* and *v*, especially in initial position. In general *v* is more common in L than in T, though there is no consistency; as *u* is the norm in both manuscripts I have standardized it unless they agree on *v* (whether for vowel or consonant). Similarly I have used capital *I* for both vowel and consonant, there being, of course, no significant difference of shape in either manuscript. In the *apparatus criticus* I do not usually record spelling variants unless I have normalized against the evidence of both manuscripts. Abbreviations (which are very frequent) are expanded without notice except occasionally in the *apparatus* when it seemed that the nature of, or reason for, a scribe's error would be made clearer by an indication that he was using a contraction; in such instances I either reproduce the abbreviation or italicize the letters supplied in expansion. Also in the *apparatus*, letters interlined by the original scribe are enclosed in caret brackets, thus ⟨a⟩. A very few explanatory notes are intermingled with the record of variants, but I have not thought it necessary to justify my editorial decisions (except for the cases discussed in Chapter III above), nor do I normally give references for the Biblical and other citations in the text; those from the Bible can be identified by the use of a concordance to the Vulgate. References to the *Moralia* are by part and chapter and the folio-numbers of L and T; those to *Ancrene Wisse* are to the folio- and line-numbers of the Corpus MS. (ed. Tolkien, E.E.T.S. 249) except in one instance where it is not running, when the reference is to the Cleopatra MS. (ed. Dobson, E.E.T.S. 267).

LIST OF PASSAGES CITED

Chapter of *Moralia*	Number of entry	Chapter of *Moralia*	Number of entry
I. 1	37	II. 16 (footnote in T)	44
8	71		
13	3	26	33
16	51	30	45
18	38	33	20
24	2	35	63
30	36	44	30
32	23	47	30
39	34	51	25
39	41	51	22
39	44		
43	54	III. 1	74
49	80	1	20
61	17	3	77
62	35	5	74
69	14	8	16
69	8	11	55
72	31	12	43
73	47	16	59
75	27	17	24
76	4	18	84
76	2	21	73
		22	29
II. 1	5	26	58
4	81	27	30
8	1	28	30
9	16	36	44
11	3	45	34
11	61	47	72

Chapter of *Moralia*	Number of entry	Chapter of *Moralia*	Number of entry
III. 48	82	IV. 9	61
52	79	10	69
52	5	11	1
54	62	15	11
56	76	16	83
61	75	17	74
63	19	17	9
66	75	18	48
68	7	22	56
69	35	24	7
71	53	28	26
71	68	29	57
75	61	30	41
79	61	33	67
82	14	37	28
82	32	38	23
83	15	38	13
83	61	38	9
84	18	41	64
85	65	44	70
86	12	46	71
88	55	50	(62,) 71
88	49	51	41
92	2	52	62
94	82	53	38
95	41	53	46
96	60	55	66
97	30	62	62
98	52	63	3
		63	39
IV. 2	6	63	19
6	10	64	13

(1) *A.W.* f. 3b/10–12 and ff. 12b/25–13a/1 (the anchoresses should be black and yet white, unattractive externally and beautiful within). Compare *Mor*. II. 8 (L f. 71^{r-v}, T f. 102^v), though the application is different:

Sicut enim per incaustum parcamenum exterius deformatur, nec ob hoc uiolatur candor interior, sic[1] et homo per peni-

[1] sic] sicut T

tentiam in corpore macie et pallore inficitur, malis etiam[1]
contemptibilis efficitur, candor tamen[2] interior non minuitur
sed potius ex pressuris suscipit incrementum. Hinc est quod
in Cantico Amoris sub typo penitentis a sponsa dicitur,
'Nigra sum sed formosa': supple[3] 'per pressuras penitentiales et malis contemptibilis, sed formosa in facie diuina'.

Compare also *Mor*. IV. 11 (L f. 194, T f. 324):

Octauus [*sc*. lapis] est[4] achates qui nigri coloris [est][5] et
ramos habet candidos, et significat sanctos pressuris et tribulationibus nigros sed decore uirtutum candidos, unde in
Canticis i, 'Nigra sum sed[6] formosa, filie Ierusalem.'

(2) *A.W.*(Corpus) f. 14a/16–14b/3 (sins caused by sight: Dina) and
A.W.(Cleopatra) ff. 25^v/20–26/1 (the windows of the eyes, through
which death enters). Compare *Mor*. I. 24 (L f. 27, T f. 31^v):

Non solum membra genitalia circumcidenda sunt, sed etiam
quinque sensus, de quibus dicit Ieremias quod mors intrat
per fenestras. [Subheading] *De circumcisione quinque sensuum:
Visus*.[7] Si uideris pauperem ad compaciendum ei, uita in te
per oculorum fenestras ingreditur. Si autem uideris mulierem
ad concupiscendam eam, mors per eorundem fenestras in
animam tuam se ingerit. Dina egressa ut uideret mulieres
alienigenas[8] corrupta est a Sichem filio Emor. Seniores quos
condempnauit Daniel species muliebris decepit,[9] et de Iudith
et de Holoferne legitur, 'Sandalia eius rapuerunt oculos eius;
pulcritudo eius captiuam fecit[10] animam eius.'

Compare also *Mor*. I. 76 (L ff. 63^v–4, T ff. 90^v–1):

Fenestre nostre quinque sunt sensus. Ad illas[11] sedemus cum

---

[1] etiam] et L   [2] tamen] iñ T   [3] supple] suple LT   [4] est]
om. L   [5] est] *om*. LT   [6] sed] et T   [7] Visus] *om*. L
[8] alienigenas] *so A.W.*; regionis illius *Vulgate* (*Gen. 34: 1*)   [9] decepit]
interlined by original scribe L *om*. T   [10] captiuam fecit] fecit captiuam
T   [11] illas] illam T

easdem ita custodimus, oculos ne uideant uanitatem, aures ne audiant[1] detractionem, et ita de aliis. De istis fenestris dicit Ieremias, 'Mors intrat per fenestras.'

Compare further *Mor*. III. 92 (L f. 180[v], T f. 300[v]):

Virgines de quibus in themate proposito mentio facta est merito per quinarium numerantur, eo quod (considerando propheticum illud quo[2] dictum est, 'Mors intrat per fenestras'), fenestris quinque sensuum continentie pessula apponendo, uiciis in ipsas aditus obstruxerunt;[3] eo etiam quod quinque uulnera Cristi ad mentem frequenter reduxerunt.

(3) *A.W.* ff. 18b/4–20a/20 (on the virtue of silence) combines citations found in several passages in the *Moralia*. *Mor*. I. 13, 'De approbatione silentii et suggilatione multiloquii . . .', takes as its starting-point Mary's silence after the angelic salutation (cf. *A.W.* f. 16a/13–15) and includes the passage (L ff. 19[v]–20, T ff. 18[v]–19):

Hinc propheta ait, 'In silentio et spe est fortitudo nostra', et item, 'Cultus (scilicet[4] custos) iusticie silentium.' Et iterum Ieremias:[5] 'Bonum est cum silentio prestolari salutare dei.' Sit igitur tibi[6] collum [arte anctum][7] ne sis preceps in sermone. Multiloquium enim non declinat peccatum; fluuius exundans cito colligit lutum ultra modum, flatus maris periculum parit . . . Alliga sermonem tuum ne luxuriet,[8] ne lasciuiat[9] et multiloquio sibi peccata colligat. Sit restrictior,[10] et ripis suis coerceatur . . . Sicut urbs patens et absque murorum ambitu, ita uir qui non potest in locutione cohibere spiritum suum.

---

[1] audiant] audeant L   [2] quo] de quo T   [3] obstruxerunt] *corr. from* obstrixerunt T   [4] scilicet] fuit L   [5] Ieremias] Interius L   [6] tibi] *interlined* T   [7] arte anctum] artee·L aror T   [8] luxuriet] luxuriat *corr. by later hand to* -et L   [9] lasciuiat] laciuiet L   [10] restrictior] restrictor L

Mor. II. 11, 'De septem que uiam diabolo in homine pariunt et eorundem remediis' (cf. *A.W.* f. 18b/12–14), contains the sentences (L f. 73, T f. 106):

Quartus modus corruptela est praue locutionis. Apostolus: 'Corrumpunt bonos mores colloquia praua.' Praua uerba praua sunt incitamenta peccatorum. Salomon: 'Mors et uita in manibus lingue.'

Compare further *Mor.* IV. 63 (L ff. 246ᵛ–7, T f. 404):

De lingua igitur oris nobis ad presens erit sermo, cuius circumspectionem et nouitatem affectans Ecclesiasticus xxii dicit, 'Quis dabit ori meo custodiam, et super labia mea signaculum[1] certum, ne cadam in ipsis et lingua mea perdat me?' Ne mireris si custodiam lingue affectauerit Iesus filius Syrach, cum per linguam inconsideratam et precipue adulatoriam multi occiderint; plus enim nocet lingua adulatoris quam gladius interfectoris.

(4) *A.W.* f. 21b/11–12, 25–6 (in the passage concerning the backbiter). Compare *Mor.* I. 76 (L f. 63ᵛ, T f. 90ʳ⁻ᵛ):

[Subheading] *Detractio* . . . Salomon in Parabolis xxiii: 'Noli esse in conuiuiis[2] potatorum, nec in commessationibus eorum qui carnes ad uescendum conferunt, quia uacantes potibus et dantes[3] symbola consumentur, et uestietur pannis dormitatio.' 'Carnes ad uescendum conferre' est alicui aliquem detrahere, et alium ad detrahendum eidem associari, et eundem proximum[4] decerpendo[5] iuuare. 'Potibus uacare' est de opprobrio aliene uite sese inebriare, id est in ipso delectari . . . Item Ecclesiasticus:[6] 'Uentus aquilo dissipat pluuias, facies tristis linguam detrahentem', id est, sicut aquilo

---

[1] signaculum] signaculun L   [2] conuiuiis] conuiuio L   [3] dantes] diuites T   [4] proximum] *corr. from* proximo L proximo T   [5] decerpendo] *corr. from* deturpendo T   [6] Ecclesiasticus] *in fact Prov. 25: 23; but cf. Ecclus. 43: 22*

pluuias, sic et tristicia que detracto ingeritur detrahentem
ad nichilum rediget.

(5) *A.W.* ff. 24b/16–25a/7 deals with the two wedding-gifts that
anchoresses receive, 'swiftness and the light of clear sight'. Two
passages in *Mor.* similarly speak of a double dowry, but the
qualities conferred are different. The first is in *Mor.* II. 1 (L
f. 66[v], T f. 95):

[Subheading] *De desponsatione Cristi et fidelis anime, et
de dote quam in ipsam dat deus fideli anime, et de maritagio
quod Cristus ab homine deposcit* . . . Scio quod a uiro mulieri
datur dos, uiro maritagium ab illo qui dat uxorem. Quando
confitetur quis,[1] contrahit[2] matrimonium cum deo,[3] cui dat
Cristus duo in dotem, scilicet ut oculo clementie eum respi-
ciat[4] et conferat ei gratiam penitendi, secundo remissionem
peccati. Ecce dos. Dominus etiam[5] a te[6] maritagium deposcit,
quod in Michea hiis exprimitur: 'Indicabo[7] tibi, o homo,
quid requirat deus a te, facere iudicium et iusticiam.'

The second is in *Mor.* III. 52 (L f. 147[v], T f. 241[v]):

Dos igitur duplex est, scilicet gratia in presenti et gloria in
futuro. Unde Psalmista: 'Gratiam et gloriam dabit dominus.'

(6) *A.W.* f. 28a/15–16 (which says that Christ wept thrice) depends on *Mor.* IV. 2 (L f. 187[v], T f. 312[r–v]):

Ipse enim ait per Ieremiam prophetam, 'Tu polluta es cum
amatoribus multis, reuertere tamen et reuertar ad te ut
sordes tuas abluam et[8] triplici aqua ablutam[9] te[10] mihi con-
federem.' Legimus de triplici aque effusione per Cristum

---

¹ quis] qui T   ² contrahit] trahit T   ³ deo] Cristo L
⁴ respiciat] respiciant T   ⁵ etiam] *interlined* T   ⁶ a te] *corr.
from* ait T   ⁷ Indicabo] Iudicabo T   ⁸ et] *erased in* L   ⁹ ab-
lutam] abluite (-ite *over erasure*) L   ¹⁰ te] et *interlined by later hand
before* te L

facta: prima cum uidens ciuitatem fleuit super eam; secunda in suscitatione Lazari; tercia cum aquam misit in peluim.[1] Prima contritionis significatiua est; secunda confessionis, ratione clamoris fletui[2] secundo annexi (unde legitur quod lacrimatus est[3] et clamauit, 'Lazare, ueni foras'); per terciam aquam satisfactio exprimitur . . . Tercia lauat manus; unde illud, 'Lauabo inter innocentes[4] manus meas.'

(7) *A.W.* f. 30b/2–12 (Christ sweated blood on the Cross). Compare *Mor.* III. 68 (L f. 160, T f. 264ᵛ):

Ut dicit Ysaias, Cristus fuit 'uir dolorum', nam 'in agonia factus est sudor membrorum quasi gutte sanguinis decurrentis in terram'. Super quem locum dicit [Bernardus],[5] 'Non solum oculis sed omnibus membris Cristus fleuisse uidetur, ut totum corpus eius, quod est ecclesia, tocius corporis lacrimis rigaretur.'

The ideas, and the erroneous ascription, are repeated in *Mor.* IV. 24 (L f. 205, T f. 343):

'Et factus est sudor eius sicut[6] gutte sanguinis decurrentis in terram.' . . . Ratione huius sanguinis dicit [Bernardus][7] de Cristo, 'Non solum oculis sed etiam[8] omnibus membris Cristus fleuisse uidetur, ut totum corpus eius, quod est ecclesia, tocius corporis lacrimis rigaretur.'

(8) *A.W.* f. 30b/14 ff. (Christ's tender flesh). Compare *Mor.* I. 69 (L f. 59ʳ⁻ᵛ, T f. 83):

'Attendite et uidete si est dolor sicut dolor[9] meus.' Quod bene uideri potest per assimile,[10] quia caro mortua, lesa et percussa,

---

[1] peluim] peluem L　　[2] fletui] fletu L　　[3] est] *om.* L, *supplied by later hand*　　[4] innocentes] innocentem T　　[5] Bernardus] Beda LT　　[6] sicut] sucut T　　[7] Bernardus] Beda LT　　[8] etiam] *om.* T　　[9] sicut dolor] *om. but supplied in margin in plummet by original scribe* L　　[10] assimile] simile T

non sentit penam tam acerbam sicut et caro[1] uiua. Sic[2] caro
nostra, per peccatum mortificata,[3] passionem sibi illatam non
sentit sicut et caro Cristi, que uiua fuit et, immunis a peccato,
preciosa fuit[4] et attrahens, unde 'Cum exaltatus fuero a terra',
etc. Ita,[5] sicut adamas ferrum, et[6] [Cristus attrahit][7] nos, qui
sumus ferrei, id est ad bonum duri et ad malum acuti.
Cum[8] enim deus per alia opera nos moneat et moueat, per
passionem suam nos attrahit, [quis][9] non est tam durus (si[10]
bene attendat et recolat passionem Cristi et si recordetur
quantum biberit ad patibulum qui nos inuitat[11] ad celum)
quin cor eius per dilectionem attrahatur, et omnes penas
quas sustinet pro eo paruipendat?[12]

(9) *A.W.* ff. 30b/23–31a/14 (Christ's bloodletting on the Cross).
Compare *Mor.* IV. 17 (L f. 198[v], T f. 332[v]):

Ipse potatus est aceto cum felle mixto in minutione[13] sua,
nos [in minutione][14] nostra uino gariophylis condito contra
eum potamur.

Compare also, and more importantly, *Mor.* IV. 38 (L f. 220[v],
T f. 366[v]):

[Subheading] *De statu Cristi in cruce et quod fleobotomia ipsius
e diuerso fleobotomie nostre respondeat.* Item ad sumptionem
crucis nos inuitat passio Cristi, que ex contrariis que fleubo-

---

[1] caro] *om.* T   [2] Sic] Sic et T   [3] mortificata] *before* per
peccatum T   [4] immunis . . . fuit] *om. but* supplied in margin by
original scribe T   [5] Ita] *erased by later hand* L   [6] et] *altered
to* ita *by later hand* L *interlined* T   [7] Cristus attrahit] *om.* LT
[8] Cum] cum L   [9] quis] Quia L quia T   [10] si] qui L   [11] inuitat]
mutat L   [12] paruipendat] paruipendet L   [13] minutione]
municione *struck through and replaced by* minutione *in margin in later
hand* L   [14] in minutione] in municione *altered to* in minicione L
iminutione T

tomia deposcit perspicua erit. Quibus autem eadem gratuletur
ex uersibus subscriptis elicias:

> Iuncta quies[1] tenebris est grata cruore minuto;
> [Solem][2] deuitat, baculum tenet, utitur idem
> Deliciis. Posito secus accidit in cruce Cristo:
> Expositus uentis et soli fleubotomatur.
> In cruce plus aliis premitur[3] caro uiuida[4] Cristi.
> Cur? Quia peccatum numquam corrupit eandem.
> Hanc etiam [querit][5] de uirgine, cui caro queuis[6]
> Mollicie minor est. Tumulo dormitat ad horam.[7]
> Nec crux sed[8] claui,[9] [baculi][10] uice, sustinet ipsum;
> In cruce cum felle mixto potatur aceto.

(10) *A.W.* f. 32a/19 ff. (the pelican). Compare *Mor.* IV. 6 (L
f. 190, T f. 317ᵛ):

Hiis aditias quod pellicanus[11] pullos suos interficit et post
biduo deplorat et tercia die sanguine a se fuso uiuificat. Sic
et Cristus Saulum occidit et Paulum suscitauit et sanguine
suo uiuificauit, id est, fide[12] passionis sue corroborauit.

(11) *A.W.* ff. 32b/2c–33a/16 (wrath transforms human nature).
Compare *Mor.* IV. 15 (L f. 196ᵛ, T f. 329):

Ad suggillationem ergo iracundie facit quod non est aliquod
uicium quod ita hominem transformet et exterminet sicut
uicium ire. Cum enim iuxta Philosophum hominis[13] magis
proprium sit quam alterius animalis esse mansuetum natura,

---

[1] quies] qui es *altered from* qui es*t* T   [2] Solem] Sompnum LT
[3] premitur] *altered by later hand to* preeritur (*preerit intended?*) L
[4] uiuida] in uida *corr. to* uiuida *by hair-strokes over third and sixth minims*
T   [5] querit] q. arit L q̄ arit T   [6] queuis] q*uis* T   [7] horam]
oram L   [8] sed] nec T   [9] claui] clauis T   [10] baculi] baiuli L
baculis T   [11] pellicanus] pellanus *corr. in margin by later hand to*
pellicanus L   [12] fide] fidem L   [13] hominis] hominum T

ira hominem[1] furibundum facit. Unde et ratione effectus dicit Philosophus, 'Ira furor breuis est', etc.

(12) *A.W.* ff. 33b/1–19 and 34a/4–10 (a word is only wind). Compare *Mor.* III. 86 (L f. 174ᵛ, T f. 291):

Item debilis censendus est qui modico flatu uenti deicitur. Uerbum autem non est nisi uentus quidam. Bene ergo se debilem demonstrat si per aliquod uerbum iratus cadat.[2] Mirum est enim, cum pro domino sancti[3] sustinerent plagas corporis, quod nos sustinere refutamus quasdam plagas aeris. Ut autem plagas a deo illatas pacienter feras, consideres quod deum multociens[4] offendisti, et quod deus offensas suas hic punit uel alibi; et si hic,[5] non alibi, quia non punit deus bis in id ipsum.

(13) *A.W.* f. 36a/6–10 (similitude from a bird flying in the form of a cross). Compare *Mor.* IV. 38 (L f. 220, T f. 365ᵛ), which has a series of bird similitudes:

Auis non nisi cruciata ad superiora prouehitur, nec homo nisi cruce signatus ad celum promouetur. Auis cruciata laqueos declinat, et homo cruce signatus de facili laqueos diaboli deuitat. Columba alis expansis, rostro mediante, ab hoste defenditur, et homo signaculo crucis ad hec uerba, 'In nomine patris, etc.', a demonibus sese conseruat illesum. Auis uolando aliam intercipit, et homo cruce signatus diabolum disconficit.

Another comparable instance is in *Mor.* IV. 64 (L f. 248, T f. 405ᵛ):

Et notandum quod, sicut uulgariter dicitur, auis in alto uolans alas habet extensas, quarum una erat iusticia et altera miseri-

---

[1] hominem] *corr. from* hominum T   [2] cadat] *corr. from* cedat T
[3] sancti] *before* pro domino T   [4] multociens] multocies *altered by faint plummet mark* L   [5] hic] hic et *altered to* hic: et T

cordia, que inuicem in Cristo fuerunt annexe, ita quod numquam fuit in eo una sine altera. Has extendit Cristus in
cruce . . .

(14) *A.W.* f. 36a/12–21 (the worldly anchoress compared to the
ostrich, which cannot fly). Compare *Mor.* I 69 (L ff. 58ᵛ–9,
T f. 82ᵛ):

Penne igitur siue ale quibus ad deum querendum prouehimur[1] sunt amor et timor. Quorum utrumque per se infructuosum:[2] amor enim sine timore erigit in presumptionem,
timor uero[3] sine amore deicit in desperationem. De pennis
siue alis propositis dicit Ezechiel x quod uidit hominem
habentem duas alas[4] et manus[5] hominis subtus pennas eius . . .
Manus hominis sunt opera bona, scilicet opera rationis, ut
ieiunium, oratio, elemosina, et huiusmodi. Sed multi habent
alas sed non habent subtus manus[6] hominis sed bestie, et
ideo non possunt ascendere, sicut[7] struccio[8] qui[9] habet alas,
nec tamen potest uolare. Manus bestie sunt opera mala,[10] ut
carnales uoluptates etc., ut qui rapit aliis uel luxuriatur uel
superbit.

Compare also *Mor.* III. 82 (L f. 171, T ff. 284ʳ⁻ᵛ):

'Ue uobis scribe et pharisei, ypocrite . . .' . . . Quid struccionum[11] nomine nisi ypocrisis designatur? Struccio[12] speciem[13]
uolandi[14] habet sed uim uolandi non habet, [quasi][15] ypocrisis
cunctis[16] uidentibus ymaginem sanctitatis de se insinuat, sed
uitam tamen sanctitatis non seruat.

---

[1] querendum prouehimur] prouehimur querendum *but marked for
transposition* L   [2] infructuosum] infructuosum est T   [3] uero]
enim T   [4] alas] pennas *with* siue alas *above* L   [5] manus] *corr.
from* minus T   [6] manus] *interlined* T   [7] sicut] sed T   [8] struccio] strucio L structio T   [9] qui] *om.* L   [10] opera mala] mala
opera T   [11] struccionum] strucionum T   [12] Struccio] Strutio T
[13] speciem] spēm *in margin replacing* spm̄ *deleted in text* L   [14] uolandi]
corr. from uolendi L   [15] quasi] quia LT   [16] cunctis] cuntis T

(15) *A.W.* f. 37a/8–22 (the eagle puts in his nest a stone called *achate*). Compare *Mor.* III. 83 (L f. 172, T f. 286):

[Subheading] *De efficacia lapidis qui echites dicitur.* Adiecto quod, sicut aquila echitem siue amatistam defert ab oriente in[1] nidum suum ut reprimat uirus, sic et Cristus corpus suum in fideles deportat[2] ut uirus peccati ab ipsis repellat. Uersus de echite:

> Eximie lapis est uirtutis quum Iouis ales,
> Ut uirus perimat, solis deportat ab ortu.
> Hunc si leua gerat lapidem cui nomen echites
> Auget opes, confert palmam, largitur amorem,
> Mensuramque parit lapis hic, regumque fauorem.

(16) *A.W.* f. 37b/6–18 (the interpretation of the name *Olofernes*). The interpretation, which comes from the later lists of *Interpretationes nominum hebraicorum*, is similarly used in *Mor.* II. 9 (L f. 71[v], T f. 103[r–v]):

Nabugodonosor diabolum, Olofernes mundum significat,[3] et merito. Olofernes enim interpretatur 'infirmitas discessionis uel infirmans uitulum saginatum'. Hoc competit mundo, quia omne quod in eo est, instabile est et transitorium ... Uitulus saginatus est qui in mundialibus[4] excrescit et a mundialibus[4] suffocatur, ne ad eterna queat assurgere. Uitulum huiusmodi mundus ita[5] infirmat et dissoluit ut qui uictima dei esse debuerat, uictima mundi et diaboli efficiatur ... Mundus est princeps milicie diaboli, quia per amorem mundi plurimos sibi subiugauit diabolus.

Compare also *Mor.* III. 8 (L f. 114[v], T f. 175):

Olofernes interpretatur 'infirmans uitulum saginatum', in quo

---

[1] in] in *corr. from* ut T   [2] deportat] deportet T   [3] significat] signat T   [4] mundialibus] mundalibus L   [5] ita] *om.* T

notatur potestas diaboli, quam habet maxime in eos qui sunt
uituli per lasciuiam[1] et saginati per temporalem habundan-
tiam.

(17) *A.W.* f. 40a/11–27, 40b/11–12 (good deeds should not be
done for worldly praise). Compare *Mor.* I. 61 (L f. 53, T f. 73):

[Heading] *Circa suggillationem*[2] *ypocrisis versatur.*[3] 'Cum facis
elemosinam, noli tuba canere ante te sicut hypocrite faciunt.'
. . . Iob contra ypocrisim[4] loquens ait, 'Non ei placebit
uecordia ypocrite, et sicut tela aranearum fiducia eius.'
Gregorius: 'Uecordia est magnam rem uili precio uendere,
id est bona laboriosa agere pro fauore.' Hoc modo delectatur
sed in pena displicebit, et tunc sciet nichil fuisse[5] omnia que
transierunt. Unde 'sicut tela aranearum':[6] tela aranearum
studiose texitur, flatu uenti dissipatur.

(18) *A.W.* f. 40a/27–40b/4 (Moses' hand, withdrawn from his
bosom, seemed leprous). Compare *Mor.* III. 84 (L f. 172[v], T f.
287):

Opulentus enim in operatione sua gloriam mundi querit,
et ad ipsam[7] assequendam opus suum publicare desiderat.
Recolat igitur huiuscemodi quod Moysi a domino dictum est:
'Mitte manum tuam in sinum.' Quamdiu manus est in sinum,
id est in occulto, munda est; prolata extra sinum per glorie
manifestationem, leprosa est. Retrahatur ergo ad sinum, id
est[8] ad occultationem, et ad mundiciam reuertetur. Sicut ergo
leprosus in corpore ab obsequiis humanis, sic et leprosus in
mente ab obsequiis dei repellitur.

---

[1] lasciuiam] laciuiam LT   [2] suggillationem] siggillacionem *corr. to*
sugg- L singillationem T   [3] versatur] *om.* T   [4] ypocrisim]
apocrisim T   [5] nichil fuisse] quia nichil fuerunt T   [6] ara-
nearum] ara. LT   [7] ipsam] *corr. from* ipasam T   [8] id est]
om. T

(19) *A.W*. ff. 40b/12–41a/13 (similitude of the fig-tree). Compare *Mor*. III. 63 (L f. 156ᵛ, T f. 258):

Qui enim opera sua ad¹ ostentationem magnificant, ficum fructiferam decorticant et eam spoliant. Iohel: 'Gens innumerabilis ascendit super terram meam; ficum decorticauit, nudam spoliauit,² albi³ facti sunt rami eius.' Mala est ista dealbatio. Tales hic mercedem accipiunt: fauorem et laudem humanam quam querunt.

Compare also *Mor*. IV. 63 (L f. 247ʳ⁻ᵛ, T ff. 404ᵛ–5), where the text is applied against flatterers but details of the exposition correspond to the passage in *A.W*.:

Item contra adulatores facit illud Iohelis, 'Ficum meam⁴ decorticauit, nudans⁵ spoliauit eam, proiecit eam, rami eius facti sunt albi.' Nudans adulator spoliauit eam bonis suis⁶ per adulationem, et sic a bono statu⁷ proiecit eam. Rami eius, id est opera bona, uirore humilitatis prius obducta, facti sunt albi et ita aridi. Ablato enim cortice, non potest ramus uirorem suum seruare⁸ sed arescit; sed quam diu cortex ramo in suo trunco manente adheret, uiror rami interius conseruatur. Sic quam diu humilitas adheret operi, uiror operis conseruatur; sed recedente per propallationem, bonum opus arescens mortificatur. Pulcritudinem tamen exterius pretendit, et albi⁹ facti sunt rami eius, ut enim dicit Gregorius, 'Hostes ad rapinam prouocat, qui suas eorum noticie diuicias denudat.'

(20) *A.W*. f. 41a/18–21 (citation of Gregory). The same sentence is twice cited in the *Moralia*; so II. 33 (L f. 89ᵛ, T f. 133ᵛ):

Gregorius: 'Depredari desiderat qui puplice [publice T] thesaurum in uia portat.'

¹ ad] ab T   ² spoliauit] *corr. from* sploliauit L   ³ albi] *corr. from* alibi T   ⁴ meam] meum L   ⁵ nudans] *corr. from* nudatis T   ⁶ suis] *om.* T   ⁷ bono statu] statu bono T   ⁸ seruare] *after* serrorem *deleted* T   ⁹ albi] *corr. from* alibi T

and *Mor.* III. 1 (L f. 110, T f. 167ᵛ):

Iustus autem tondetur[1] in hyeme huius mundi quando facit opus bonum propter uanam[2] gloriam et sic[3] spiritualiter morietur. Unde Gregorius: 'Depredari desiderat qui thesaurum puplice [publice T] in uia portat.'

(21) *A.W.* f. 42a/27–8 (citation of Jeremiah 9: 1); see entry no. 36 below.

(22) *A.W.* f. 43b/11–16 (our Lady was found in solitude by Gabriel). Compare *Mor.* II. 51 (L f. 102ᵛ, T f. 155ᵛ):

Legitur quod beata uirgo ab angelo sola inuenta est, et ab angelo salutari meruit. In signum quod in solitudine mentis constituti a magni[4] consilii angelo salutem consequentur.

(23) *A.W.* f. 44a/27–44b/7 (a wise woman would take refuge from a roaring lion). Compare *Mor.* I. 32 (L f. 34, T f. 43):

Si bestia inmanis et truculenta quempiam ad deuorandum quereret, ad locum munitum in quo immunis a bestie lesione delitescere posset sese transferret.[5] Quis diabolo truculentior? De quo Petrus: 'Aduersarius noster diabolus tanquam leo rugiens circuit, querens quem deuoret.' . . . Nobis ergo, tociens a diabolo ad deuorandum quesitis, ad locum munitum, Cristum[6] scilicet, confugiendum est.

A more martial version comes in *Mor.* IV. 38 (L f. 220, T f. 365ᵛ):

Si bestia inmanis ad quemuis deuorandum accederet, ad se ipsum conseruandum armis se indueret quibus se ab aduersario tueri[7] posset. Aduersarius noster diabolus est, de quo

---

[1] tondetur] *corr. from* tonditur L   [2] uanam] ua⟨na⟩m T   [3] et sic] *om.* L   [4] magni] *corr. from* maligni L   [5] transferret] transferet L   [6] Cristum] *before* munitum *but marked for transference* L   [7] tueri] tue⟨r⟩i T

dicitur: 'Aduersarius noster tanquam leo rugiens circuit, querens quem deuoret.' Arma sunt signacula[1] crucis, quibus multociens diabolus in bello[2] subcumbit; unde et eadem diabolus pre ceteris rebus formidat.

This, in the use of the sign of the cross as a weapon against the devil in the form of a beast, resembles the 'dog of hell' passage in *A.W.* f. 79a/3–12 but is not otherwise parallel to it.

(24) *A.W.* f. 45a/14–15 (worldly things compared to the moon). The idea is commonplace, but perhaps compare *Mor.* III. 17 (L f. 121, T f. 187ᵛ):

Stultus ut luna mutatur. Stultus lune simulatur, et merito: sicut enim luna crescit et decrescit, sic et[3] stultus in temporalibus augetur et in uirtutibus minoratur.

(25) *A.W.* f. 46a/18–46b/23 (Semei and his significance). The same moral is more concisely drawn in *Mor.* II. 51 (L f. 102ᵛ, T f. 155ᵛ):

Semey[4] secutus seruum fugitiuum extra Ierusalem interfectus est. Eodem modo multi qui requiescere deberent in Ierusalem, hoc est in claustro uel in scolis, dum secuntur seruum fugitiuum, scilicet redditum aliquem, sepe [intercipiuntur et interficiuntur].[5] Dina egressa a Sichem[6] oppressa est. Per Dinam intelliguntur uagabundi; unde bene Dina interpretatur 'iudicium', et uagabundi iusto iudicio dei a demonibus rapiuntur.

(26) *A.W.* f. 46b/15–23 (part of preceding passage; the five wits should stay at home and serve their lady). Compare *Mor.* IV. 28

---

[1] signacula] signaculum T   [2] in bello] *om.* L   [3] sic et] et sic *but marked for transposition* T   [4] Semey] Symeon L   [5] intercipiuntur et interficiuntur] interficiuntur et intercipiuntur L intercipiuntur T   [6] Sichem] Sychē L sichen T

(L f. 209, T f. 349^(r–v)), though in it the example is Ysboseth's
handmaid:

Ancilla est caro uel sensualitas, que subesse debet non pre-
esse, ut sit ancilla, non domina. Hec est ancilla que dum
male custodiuit hostium, interfectus est Ysboseth.[1]

(27) *A.W.* f. 47a/6–18 (the anchoresses should be like a thief
who has taken refuge in a church). The similitude is very briefly
stated in *Mor.* I. 75 (L f. 62^v, T f. 89):

Fur, ut suspendium deuitet, ad ecclesie se[2] transfert sub-
sidium.

(28) *A.W.* f. 48a/21–2 (temptations are exterior and interior).
So *Mor.* IV. 37 (L f. 219^v, T f. 364^v):

Et nota quod omne genus peccati in hiis duobus consistit,
scilicet in mala operatione exterius et in mala uoluntate
interius.

(29) *A.W.* f. 50b/23–4 cites 'Salomon' (in fact Ecclus. 21: 11),
'Via impiorum complantata est lapidibus, id est, duris afflictionibus.' Miss Salu, op. cit., p. 83 n. 1, rejects *complantata* for the
standard Vulgate reading *complanata*, but the author certainly
meant *complantata*, which was a common variant. So in *Mor.*
III. 22 (L f. 125^v, T f. 196^(r–v)):

In miseria et pena et afflictione sunt in hoc mundo omnes[3]
tam diuites quam pauperes, et omnes moriuntur. Unde
Ecclesiasticus . . . Item: 'Uie impiorum complantate sunt
lapidibus[4] quadris, et finis illorum tenebre et mors.'

A.W.'s gloss, 'id est, duris afflictionibus', may have been suggested by the first part of this.

---

[1] Ysboseth] Ysbo(s)eth T   [2] se] si *subpuncted and the* i *erased before*
se T   [3] omnes] *om.* L   [4] lapidibus] lapibus L

(30) *A.W.* f. 58a/4–9 (in hell the coverlet and the blanket of the covetous will consist of worms). The *Moralia* has a series of comparable passages. *Mor.* II. 44 (L f. 97ᵛ, T f. 147ᵛ):

Audi prophetam quid dixerit: 'Uermis', inquit, 'eorum[1] non morietur, et ignis eorum non extinguetur.' Isti sunt uermes quos gignit auaritia, quos generat diuiciarum ceca cupiditas.

Mor. II. 47 (L f. 99ᵛ, T ff. 150ᵛ–1):

In aqua[2] stante, que uermes generat, figurantur diuicie terrene que, cum egenis non disperguntur, in uermes eterne dampnationis conuertuntur . . . Spargi[3] quoque debent diuicie ne uermes generent conscientie si quiescunt et ne ex earum accumulatione uana gloria fiat.

Mor. III. 27 (L f. 128ᵛ, T f. 202ʳ⁻ᵛ):

'Homo quidam erat diues et induebatur purpura et bysso, et epulabatur cotidie splendide.' . . . De primo,[4] scilicet de[5] concupiscentia carnis, ait Ysaias: 'Subter te sternetur tinea et operimentum tuum uermes.' Ecce culcitra[6] et operimentum nostrum.

Mor. III. 28 (L f. 130, T ff. 205ᵛ–6):

Lintheamen erit tinea, operimentum erunt uermes. Vnde Ysaias: 'Subter te sternetur tinea et operimentum tuum uermes.'

Mor. III. 97 is on the Pains of Hell; under the third and fourth (hunger and thirst) the author cites (L f. 185, T f. 308) the text 'Serui mei comedent et uos esurietis' (cf. *A.W.* f. 58a/17–19), and the seventh is thus described (L f. 185, T f. 308):

Septima est uermes, serpentes, colubri, et alii uermiculi. Unde Ysaias, lectum diuitis qui delicate in hoc seculo uiuit

---

[1] inquit eorum] eorum inquit T   [2] aqua] qua T   [3] spargi] spergi T   [4] primo] primo dicitur L   [5] de] *interlined* T
[6] culcitra] *corr. from* culcitur T

describens,[1] ait 'Subter te sternetur tinea et operimentum tuum uermes.' Loco enim culcitre quam habuit diues ex plumis, dabuntur ei[2] culcitre ex tineis et aliis uermiculis; loco operimentorum que hic habuit ex uario et grisio, dabitur ei operimentum contextum ex serpentibus. Durus est iste lectus delicatis.

(31) *A.W.* f. 58b/2–11 (the lecher stinks before God). Compare *Mor.* I. 72 (L f. 61, T f. 86):

Sic et quanto quiuis plus feruet estu libidinis, tanto ante deum magis putet et fetidius.

(32) *A.W.* f. 60a/19–60b/21 (the devil, giving speciously good advice, may make charity the occasion of cupidity and other sins). Compare *Mor.* III. 82 (L f. 171ᵛ, T f. 285):

Item per strucciones[3] demones transformantes se in angelos lucis signantur, qui sub specie[4] boni aliis mala suggerunt. Huiuscemodi quosdam ad curiam sectandam inuitant ut parentibus et pauperibus profusius[5] largiantur. Quod quidem a demonibus non ob hoc persuadetur, scilicet ut detur pauperibus, sed ut cupiditati solito curiosius inuigilent.

(33) *A.W.* f. 61b/20–6 (a stronghold that has been taken is not attacked). For a different similitude, but of the same type, see *Mor.* II. 26 (L f. 84ᵛ, T f. 125ᵛ):

Nostis quod id moris est[6] in castri obseditioni ut, si uicti sint qui in castro sunt, uictor post castri redditionem statim[7] in eius eminentiori loco signum suum ponit, ut per hoc innotescat omnibus sibi redditum. Nostis item quod homo,

---

[1] describens] descri *with* bens *added in red* T   [2] ei] eis L
[3] strucciones] structiones L strutiones T   [4] specie] spe T   [5] profusius] perfusius *with abbreviation for* pro *in margin in plummet* L
[6] est] sit *after* obseditioni T   [7] statim] *corr. from* statum T

dum in mortali peccato est, est castrum diaboli, nec prius
castrum dei efficitur antequam per confessionem expellatur
ipse diabolus.

(34) *A.W.* f. 62b/6–16 (the similitude of the mother hiding in
play from her child and then running to him with spread arms).
There is no parallel in the *Moralia*, but there are two similitudes
of the same type. The first is in *Mor.* I. 39 (L f. 39ᵛ, T f. 52):

Sic mater paruulo delinquenti irata, si uidet eum ire in preceps, ne cadat occurrit, ire oblita, pietate plena. Est igitur opus
dei proprium misereri,[1] parcere, et condonare. Non suum est
sed alienum irasci et punire.

The other is in III. 45 (L f. 142ᵛ, T f. 231):

Ibi [*sc.* in cruce] enim extendit dominus brachia sua ad nos
amplectendos et portandos,[2] et sicut nutrix ad alliciendum
puerum plene extendit brachia sua quantum potest, cum
tamen modica et paruula extensione eum possit colligere et
amplecti,[3] sic dominus in cruce.

(35) *A.W.* f. 66a/24–6 (the verses *Oratio lenit* . . . and their
translation). Compare *Mor.* I. 62 (L f. 54, T f. 74):

Oratio autem dominum[4] delinit, lacrima cogit; illa ungit, ista
pungit.

The same idea, differently expressed, comes in *Mor.* III. 69
(L f. 161, T f. 267):

Item deuota debet esse oratio in lacrimis. Vnde Beda: 'Lacrime pondera uocis habent; non supplicant sed imperant.'

---

[1] misereri] misseri T   [2] et portandos] et portantos L *om.* T
[3] et amplecti] *om.* T   [4] dominum] dm̄ *over erasure* L domini T

(36) *A.W.* f. 66b/9–14 (tears compared to a castle's moat). So in *Mor.* I. 30 (L f. 33ʳ⁻ᵛ, T f. 41ᵛ):

Non igitur¹ ad abluendum sed ad castri nobis commissi munimentum lacrime necessarie² sunt. Castrum materiale, quo aquis profundioribus cingitur, eo amplius contra hostium impetus roboratur.³ Duo autem sunt que aquas circa castra exuberare⁴ faciunt, fons scilicet et pluuia . . . Per aquas que de fontibus scaturiunt, et aquas pluuiales, duo lacrimarum genera pinguntur . . . De hiis lacrimis ait Ieremias, 'Quis dabit capiti meo aquam et oculis meis fontem lacrimarum?'

(37) *A.W.* f. 67a/22–4 (who will be proud when he considers how little the Lord made himself within a poor maiden's breast?). Compare *Mor.* I. 1, 'De remediis contra superbiam' (L f. 11ᵛ, T f. 7ᵛ):

[Subheading] *Medela⁵ superbie ad paupertatem Cristi relata.* Item cum temporalium affluentia superbiam parere soleat, subtracta causa subtrahetur effectus; memoria etenim incarnationis et natiuitatis Cristi temporalium amorem abstergit. Considerato itaque quod filius dei de paupercula uirgine fuit conceptus, in diuersorio pauper natus, pannis inuolutus, et in presepio reclinatus, mundialium sordebit affectus et paupertas quam Cristus elegit in corde tuo florebit.

See also no. 41 below.

(38) *A.W.* f. 67b/4–9 (God came to earth to make a threefold peace and after his resurrection greeted his disciples with 'Pax vobis'). Compare *Mor.* IV. 53 (L f. 236, T ff. 389ᵛ–90):

[Heading] *De multiplici pacis reformatione, inter deum et hominem, angelum et hominem, [hominem et hominem, id est*

---

¹ igitur] ergo tamen L   ² necessarie] necesse L   ³ roboratur] roborabitur L   ⁴ exuberare] *corr. from* exuberate T   ⁵ Medela] De Medela T

inter iudeum et gentilem uel inter][1] *carnem et spiritum; et de*
triplici pace in triplici uita necessaria; et de tribus perturbanti-
bus pacem, disseritur. 'Pax uobis.' . . . Per peccatum autem
hominis[2] facta est rebellio inter deum et hominem . . . Que
[*sc.* Pax] quidem ab ipso reformata est in domini[3] conceptione, acclamata in eius natiuitate hiis uerbis 'Pax hominibus
bone uoluntatis', firmata in[4] eius passione, quando porte celi
aperte sunt . . . Et erupit hostilitas inter angelum et hominem,
et in conceptione Cristi pax inter eos restituta est. Facta
etiam est[5] pax inter iudeum et gentilem per Cristum . . . ad-
ueniente noua lege per Cristum, conuersi sunt ad fidem . . .
unde et[6] pax inter eos reformata est.

Compare also *Mor.* I. 18 (L f. 23, T f. 24):

[Heading] *De triplici pace*[7] *reformata per Cristum* . . . Salomon interpretatur 'pacificus' et significat Cristum, qui uenit
reformare pacem inter deum et hominem, inter[8] angelum et
hominem, inter hominem et hominem (id est inter iudeum
et gentilem uel inter carnem et spiritum).

(39) *A.W.* f. 68b/8–12 (examples of the advantages of unity:
dust and grit are dispersed by a little puff of wind, but not if
mortared together in a lump). A similar image is used in *Mor.*
IV. 63 (L f. 247, T f. 404[v]) but is very differently applied in a discussion of the evil effects of flattery:

Sicut dicitur in Psalterio, 'Impii sicut[9] puluis quem proicit
uentus a facie terre.' Puluis cum in altum erigitur facilius a
uento rapitur quam [si][10] in terra dimittatur; similiter et
peccatores, qui puluis sunt, facilius a turbidine temptationum

[1] hominem . . . inter] *om.* LT; *see pp.* 57–8 *above*   [2] hominis]
om. L   [3] domini] deum T   [4] firmata in] firmatas T   [5] est]
om. T   [6] et] *om.* L   [7] triplici pace] pace triplici T   [8] inter]
et inter L   [9] sicut] sunt T   [10] si] *om.* LT

proiciuntur et rapiuntur cum per adulationem in altum sub-
leuantur.

The two passages are probably independent.

(40) *A.W.* f. 70b/3–13 (remedies against sloth: others seek rest
during bloodletting, Christ had none). See the passages from the
Moralia quoted under no. 9 above.

(41) *A.W.* ff. 70b/15–71a/17 (remedies against covetousness:
Christ's poverty on earth, from his birth to his death). The
Moralia has several discussions of *paupertas Cristi*, of which
that in I. 1 (specifically adduced as a remedy for pride) is quoted
under no. 37 above. There is another brief reference to the topic
in III. 95 (L f. 183, T f. 305):

Turtur, amisso compare suo, ramo emortuo insidet. Sicut
per columbam mentis simplicitas, sic et per turturem corporis castitas, per ramum uero emortuum paupertas exprimitur. Quam exquisitam habet sedem continentia, si
aride[1] paupertati insideat. Liber experientie[2] quemque nostrum docuit quam amica sit continentie ciborum ariditas,[3]
quam contraria eorum mollicies et ingurgitatio. Omnem
reuoluite uitam saluatoris ab utero uirginis usque ad patibulum crucis, non inuenietis in eo nisi stigmata paupertatis.[4]

A closer parallel to part of the passage in *A.W.* is in *Mor.* IV. 30
(L f. 211ᵛ, T f. 353):

Sequitur [*i.e. after* humilitas] paupertas. Non enim habuit
tantum spacium in toto globo terre filius dei in quo nasce-
retur . . . Ita erat[5] locus artus in diuersorio quod uix cape-
ret Mariam et Ioseph; unde regredienti ex matris utero
non fuit locus in diuersorio, sed reclinauit eum in presepio.

---

[1] aride] arride L
crossed through T
pa⟨u⟩pertatis T

[2] experientie] experientientie *with final* ntie
crossed through T

[3] ariditas] arriditas LT

[4] paupertatis]

[5] erat] *corr. from* erit T

Non habuit in cruce ubi caput suum reclinaret.[1] Non habuit[2] sepulcrum nisi mutuatum, nec sudarium nisi misericorditer[3] ei[4] datum.

Other significant details occur in a passage which comes, in only slightly different forms, at two widely separated points in the *Moralia*. The first is in I. 39 (L f. 39ᵛ, T f. 52):

Duo sunt que hominem precipue dilectione dignum efficiunt, humilitas scilicet[5] et misericordia. Hec duo pre ceteris in Cristo enituerunt. De humilitate patet, considerato que pro nobis Cristus suscepit.[6] Ipse quidem cuius celum sedes est exiguum intemerate uirginis uterum uice hospicii[7] inhabitare[8] dignatus est. Qui etiam, relicta palacii celestis gloria, artum[9] elegit presepium. Ille etiam cuius indumentum erat lux et pulcritudo panniculis inuolutus est, et qui ratione heredi-tatis omnia habuit in manu, in[10] terris non habuit ubi caput suum reclinaret,[11] ut habetur in Euangelio.

The second is in *Mor*. IV. 51 (L f. 234, T f. 387):

Ut igitur sub ipso humiliemur, et ne ipsum detruncemus, consideremus illa que pro nobis suscepit. Ille cuius 'celum sedes' est, ut dicit propheta, tam amplum habens hospicium, in artum hospiciolum, scilicet intemerate[12] uirginis uterum, intrare dignatus est. Qui et, relicta palacii gloria celestis, elegit artum presepium. Ille etiam cuius indumentum erat lumen et pulcritudo inuolutus est panniculis. Ecce quantus erat qui descendit:[13] qui [ratione][14] hereditatis omnia creata habuit in manu, in terris non habuit ubi caput suum re-clinaret. Vnde Euangelium, 'Uulpes foueas habent, etc.'

[1] reclinaret] *corr. from* inclinaret T   [2] habuit] *in part over erasure, with* habuit *in plummet in margin as note for correction* L   [3] miseri-corditer] misercorditer L miscditer T   [4] ei] *after* nisi T   [5] scilicet] *om.* L   [6] suscepit] susceperit L   [7] hospicii] hospicis T [8] inhabitare] in humilitate T   [9] artum] arcum T   [10] in] et in L [11] reclinaret] reclinauit T   [12] intemerate] intermerate L   [13] de-scendit] de⟨s⟩cendit L   [14] ratione] eterne LT

(42) *A.W.* f. 71a/18–22 (against gluttony: Christ, when he laboured and suffered bloodletting on the Cross, had as his pittance only a sponge of gall). See the passages cited under no. 9 above.

(43) *A.W.* f. 73a/1–19 (in the subsection 'Against lechery': the devil seeks to ride mankind like a horse). Compare *Mor.* III. 12 (L f. 117ᵛ, T f. 180ᵛ):

Per luxuriam etiam efficitur homo equus diaboli, et de hoc equo in Exodo: 'Equum et ascensorem[1] proiecit in mare.' Si pro infelice[2] habendus est qui per caudam equi trahitur ad furcas materiales, pro multo infeliciore habendus est qui per caudam equi diaboli trahendus est ad furcas infernales. Equus diaboli, ut dictum est, corpus hominis est; lumbi hominis luxuriosi lumbi diaboli sunt . . . Hos lumbos, qui posteriora sunt hominis, ligat diabolus fune luxurie[3] . . . Hoc fune per posteriora trahuntur luxuriosi ad furcas infernales.

(44) *A.W.* f. 77b/14–27 (metals are cleansed of dross by the file and by fire; God must have fire and bellows and hammers in his smithy). Similar ideas come in several passages in the *Moralia*. So briefly in I. 39 (L f. 40, T f. 53):

Sed tamen scriptum est, 'Qui approximant[4] michi, approximant[4] igni.' Si aurum et argentum fueris et igni appropinquaueris, clarius per ignem effulgebis.[5]

At II. 16, T (f. 112ᵛ) has a footnote (not in L) which reads:

Nota quod [quadrupliciter][6] formantur vasa, scilicet manu,

---

[1] ascensorem] assessorem L   [2] infelice] infice *but after* f *insertion-mark and* feli *added in margin to make* (*strictly*) inf⟨feli⟩ice T   [3] ligat . . . luxurie] diabolus precingit furce luxuriose T   [4] approximant] approximat T   [5] effulgebis] effulgebit T   [6] quadrupliciter] tripliciter T

flatu, fusione, malleactione. Sic et dominus quos uult reformat tanquam bonus artifex, quandoque manu ... quandoque flatu ... quandoque per modulum ... quandoque per
malleum aspere tribulacionis.

In III. 36 (L f. 135^{r-v}, T f. 216^{r-v}) there is a sequence of such
similitudes:

Miles equum quem pungit, faber ferrum quod tundit, fullo
pannum quem calcat, permentarius pellem quam percutit,
vinitor uuam quam calcat, non odit. Sic nec Cristus quos
cruciatibus exponit odio habet;[1] sed quos in usus suos
conuerti affectat cruciari permittit, ut si quid[2] ineptum in
ipsis effrenata delectatio pepererat, tribulationis lima matu-
rius[3] [resecetur].[4] Propinauit nobis ergo[5] Cristus de calico
passionis[6] pleno ut ipsum totum hauriamus uel, si ipsum
totum[7] haurire non possumus, saltem aliquid modicum de
ipso gustemus. Super incudem paciente denario ictibus
malleorum caracter[8] regis imprimitur;[9] sic et qui crebro
tribulationibus atteritur, dum modo paciente uigor non de-
fuerit, summi regis ymagine insignietur.[10] Tribulatio casti-
moniam parit. Unde in Apocalypsi: 'Ego quos amo castigo.'

A footnote in both L (f. 135) and T (f. 216^v) gives the following
versified summary:

Non faber incudem, non pannum fullo, uel uuam
Vinitor, aut mannum miles, pellemve minister
Quam cedit, uel Cristus eum[11] quem percutit, odit.

---

[1] habet] et non habet *with* et *subpuncted* T   [2] quid] quod T
[3] maturius] *om.* L   [4] resecetur] recesetur L reseretur *but perhaps
with attempt to alter second* r *to* c T   [5] nobis ergo] ergo nobis T
[6] passionis] passione T   [7] totum] *om.* L   [8] caracter] *written
above subpuncted* extractet T   [9] imprimitur ... summi regis] *om.
but added in margin by original scribe, preceded unnecessarily by* regis *and
with* si *for* sic L   [10] insignietur] insignetur T   [11] eum] eam T

(45) *A.W.* f. 79b/4–6 (she is altogether too miserable who can overcome her foe by lifting up three fingers and will not because of sloth). So in *Mor.* II. 30 (L f. 87ᵛ, T f. 130):

Item miserrimo[1] maius miser censendus esset siquis in bello hosti subcumberet, de quo trium digitorum motu triumphare posset. Pro miserrimis[2] ergo habendi sumus qui, cum tribus digitis nobis signaculum fidei imprimere possumus, hosti nobis noxio et pernicioso subcumbimus, cum ad crucis signaculum, fide cooperante, omnes uersutie eius euanescunt.

(46) *A.W.* f. 80b/4–16 (crush the beginnings of temptation, break on the stone the first stirrings of the flesh, catch the little foxes that destroy the vineyards). So in *Mor.* IV. 53 (L f. 236ᵛ, T f. 390ʳ⁻ᵛ):

Primi motus, ubi insurgunt in nobis uelimus nolimus, héé[3] sunt uulpecule de quibus in Canticis, 'Capite uulpeculas que moliuntur uineam domini.' Capite scilicet resistendo eis, cum Psalmista dicendo, 'In matutino interficiebam omnes peccatores terre.' Uinea domini est fidelis anima, quam primi motus demoliuntur, id est perturbant, dum in actus et sermones illicitos uel diuturnas cogitationes cogunt erumpere. Sicut ergo docet Psalmista, 'Allide paruulos tuos ad petram', id est Cristum, habendo eius mortem et passionem pre oculis.

(47) *A.W.* ff. 80b/25–81a/5 (a great fire comes from a little spark). The same proverb is used in *Mor.* I. 73 (L f. 61ᵛ, T f. 87ʳ⁻ᵛ), but whereas in *A.W.* it is applied to the beginnings of sin, in the *Moralia* it illustrates how a little word may inflame men to virtue:

Item sicut ad modicam scintillam aliquotiens domus ampla comburitur, sic et ad modicum uerbum, igne spiritus sancti inflammatum, multi ad rectitudinis statum conuertuntur.

---

[1] miserrimo] miserimo LT   [2] miserrimis] miserimis L   [3] héé] so LT *for classical* hae

(48) *A.W.* ff. 82b/1–92b/26 (the sixteen qualities that confession should have). The English author rearranges the order of the points (advantageously), replaces *Certa* by *Studeuest* 'Steadfast' (Latin version *Stabilis*), and shifts and alters and greatly adds to the material (partly from other passages in the *Moralia* itself), but it is nevertheless clear that the main source for the out-line of his discussion and for much of the detail is *Mor.* IV. 18 (L ff. 199–200ᵛ, T ff. 333ᵛ–5ᵛ):

[Heading] *Penitentem mulieri parienti*[1] *equiperat; in ipso etiam de penitentia et confessione*[2] *agitur.* 'Mulier cum parit tristi-ciam habet,[3] quia uenit hora eius; cum autem pepererit filium, iam non meminit pressure propter gaudium, quia natus est homo in mundum.' Non ab re est quod per mulierem[4] penitens exprimitur; sicut enim pariens in partu tristatur, et post partum pre gaudio fructus pressure pre-cedentis non meminit, sic et penitens, cum Cristum per bonum opus parit, dolet quidem et ingemiscit, sed cum Cristum pepererit, fructus impreciabilis gaudii[5] omnem doloris in penitente scintillam extinguit . . .

Que [*sc.* Confessio] cuiusmodi debeat esse ex dicendis aduertas. Versus:[6]

> Integra, certa, frequens, humilis, cita, fusa rubore,
> Plena metus, discreta, uolens, sua, nuda, morosa,
> Fidens, uera (prius totum, post singula signans),
> Accusans et amara rei confessio fiat.

Integra debet esse confessio.[7] Satagendum est homini ut

---

[1] parienti] parturienti T   [2] confessione] de confessione T
[3] tristiciam habet] habet tristiciam T   [4] mulierem] mulieram *im-perfectly altered to* mulierem T   [5] gaudii] gaudium L gaudium *corr. to* gaudii T   [6] *For these verses see Hans Walther,* Initia Car-minum, *no. 9431; they occur in exactly this form in Oxford MS. Rawlinson C. 22 (s. xii–xiii), f. 132. Variants occur elsewhere; one (Walther, no. 14859) was written into Cotton MS. Cleopatra C. vi, f. 138, by scribe D (late s. xiii)*   [7] Integra . . . confessio] *written in both MSS. as marginal subheading but probably intended by author as part of text; cf. following paragraphs*

integre et plene et uni omnia peccata confiteatur.[1] Peccant
enim quidam qui, ut innocentes uideantur, non omnia uni,
sed eadem diuisim pluribus confitentur, sperantes se per
particularem confessionem plenam indulgentiam assequi
posse; et falluntur, cum summe crudelitatis sit ab eo qui
summe bonus est[2] dimidiam[3] sperare ueniam. Non enim
particulariter[4] remittit deus, [atqui][5] simul aut[6] omnia peccata mortalia[7] aut nulla.[8]

Certa etiam uel saltem estimata debet esse confessio.
Tenetur enim homo confiteri quotiens peccatum suum com-
misit. Puta, si fecerit fornicationem, tenetur numerum[9]
exprimere, vel si incertus sit numero tenetur estimare et
potius plus quam minus exprimere; et sic certa debet esse
confessio.

Frequens etiam debet esse confessio; frequenter enim
super peccatis nostris sacerdotes consulere debemus, et quociens labimur, tociens resurgendo ad eosdem recurrere, et
non per totum annum usque ad Quadrigesimam peccati
medicinam prolongare. Unde quidam, caute agentes, suis
iniungunt ouibus ut quociens innocentie uellus a nephandis
lupi dentibus distrahitur, tociens, sublata[10] dilatione, ad
pastorem recurrant ut redintegretur.[11]

Humilis tenetur esse confessio. In maxima enim humilitate confiteri[12] debemus et ad uicarium dei accedere, quia
per superbiam peccando a deo discessimus. Cum superbia
confessus est Saul, et ideo audiuit a domino, 'Transtulit
dominus regnum tuum a te.' In humilitate confitebatur
Dauid, et ideo meruit audire a domino per Nathan pro-

---

[1] confiteatur] confiteantur T   [2] est] *om.* L   [3] dimidiam]
dimi⟨di⟩am L   [4] particulariter] *corr. from* particulanter T
[5] atqui] quia L qui T   [6] simul aut] aut simul T   [7] mortalia]
peccata (*repeated*) T   [8] *For L's footnote to this paragraph see below*
[9] numerum] *corr. from* numero T   [10] sublata] *preceded by* dilata
subpuncted L   [11] redintegretur] *corr. from* redigtegretur T   [12] con-
fiteri] *corr. from* conferri T

phetam, 'Transtulit dominus peccatum[1] tuum a te.' Item
superba[2] fuit confessio pharisei, ideo descendit iniustifica-
tus; humilis fuit[3] confessio publicani, et ideo[4] recessit[5] iusti-
ficatus. Hanc humilitatem representat ecclesia cum dicit[6]
in aspersione cinerum super capita nostra—[quo][7] enim
poterit in te extolli[8] superbia cum audis—'Memento homo
quia cinis es, etc.'; cum statum tuum recolis, quid eras
(sperma), quid es (uas stercorum), quid eris (puluus et esca
uermium, quia merces carnis uermes et ignis). Qui quidem
cineres in capite non in manibus ponuntur? Ut ubi magis
apparet hominis decor, quia ibi uigent quinque sensus
hominis, ibi magis humilietur homo, et dicat cum propheta, 'Humiliata est in puluere anima mea[9] etc.'

Festinata debet esse confessio, quia mora in hac secum
trahit[10] periculum. Peccatum enim quod cito per penitentiam non deletur, mox[11] pondere suo trahit ad aliud. Peccatum enim est moneta diaboli quam tradit[12] nobis ad usuram,
quod quidem semper[13] penes debitorem multiplicatur, nisi
citius pessimo creditori persoluatur.

Uerecunda: in confessione enim peccati debet erubescentia adiungi. Per Mare enim Rubrum fugerunt filii[14] Israel
Pharaonem insequentem; et nos similiter, spiritualem fugi-
entes Pharaonem quasi per Mare Rubrum (id est, amaritudinem penitentie transeundo), pro peccatis faciem rubore
erubescentie tinctam habere debemus. Et tunc submergitur
Pharao, precipue cum ipsa erubescentia sit potissima pars
satisfactionis. Unde consulendum est penitenti ut pluribus
confitetur, ut sic pluries[15] erubesceret.

[1] peccatum] *interlined* L   [2] superba] *corr. from* superbia T
[3] fuit] *interlined* L   [4] ideo] *om.* L   [5] recessit] *corr. from* resessit
T   [6] cum dicit] *om.* T   [7] quo] Que LT   [8] te extolli]
textolli T   [9] mea] nostra L   [10] secum trahit] trahit ⟨secum⟩ T
[11] mox] *after* pondere suo *but marked for transposition* L   [12] tradit]
corr. from trahit T   [13] semper] *om.* T   [14] filii] *om.* T   [15] pluries]
plures T

Meticulosa: semper enim timere debemus ne minus suffi-
cienter facta sit peccati confessio, ne aliqua peccati circum-
stancia taceatur. Bonarum etiam[1] mentium est ibi culpam
agnoscere ubi culpa non est.

Discreta: ut locum scilicet et numerum et tempus et
diurnitatem et alias circumstantias peccatum aggrauantes
reuelare. Que in hiis uersibus notantur:

Etas, ordo, locus, cur,[2] quomodo, quanta uoluptas,
Cum numero[3] tempus, uotum, discretio sexus.[4]

Uoluntaria debet esse, ut sicut propria uoluntate se reum
fecerat, ita proprie uoluntatis arbitrio se reum ostendat;
maxime cum coacta seruicia deo non placent.

Propria: multi enim cum[5] propria confitentur peccata,
illos siue illas cum quibus peccauerunt nominare et detegere
non uerentur cum illud non opporteat. Quos instruens,
propheta[6] ait de se, 'Deus, uitam[7] meam annuntiaui[8] tibi',
quasi diceret 'non alterius proditor fui[9] sed mei[10] correptor'.

Nuda: non enim debemus palliare[11] peccatum, sed quam
detestabile, quam terribile[12] sit denudare debemus.

Morosa: cum mora enim et dilatione peccata[13] confiteri
debemus et cum magna animi deliberatione, et sic mora debet
esse in confessione peccati; precipites autem esse debemus
ad confessionem peccati.

Fidens[14] debet esse confessio, id est cum fiducia et spe
uenie. Sine fiducia autem erat[15] confessio Caym, qui, licet
amarissime peniteret, ueniam non est consecutus, quia, de-
sperans de dei misericordia, ueniam se consecuturum non

---

[1] etiam] enim T   [2] cur] crux T   [3] numero] nuero T   [4] *For
L's footnote giving a shorter version of these verses see below*   [5] multi
enim cum] cum multi enim T   [6] propheta] *i.e. David in Ps. 55: 9*
[7] uitam] uitam uitam T   [8] annuntiaui] *corr. from* annuntiabo T
[9] fui] sui T   [10] mei] me⟨i⟩ L   [11] palliare] palpare L   [12] ter-
ribile] horribile T   [13] peccata] *corr. from* peccati T   [14] Fidens]
Fidens autem L   [15] erat] *interlined* T

credebat, dicens 'Maior est iniquitas mea quam ut ueniam
merear.' Talis erat confessio[1] proditoris, qui penitens de
peccatis dixit, 'Peccaui tradens sanguinem iustum', et abiens
de uenia diffisus laqueo se suspendit.

Uera debet esse confessio. Non enim debet aliquis aliud
uel aliter peccatum confiteri quam actum sit, sciens et prudens, nec etiam enormius. Quia cum humilitatis causa men-
tiris, si non eras peccator antequam mentireris, mentiendo
efficieris[2] quod euitaras. Multi enim de se falsa confitentur
ut ceteros per confessionem suam reddant infames.

Generalis: primo enim peccator in genere confiteri debet,
ne cita morte preuentus specialiter confiteri[3] non possit, et
ne pre multitudine aliqua obliuioni tradantur.[4]

Specialis: facta enim generali confessione, descendere debemus ad specialem confessionem,[5] specialiter confitendo
singula mortalia que memorie accurrunt.[6]

Accusatoria tenetur esse. In confessione enim debet
homo[7] accusare se ipsum et non excusare, quia si excusat,
deus accusat; si [ipse][8] peccatum diminuit, deus amplificat.
Sic Adam refudit culpam in mulierem, muliere effundente
in serpentem; sic magis peccabant,[9] quia sic per con-
sequens creatorem suum infamare uolebant. Contra quod
dicit Dauid: 'Ne declines cor meum in uerba malicie, etc.'

Amara etiam debet esse.[10] In amaritudine namque magna
peccata nostra numerare debemus. Sed sunt nonnulli qui,
cum peccata confitentur, non magis faciem lacrimis irrigant,
nec etiam uultum[11] magis exhibent humiliatum, quam si[12]

[1] confessio] *followed by* Caym qui licet amarissime *but with* va . . . cat
written above T   [2] efficieris] efficeris T   [3] debet . . . confiteri]
om. but supplied in margin by original scribe T   [4] tradantur] *corr.
from* tradentur T   [5] descendere . . . confessionem] *om. but supplied
in margin by original scribe* T   [6] accurrunt] *altered to* occurrunt *by
later hand* L   [7] homo] *followed by* esse *subpuncted* T   [8] ipse]
ipsum LT   [9] peccabant] peccabunt T   [10] debet esse] esse
debet T   [11] uultum] *interlined* T   [12] si] *preceded by* ci *subpuncted* L

cum procuratore expensarum pecunias numerando computarent—immo, ut uerius dicam, quidam magis pro sumptuosa expensarum superfluitate quam peccatorum pondere contristantur.[1]

L has two footnotes to this chapter which are not in T. The first, on f. 199ᵛ, gives a versified summary of the latter part of the paragraph 'Integra debet esse confessio'; correcting the scribe's *lacmante* to *lacrimante*, it reads:

> Magna dei pietas veniam non dimidiabit;
> Aut nichil aut totum te [lacrimante] dabit,

with the gloss 'id est condonabit' interlined above *dabit*. But the second line scans as a pentameter not as a hexameter (the normal metre of the verses in the *Moralia*); this, and the presence of rhyme (though inexact in quantity), may suggest that the scribe of L did not get the couplet from his exemplar but from some other source, though the method of glossing is the same as the author's. The second note, on f. 200, gives a one-line version of the verses at the end of the paragraph 'Discreta', thus:

> Quis, quid, vbi, quibus auxiliis, cur, quomodo, quando.

This is nearer to the list of the circumstances, or *totagges*, of sin given in *A.W.* f. 86b/4–7.

(49) *A.W.* ff. 82b/28–83a/10 (Anselm on the Last Judgement). *Mor.* III. 88 cites the same passage from Anselm (L f. 176ᵛ, T f. 294ʳ⁻ᵛ):

Sextus domini aduentus erit ad iudicium, in quo quidem terribilis erit impiis. De circumstanciis huius aduentus dicit sanctus Anselmus:[2] 'Hinc erit accusancia peccata, illinc terrens iusticia; subtus patens chaos inferni, super iudex iratus; intus conscientia urens, extra mundus ardens. Miser homo sic deprehensus in quam partem se premet? Latere erit impossibile, apparere intolerabile.'

---

[1] contristantur] contrista⟨n⟩tur T   [2] Anselmus] anselinus L

(50) *A.W.* f. 84a/23–6 (God does not punish twice for the same offence). The citation was a commonplace at this time, but see no. 12 above (end).

(51) *A.W.* f. 84a/6–7, 11–16 (the significance of Thamar and Judas). The source is the *Glossa Ordinaria*, but compare also *Mor.* I. 16 (L ff. 21ᵛ–2, T f. 22):

[Heading] *De penitentia per Thamar, ratione*¹ *duplicis nominis propositi* [*interpretationis*],² *signata*. 'Iudas autem genuit Phares et Zaram de Thamar.' Thamar interpretatur 'amaritudo', que iuncta confessioni parit Phares, id est diuisionem peccati; amaritudo enim contritionis, cum confessione, peccati retundit amaritudinem. Confessio etiam³ iuncta amaritudine gignit⁴ Phares, id est Cristum, qui in presenti merito bonos separans a malis, ipsos in futuro ab eis loco et merito separabit. 'Iudas autem [genuit]⁵ Zaram', id est orientem Cristum,⁶ de quo scriptum est, 'Ecce uir, oriens est nomen eius.'

(52) *A.W.* f. 84b/16–22 (how would a man's heart stand who had been sentenced to be burned alive for a wicked murder? You, when you murdered your soul through sin, were sentenced to be hanged on a burning gallows in hell). Compare *Mor.* III. 98 (L f. 186, T f. 309ᵛ):

Item dictum est quod dolere debet homo in presenti; nec mirum! Siquis enim⁷ meruisset suspendium et ignarus⁸ utrum proxima hora suspendendus esset, nullus illum letificare posset. Sed peccans mortaliter meretur furcas infernales; cum ergo ignoret utrum suspendendus sit in illis proxima⁹ hora, nullo modo, si sane mentis est, gaudere poterit.

¹ ratione . . . signata] *om.* T   ² interpretationis] *om.* L   ³ etiam] enim T   ⁴ gignit] gign *subpuncted and replaced by* genuit *in margin* L   ⁵ genuit] *om.* LT   ⁶ Cristum] *om.* L   ⁷ enim] *om.* T ⁸ ignarus] *so MSS.; read perhaps* ignarus esset   ⁹ proxima] *written above* propria *subpuncted* T

Compare also the reference to *furcas materiales* and *furcas infernales* in no. 43 above.

(53) *A.W.* f. 85a/7–11 (similitude of a knight who allows a king's son entrusted to his care to be captured). A different but comparable similitude is used in *Mor.* III. 71 (L f. 163, T f. 270):

Item si dolendum est homini eo quod castrum, sibi a rege terreno traditum, hostium ipsius tutele committit, multo fortius tibi dolendum est si castrum tibi a rege celesti commissum, corpus scilicet et animam, per peccatum diabolice subicis potestati uel dicioni.[1]

(54) *A.W.* f. 85b/9–10 (confession, beyond childhood, must be complete, i.e. made to a single man) and f. 85b/18–25 (a man who allows the physician to heal all his wounds but one dies just the same, and shipmen drown who stop all the holes in their ship but one). Compare *Mor.* I. 43 (L f. 42ᵛ, T f. 56ᵛ):

Item in ii Regum: 'Sola autem domus Iuda sequebatur Dauid', id est deum. Quasi diceret: illi soli (adulte etatis dico) secuntur Cristum et[2] sunt de familia eius (id est participant[3] suffragiis ecclesie et habebunt uitam eternam) qui conteruntur de peccatis et confitentur. Et hoc dico si habeant[4] copiam sacerdotis. Si uis deum imitari, si familie eius ascribi, confitearis omnia peccata tua. Qui enim omnia uno excepto confitetur, homini assimulandus est, multis cathenis astricto,[5] cui omnia uincula soluuntur preter unum, quod ad ipsum sufficit retinendum. Similis est naui in pluribus locis perforate, quorum singula[6] obstruuntur, uno foramine superstite,[7] per quod nauis periclitari potest. Similis etiam[8] est homini pluribus uulneribus sauciato, quorum, singulis

---

[1] uel dicioni] *interlined above* potestati L   [2] et] i. (*for* id est) L
[3] participant] participent L   [4] habeant] habent T   [5] astricto] afflicto L   [6] singula] *sc.* foramina; singule T   [7] superstite] superstice (*perhaps altered from* superstite) T   [8] etiam] *om.* T

curatis, unum restat incuratum, quod ad hominis sufficit interemptionem.

(55) *A.W.* f. 85b/9–18 (confession compared to a woman sweeping a house and finally sprinkling water, i.e. tears, on the fine dust). Similarly in *Mor.* III. 11 (L f. 117, T f. 179ᵛ):

Conscientia etiam uicem domus materialis rependit. Nostis quod, siquis paterfamilias ancille sue preciperet ut domum suam scopa mundaret, deinde etiam minutissimum puluerem proiceret, si precepto ipsius[1] non pareret, utique[2] ipsam affligeret. Paterfamilias spiritus est, ancilla autem[3] ipsa caro; spiritus ergo precipit carni ut mundet domum suam, id est conscientiam,[4] scopa, id est lingua, a sordibus peccati. Postmodum aquam, id est fletus penitentiales, super infundat, ut per fletus penitentiales etiam minutissime circumstantie peccati diluantur ... Dicto igitur modo, a pauimento consciencie luto uitiorum eiecto et puluere carnalium desideriorum abstracto, conscientia in statum pristinum reformabitur.

There is a variant of the similitude in *Mor.* III. 88 (L f. 176, T f. 293ᵛ), but it does not correspond in detail with the passage in *A.W.*:

Sicut igitur ad cuiusuis diuitis aduentum domus materiales scopis mundantur, ne quid in ipsis inueniatur quod potentie ipsius oculos offendat, sic etiam ad tanti hospitis [*sc.* Cristi] aduentum mens hominis penitentie scopa mundanda est, que id quidem efficacie habet ut animam soli[5] materiali in claritate equiparet. Vnde illud Ecclesiastici,[6] 'Iustus in sapientia sua manet ut sol, stultus autem ut luna mutatur.'

---

[1] ipsius] ipsi T   [2] utique] ut⟨i⟩que T   [3] autem] an*te* T
[4] conscientiam] conscientia *with* m *interlined by later hand* L   [5] soli
. . . mutatur] *om. but supplied at top of page by original scribe* T
[6] Ecclesiastici] ecc*lesi*as*te*s T

(56) *A.W.* f. 86a/15–28 (shameful things should not be disguised by fair phrases, but the words must correspond to the deeds). Compare *Mor.* IV. 22 (L f. 202[v], T f. 339[v]):

Medela autem peccati penitentia est. [Iniqua][1] confitendo,

Noris[2] [signari][3] deformia[4] nomine turpi,

unde et peccata eadem deformitate qua fiunt in confessione exprimi debent:

Si quid [habes][5] odio, dices deformiter ipsum.

In Matheo legitur quod surdus et mutus, a domino curatus, recte loquebatur. Ille autem recte loquitur, et non per modum blandientis, qui res appellat propriis nominibus. Si quis odio haberetur letaliter, odio habentur sua. [Sicut][6] peccata odio habenda sunt, sic et eorum circumstancie.

(57) *A.W.* f. 87a/23–8 (pour out your heart like water which, unlike oil or milk or wine, leaves no trace or colour or smell in the vessel). Compare *Mor.* IV. 29 (L f. 210[v], T f. 351[r–v]):

Qualiter igitur iterum aquis penitentialibus[7] affluenti negotiandum sit, docet Ieremias hiis uerbis: 'Effundite corda uestra sicut aquam[8] in conspectu dei.' Per aquam ipse peccator siue ipsa peccata[9] intelligitur. Bene ergo dicit 'sicut aquam'.[10] Aqua enim bene sanis non uidetur multum sapida siue saporata, febribus uero estuantibus multum delectabilis uidetur et sapida. Sic et peccata spiritualiter infirmis multum sapiunt, sanis autem mente uidetur quod qui in hiis delectantur desipiunt. Preterea cum aqua plene effunditur, neque[11]

---

[1] Iniqua] In qua LT   [2] Noris] floris T   [3] signari] signanda LT   [4] deformia] *over erasure* L deforma T   [5] habes] habet LT [6] Sicut] Sic et LT   [7] penitentialibus] spiritualibus T   [8] aquam] aqua L   [9] ipse . . . peccata] ipsa peccata siue ipse peccator T [10] aquam] aqua T   [11] neque . . . odor] ita ut ⟨neque⟩ eius sapor remanet uel odor (*with* neque *apparently first marked for insertion after* eius *but then put in before it*) L

sapor eius remanet uel odor.[1] Similiter uult deus ut in confessione peccatum effundatur,[2] ita ut eius nec remaneat sapor
uel odor.[3] Sapor autem peccati est delectatio que remanet
etiam post experientiam facti; odor autem, qui non intrin-
secus sicut sapor sed extrinsecus sicut odor[4] sentitur, est
habitus inordinatus aut sermo incompositus aut gestus in-
conueniens. Quomodo enim [erit][5] immunis a[6] libidinis
culpa cum adhuc eius uestigium remanserit[7] in lingua?

(58) *A.W.* f. 87b/8–10 (load your shame on your own neck, as is
done to the thief who is led to judgement). Compare *Mor.* III. 26
(L f. 128, T f. 201ᵛ):

Sicut fur cum furto suo ad iudicium prodit, sic et nos cum
bene uel male gestis ad iudicium ueniemus.

(59) *A.W.* f. 87b/17–21 (at the Last Judgement, St. Anselm says,
an account will be required of how each hour here was spent).
So in *Mor.* III. 16 (L f. 120ʳ⁻ᵛ, T f. 185ᵛ):

Qualiter autem pro[8] elapsis a memoria satisfaciemus? Sin-
gulorum tamen que gessimus nobis in die iudicii occurret
noticia, nec[9] eadem a noticia dei poterunt abscondi (iuxta
illud Sophonie, 'Mane, mane iudicium suum[10] dabit et non
abscondetur').[11] 'Mane, mane', id est cito et manifeste,[12] et
non erit quod ab eo possit abscondi. Formidinem nobis in-
cutere potest illud Anselmi[13] quo dictum est, 'Quid faciet
miser[14] homo quando ab eo[15] exigetur[16] omne tempus ipsi
impensum, qualiter ab eo fuerit expensum?'

---

[1] odor] *corr. from* odo T   [2] Similiter . . . effundatur] *om. but supplied in margin by original scribe* L   [3] ita . . . odor] *om.* L   [4] sed
. . . odor] *om. but supplied in margin by original scribe* T   [5] erit] ē
(*i.e.* est) LT   [6] a] *om.* T   [7] remanserit] remansit T   [8] pro]
corr., probably from per T   [9] nec] ne T   [10] suum] *interlined* T
[11] abscondetur] *corr. from* absconditur T   [12] manifeste] manifesto L
[13] Anselmi] Anselini L   [14] miser] *om.* T   [15] eo] *followed by*
fuerit expensum *deleted* T   [16] exigetur] *corr. from* exigitur T

(60) *A.W.* f. 88b/1–5 (reasons for speedy confession: sin is the devil's money which he lends at interest). So *Mor.* IV. 18 (see no. 48 above, in the paragraph 'Festinata') and similarly *Mor.* III. 96 (L f. 184, T f. 306):

Item usura hominem diabolo assimulat. Sicut enim diabolus pecuniam suam, peccatum scilicet, homini commodat, ut magis recipiat, sic et usurarius. Idem etiam diabolo peior est: diabolus enim quod suum est, peccatum scilicet, homini commodat,[1] usurarius alienum; pecunia[2] quam dat mutuo non sua sed dei est.

See also no. 62 below (*Mor.* III. 54).

(61) *A.W.* f. 88b/7–12 (reasons for speedy confession: unexpected death and sickness). So *Mor.* II. 11 (L f. 73ᵛ, T f. 106ᵛ):

Quam [*sc.* confessionem] quidem[3] accelerant tria. Primum est incertitudo mortis—morte enim nichil cercius,[4] hora mortis nichil incercius.[5] Secundum est quod peccatum quod mox non diluitur per penitenciam pondere suo trahit ad aliud. Tercium est dolor egritudinis, que totam sibi mentem[6] uendicat et ipsam ad peccati confessionem transferri non sinit.

That the hour of death is uncertain is an idea expressed several times elsewhere in the *Moralia*. So III. 75 (L f. 166, T ff. 275ᵛ–6):

Cum[7] igitur nulli[8] constat de fine suo utrum post tempus presens immineat,[9] semper igitur dolendum est; morte enim nichil certius, hora mortis nichil incertius.

More briefly in III. 79 (L f. 169ᵛ, T f. 281ᵛ):

Dic ei nichil certius morte, nichil incertius hora mortis.

---

[1] ut magis . . . commodat] *om.* T   [2] pecunia] pecuniam *altered (by later hand?) from* pecunia L   [3] quidem] quidam L   [4] cercius] tercius T   [5] incercius] in-tercius T   [6] totam sibi mentem] mentem totam sibi T   [7] Cum] Dum L   [8] nulli] ulli L   [9] immineat] imineat T

And again in different words in III. 83 (L f. 172, T f. 286):

Beatus qui semper est pauidus. Timere debet homo ne subita morte preoccupetur et sic in furcis inferni suspendatur.

The application to the need for speedy confession is again explicit in IV. 9 (L f. 192ᵛ, T f. 321):

Notandum¹ quod quilibet mortaliter peccans fatuus est aut incredulus eo quod continuo post lapsum non confitetur. Si enim crederet quod hora mortis nichil incertius et quod, si post lapsum sine confessione discederet,² eternaliter periret, mox post lapsum confiteretur, quo quia non agit³ aut fatuus est aut non credit.

(62) *A.W.* f. 89a/13–17 (reasons for speedy confession: St. Gregory says that sin not washed away by confession soon by its own weight leads to another). So in *Mor.* II. 11 (quoted under no. 61 above) and in *Mor.* III. 54 (L f. 149, T f. 244ʳ⁻ᵛ):

Cum igitur insidiosus et uiolentus sit diabolus, reddenda sunt ei que sua sunt, peccata scilicet, que ab eo mutuo accepimus,⁴ que instar feneratoris a nobis⁵ diu uult detineri, sciens quod peccatum quod mox non diluitur per penitentiam pondere suo trahit ad aliud, ut ait Gregorius. Reddenda sunt igitur peccata diabolo⁶ non solum ratione sui sed ratione effectus.

There is another citation of the text in IV. 50 (quoted more fully in no. 71 below), at L f. 233ᵛ, T f. 386ᵛ:

Terra est reatus peccati, qui terra dicitur quia⁷ pre ponderositate [sua]⁸ trahit ad infima.⁹ Unde legitur, 'Pondus ad aliud trahit.'

---

¹ Notandum] nota *altered from* notum T   ² discederet] decederet T   ³ agit] *after erasure* L   ⁴ accepimus] accipimus T
⁵ nobis] vobis T   ⁶ diabolo] diaboli L   ⁷ quia] *om.* L   ⁸ sua] sui LT   ⁹ infima] imfima L

And it comes again in IV. 62 (L f. 245ᵛ, T f. 402ᵛ):

Et quid est¹ ponderosius peccato quod opprimit hominem, et
nisi diluatur per penitentiam mox pondere suo trahit ad aliud.

(63) *A.W.* f. 90a/24–90b/2 (hope and fear are two grindstones).
So in *Mor.* II. 35 (L f. 90ᵛ, T f. 135ᵛ):

Farina de qua hic fit mentio uir iustus est, qui inter duas
molas, spei et timoris, ita atteritur quod nec ad prospera
erigitur nec ad aduersa deprimitur.

(64) *A.W.* ff. 95b/17–96a/6 (among God's chosen on earth those
have the highest rank who suffer dishonour and pain with Jesus
on the Cross). There is an imperfect parallel in *Mor.* IV. 41 (L f.
223ʳ⁻ᵛ, T f. 370ʳ⁻ᵛ):

Consideratis enim ludibriis et obprobriis que Cristus pro ipsis
passus est, sancti penas quas perpessi sunt nullius momenti²
estimauerunt ut Cristum sibi lucrifacerent . . . Sunt igitur
quidam innocentes qui, innocentiam baptismalem seruando,
nichilominus tamen sese ieiuniis et aliter diuersimodo affli-
gunt; huiuscemodi sunt in cruce cum domino et cum eo erunt
in gloria.

(65) *A.W.* f. 96a/28–96b/5 (the cherubin's sword before the
gates of Paradise). Compare *Mor.* III. 85 (L f. 174, T f. 290):

Readiecto³ quod dominus collocauit ante paradisum cherubin
et gladium uersatilem.⁴ Per cherubin, quod interpretatur
'plenitudo scientie', intelligitur caritas, et merito: caritas
enim omnem scientiam plenificat et sufficientem facit ad
promerendum regnum dei; quantumlibet⁵ enim [exilis est],⁶

---

¹ est] *interlined* L   ² momenti] *interlined above* in oem *subpuncted*
T   ³ Readiecto] '*it being further added*'; re adiecto T   ⁴ uer-
satilem] uersabilem T   ⁵ quantumlibet . . . caritate] *om.* L   ⁶ exilis
est] *om.* T

et exilis scientia sufficit cum caritate.[1] Per gladium uersatilem
tribulatio temporalis signatur. Collocati sunt ergo cherubin
et gladius uersatilis ante paradisum ad designandum quod[2]
non nisi per caritatem et tribulationem temporalem in celum
regressum habemus.

(66) *A.W.* f. 97a/20–97b/10 (we must suffer on earth, as Christ
did, if we wish to share the glory of the resurrection). The same
general idea, but differently expressed, comes in *Mor.* IV. 55
(L f. 238, T f. 392ᵛ):

Illi ipsum [*sc.* Cristum] commedunt assum qui pro amore dei
cum[3] Cristo in cruce tribulationes paciuntur et ad amorem
interne[4] dulcedinis perueniunt. Qui hic assantur in tribulationibus et angustiis, in[5] eterna[6] beatitudine dulcedine[7]
resurrectionis sue saturabuntur,[8] et sic erimus participes
glorie resurrectionis si socii fuerimus eius passionis; per
duriciam exterius, participes dulcedinis misericordie interius
erimus.

(67) *A.W.* f. 98a/14–25 (the 'totoren folc' who tear their old
garments, i.e. the flesh, by the hardships of their life). The
germ of the idea seems to be in *Mor.* IV. 33 (L f. 214ᵛ, T ff.
357ᵛ–8):

Hoc uestimento paupertatis usus est dominus usque ad passionem, in qua uere apparuit uestimentum dilaceratum
quando uestimentum eius, id est caro eius beata, est dilacerata et perforata, et precipue quando Pilatus duxit eum
foras coronatum spinis . . . Hoc uestimentum reliquit dominus amicis suis et beatis pauperibus, quia diuites non

---

[1] caritate] caritate ad promerendum regnum dei T   [2] quod] *om.*,
supplied in margin by later hand L   [3] cum] pro T   [4] interne]
corr. from interm. . T   [5] in] et T   [6] eterna] interna T
[7] dulcedine] *om.* T   [8] saturabuntur] saciabuntur T

induunt uestimenta dilacerata undique perforata. Hoc uestimentum doloris recipit ecclesia[1] in uera penitentia.

(68) *A.W.* f. 98b/3–9 (ease and physical pleasure are the devil's
banners, and when he sees them displayed he knows the castle is
his; but in the 'totore folc' he sees God's banner raised up).
The source is *Mor.* III. 71 (L f. 163, T f. 270[v]):

Ad bene muniendum carnem nostram ipse [*sc.* Cristus] idem,
nisi eum eiciamus, positus est 'murus et antemurale', sicut
dicit Ysaias[2] xxv;[3] ipse autem in propria carne omnes as-
sultus nostros sustinuit. Et quod titulus domini[4] positus sit
in carne nostra habemus in Ysaia xix: 'Erit altare in medio
terre Egypti, et titulus domini iuxta turrim eius.' Titulus
domini fuit 'Iesus Nazarenus rex Iudeorum', in quo notatur
passio. In carne est titulus: maceratio et proprie carnis
afflictio.[5] Certe,[6] titulo domini cognito, non audet diabolus
insultare; sed ubi proprium carnis titulum inuenit (scilicet
delicias, luxum, pruritum), arma sua cognoscit et gentem
suam, et [it] intra[7] securus. Titulus domini est 'Rex Iudeorum', et ipse ponit signum in confitentibus.

(69) *A.W.* f. 98b/9–21 (similitude of two sick men, of whom one
forgoes the food and drink that he likes and drinks bitter potions
to recover his health, the other indulges himself and dies). So
at greater length in *Mor.* IV. 10 (L f. 193[v], T f. 323[r–v]):

[Subheading] *Quod spiritus sanctus dicitur consolator.* Quod
autem spiritus sanctus sit consolator ex subiecto[8] exemplo

---

[1] recipit ecclesia] *after* penitentia T   [2] Ysaias] *after the name,*
xix Erit altare in medio *but with* va . . . cat *written above* T   [3] xxv] *so*
LT, *but in fact xxvi. 1*   [4] domini] dominus T   [5] afflictio . . .
proprium carnis] *om. but supplied in margin by original scribe* T
[6] domini] *om.* T   [7] et it intra] et iter intra *struck through and replaced in margin by* et intra intrat *in later hand* L et iter intrat T (ant
geaδ . . . in *A.W.*)   [8] subiecto] subito L

patebit. Aliquis laborat acuta; medici prohibent ne nimium
potet,[1] precipiunt etiam ut sanatiua utatur dieta quousque in
ipso egritudinis estus deferueat. Uenit ad eum indiscretus
quiuis et dicit ei, 'Quousque medicorum uteris consilio?
Iam per abstinentiam consumeris. Epulare splendide; utere
laucioribus eduliis. Uidi quemdam esu [anguilline][2] a simili
morbo conualuisse,[3] et tu conualesces. Si quid animus tuus
appetit, pro libito gusta.'[4] Sic loquendo inducit eum ut noxia
sumat cibaria,[5] et fiat incurabilis. Ad tale nocumentum
exortatoria est consolatio seculi, que[6] inuitat[7] hominem ad
delectacionem[8] [secularem ac][9] dulcedinem. Sapiens uero
assidens egro eum consolatur utiliter, consulit breuem pati
molestiam, abstinendo a dulcibus et amaris utendo potioni-
bus, ut ciciorem percipiat sanitatem. Talis est consolatio
spiritus sancti, que monet momentaneam penitentie amaritudinem subire ut gaudium percipiat interminabile. Bene igitur
dicitur consolator quamuis luctum persuadeat, quia in presenti statu consolatur ad perferendum dolorem sub[10] dis-
ciplina penitentie, in futuro consolabitur ad omnimodam
doloris depositionem cum anima separabitur[11] a corpore.

(70) *A.W.* ff. 100b/16–101a/1 (Nicodemus brought myrrh and
aloes to anoint our Lord). The reference in *A.W.* is brief and does
not make it very clear why Nicodemus is introduced in a discussion of penance, but significantly it closely precedes the
longer discussion of the three Marys; in the *Moralia* the chapters
on the three Marys (IV. 46 and IV. 50) are similarly preceded by
one on Nicodemus (IV. 44), in which *inter alia* the significance of

---

[1] potet] *corr. from* potent L *corr. from* potat T   [2] anguilline] '*of
eel-flesh*'; augulline L angulline *altered to* angu⟨i⟩lle T   [3] a . . . con-
ualuisse] *om.* T   [4] gusta] *corr. from* gustu T   [5] sumat cibaria]
cibaria sumat T   [6] que] *corr. from* qui T   [7] inuitat] mutat L
inu⟨i⟩tat *corr. from* mutat T   [8] delectacionem] dilectionem T
[9] secularem ac] seculi non ad LT   [10] sub] dum L   [11] separa-
bitur] sepabitur T

the myrrh and aloes is made explicit. The following are extracts
(L ff. 226–7, T ff. 374–5):

'Uenit Nichodemus ferens mixturam mirre et aloes, quasi
libras centum.' . . . Nichodemus 'uictor populis' uel 'uictoria
populi' interpretatur et significat penitentem[1] qui populi
nomen ab effectu sibi usurpat . . .

De Nichodemo supra posito legitur quod ferens mixturam
mirre et aloes, id est unguentum confectum[2] ex mirra et
aloe, [uenit][3] ad unguendum[4] corpus dominicum[5] iam[6] in
monumento reconditum . . . Preter dominica unguenta est
quoddam unguentum[7] curatiuum confectum ex mirra et aloe.
Per mirram dolor siue contritio, per aloem confessio siue
labor satisfactionis exprimitur. Amaritudinem siue dolorem
parere debent in homine diuersi status Cristi: status[8] im-
becillitatis[9] ipsius, paupertatis, et pene . . . Per aloen[10] labor
qui penitenti competit exprimitur, et merito: aloe enim
odoris gratissimi est et saporis amarissimi. Sic et labor
penitentialis deo gratissimus est, eo quod ipsi quod suum
est restituit, et quod ipsi aduersa fronte repugnauerat[11]
eiusdem subicitur dicioni.[12] Labor etiam amarissimus cen-
setur, eo quod idem in penitente uarias et corporis minus
accommodas[13] parit amaritudines . . .

(71) *A.W.* f. 101a/1–101b/19 (the three Marys, the interpretations of their names, and their significance). A distinctive feature
of the passage is that it interprets the name Mary as 'bitterness',

---

[1] penitentem] *corr. from* penitentia*m* T   [2] unguentum confectum]
confectum unguentum T   [3] uenit] *om.* LT   [4] unguendum]
ung⟨e⟩undum T   [5] corpus dominicum] dominicum corpus T
[6] iam] *om.* T   [7] unguentum] ung⟨v⟩entum L   [8] status]
Sstatus L   [9] imbecillitatis] inbescillitatis L   [10] aloen] *corr. from*
aloem L aleon T   [11] repugnauerat] repungnauerat L repugnabat T
[12] subicitur dicioni] dicioni subicitur T   [13] accommodas] acco-
modas LT

though 'amaritudo' does not occur in the many lists of *Interpretationes nominum hebraicorum* that I have examined; among the
varied interpretations (including 'stella maris') the nearest is
'amarum mare'. The *Moralia*, in its discussion of the interpretations of the name of the Virgin in I. 8, follows the lists, including
'mare amarum', on which it comments (L f. 16, T f. 12ᵛ):

Hoc est mare amarum, [quod]¹ tribulationis tollit amaritudinem et umbratiles mundi delicias nobis reddit amaras.

But elsewhere the interpretation 'amaritudo' is perhaps implied
by the repeated assumption that the sea symbolizes the bitterness
of sin: so in II. 8 (L f. 71, T f. 102) and in II. 40 (L f. 94ᵛ, T f.
142), where the phrase 'mare, id est amaritudo peccati' occurs.
At T f. 43, in a marginal addition to I. 32, there is the phrase
'penitentes sicut Maria, id est in amaritudine, sed hec Maria
debet esse desponsata Ioseph, id est caritate'; and in the text of
III. 85 (L f. 173ᵛ, T f. 289) there is the comment 'amaricati qui
per Mariam signantur'. Finally the interpretation 'amaritudo' for
the name *Maria* is explicitly given in IV. 46, with the remark 'ut
sepe dictum est' (which, as far as I have observed, is not strictly
true). For this and other reasons, *Mor.* IV. 46 (L ff. 228ᵛ–9, T ff.
377–8ᵛ) must be taken as the main source of the passage in *A.W.*
The following are extracts:

[Heading] *De triplici amaritudine inscribitur, quarum prima
macerationem carnis parit,² secunda tria³ vicia principalia elidit,
tercia ex mentis tranquillitate procedit.*⁴ 'Maria Magdalene et
Maria Iacobi et Salome⁵ emerunt aromata ut uenientes un-
gerent Iesum.'... Maria ut sepe dictum est 'amaritudo' interpretatur. Per tres ergo Marias [tria]⁶ amaritudinum genera
figurantur, que⁷ nobis a domino aromata, id est uirtutum
fragrantiam, comparant; per quas idem demulcetur et de-
linitur, ne propter peccata precedentia prout meruimus quasi
feruens et iratus deseuiat.

¹ quod] q*ue corr. to* q*uod by later hand* L que T   ² parit] *om.* L
³ tria] circa T   ⁴ procedit] *om.* T   ⁵ Salome] Saloméé T
⁶ tria] trium LT   ⁷ que] *corr. by later hand from* qui T

Nota ergo[1] quod Magdalum 'turris', Magdalena 'turrita' interpretatur. Per turrim ergo uegetatio spiritus, ratione effectus, exprimitur, eo quod penitentem ad superiora monet et promouet. Huic annexa est mentis amaritudo; quo[2] enim spiritus amplius[3] roboratur, eo acerbius mens[4] de peccato compungitur. Turri proposite mortificatio carnis uice propugnaculorum subseruit, utpote per quam temptationum insultus eliduntur, ne per ipsos penitens expugnetur.

Iacob 'supplantator' interpretatur, quod quidem mentis amaritudini competit, que tria uiciorum genera supplantare non desinit: auariciam scilicet, luxuriam, et superbiam . . .

Sequitur Maria Salome. Salome 'pacifica' interpretatur, et significat tranquillitatem que, temptationibus superatis et uiciis supplantatis, in homine succedit. Huic mentis tranquillitati annexa est amaritudo ex[5] incolatu presenti procedens. De quo Zacharias, 'Erit ruina qua[6] percutiet[7] dominus omnes gentes', et paulo ante in eodem, 'Qui[8] non ascenderunt ad festiuitatem tabernaculorum, non erit super eos imber; quod et si familia Egypti non ascenderit et non uenerit, nec super eos erit.' Ascendere ad festiuitatem tabernaculi est[9] per amaritudinem separare se ab amore temporali[10] et reputare semper se[11] peregrinum. Quod non fiet si deficit[12] imber gratie et benedictionis dominice, et instat[13] ruina de peccato in peccatum.

In *Mor.* IV. 50 there is a further discussion of the three Marys, in which (inconsistently with IV. 46) they are taken as symbolizing the three vices of pride, cupidity, and lust. This symbolism was obviously not followed by the author of *A.W.*, but the course of the discussion reinforces the interpretations of the names given

---

[1] ergo] *om.* T   [2] quo] quod T   [3] spiritus amplius] amplius spiritus T   [4] mens] *interlined* L   [5] ex] et T   [6] qua] que T   [7] percutiet] percutiat *imperfectly altered to* percutiet T   [8] Qui] que L   [9] est] id est T   [10] temporali] *corr. from* temporalibus T   [11] semper se] se semper *marked for transposition* L se semper T   [12] deficit] defecit T   [13] instat] instar T

in IV. 46; in particular the unusual interpretation of *Magdaleine*
as 'tures hehnesse' (*A.W.* f. 101a/11–12), though it may be due to
misreading or misremembering the entry 'magnitudo uel turris'
given for *Magdalum* in certain lists, could be due to misunderstanding of the phrase 'hec turris est elatio' used in *Mor.* IV. 50,
and it was evidently from the latter that the English author got his
interpretation 'peace' (f. 101b/5–6) for *Salome*, in place of 'pacifica'
(Jerome) or 'pacificans eum' (in most of the medieval lists of interpretations). The following are selected passages from *Mor.* IV. 50
(L ff. 232ᵛ–3ᵛ, T ff. 385–6ᵛ):

'Noli me tangere.' . . . Legimus de tribus Mariis, quarum
una Maria Magdalene, altera Maria Iacobi, tercia Maria[1]
Salome dicta est. Maria Magdalene 'amara turris' interpretatur, et significat superbiam; Maria Iacobi, 'amara sup-
plantatio', et significat cupiditatem; Maria Salome, 'amara
pax', et significat luxuriam . . .

Maria igitur Magdalene 'amara[2] turris' interpretatur,[3]
ut dictum est. Hec est turris (id est superbia) de qua in Luca
legitur (xiii in principio) quod corruens oppressit x. et viii
uiros . . . Hec turris est elatio, sicut legitur super Matheum,
'Est primum uicium recedentibus a deo et ultimum acceden-
tibus ad deum.' . . . Per Mariam etiam Magdalenam status
penitentium designatur[4] propter prerogatiuam penitentie
quam[5] in se gessit, quia, ut ait Gregorius, 'Quot in[6] se habuit
oblectamenta, tot de se fecit holocaustomata.' Vnde propter
amaritudinem penitentie dimissa sunt ei peccata multa.
Contra superbos in temporalibus gloriantes facit illud Apocalipsis quo dictum est angelis messoribus xviii, 'Quantum
glorificauit et in deliciis fuit, tantum date illi tormentum et
luctum.' . . .

---

[1] Maria] ma *at end of line* T   [2] amara] ammara L   [3] interpretatur . . . turris] *om.* T *but supplied in margin by original scribe in form*
ut dictum est interpretatur. Hec est turris   [4] designatur] designatur
tum T   [5] quam] qua L   [6] Quot in] *corr. from* Quod in (?) L

Sequitur Maria Iacobi, que cupiditatis est signatiua, que cupidum supplantat et ipsum ad inferiora deicit et prosternit. Vnde de cupidis scriptum est, 'Oculos statuerunt[1] declinare in terram.' Hii sunt qui oculos mentales ita ad terrena incuruant quod ipsos ad celestia subleuare non possunt . . .

Sequitur Maria Salome, id est 'amaritudo tranquilla', et significat luxuriam, que pacem momentaneam et[2] penam luxurioso parit eternam . . . Unde et Beda ait, 'Breuis est uoluptas fornicationis, sed perpetua pena fornicatoris.'[3] . . . Terra est reatus peccati qui terra dicitur quia[4] pre ponderositate [sua][5] trahit ad infima.[6] Unde legitur, 'Pondus ad aliud trahit'; luxuriosus cadit . . . De[7] quibus in Euangelio, 'Qui uidit mulierem ad concupiscendam eam etc.', per quod aperte notatur, cum uisus inducat mechiam, quod multo fortius inducit cum quis earum lateribus adherere presumit. Tales enim sunt similes basilisco qui solo uisu interficit.

(72) *A.W.* ff. 104b/26–105a/17 (God has done much to win our love—by gifts, by sending messengers with the sealed letters of the Old Testament, and by coming himself with the open letters of the Gospel); *A.W.* f. 105b/13–16 ('I beseech you to love me dead when you would not living'); *A.W.* ff. 105b/21–106a/1 (Christ in a tournament had, for the sake of his beloved, his shield, i.e. his body, pierced on each side); *A.W.* ff. 106b/2–107b/3 (the four chief loves in the world: between good companions, between man and woman, between mother and child, and between body and soul). The source is *Mor.* III. 47 (L ff. 143ᵛ-4, T ff. 233ᵛ-4ᵛ):

[Heading] *Quod Cristus contracturus matrimonium cum fidelibus uices proci gesserit, et quod idem nos plusquam socius socium, plusquam mater filium, dilexerit,[8] edocetur* . . . 'Sic

---

¹ statuerunt] statuere T ² et] *repeated at turn of page* T ³ fornicatoris] fornicato⟨r⟩is T ⁴ quia] *om.* L ⁵ sua] sui LT ⁶ infima] imfima L ⁷ De] Et de T ⁸ dilexerit] dilexerat L

deus dilexit mundum ut filium suum unigenitum daret.' . . .
Unigenitus igitur, uolens in mundo cum fidelibus ipsius
matrimonium contrahere, uices proci gerendo ipsos muneribus ditari uoluit. Queque etenim animantia condidit, ut
ipsorum usibus deseruirent: oues edulio, equitatui[1] equi, et
sic de aliis. Unde Ambrosius:[2]

> Qui magna rerum corpora
> dictu iubentis uiuida[3]
> ut seruiant per ordinem
> subdens dedisti[4] homini.

Cum igitur muneribus ditati[5] ipsum minus diligerent, ut
ad ipsum diligendum magis attenderentur, scripturas pro-
phetarum uice breuis eis[6] transmisit. Ysaias: 'Erit uisio
hominis quasi uisio[7] libri[8] signati.' Liber dum adhuc signatur
hominum noticie non occurrit, reseratus[9] autem ad hominum
noticiam deuenit. Sic et Cristus in presenti minus cognosci-
tur, in iudicio autem plenius et planius cognoscetur. Minus
per litteras dilectus, homo factus ad arma recurrit, quibus
strenuitatem suam fidelibus propalaret, et nouo pugnandi
modo usus de hostibus suis triumphauit. Iudicum: 'Noua
bella elegit dominus sibi, portas hostium ipse subuertit.'[10]
Ad strenuitatis ipsius euidentiam, scutum ipsius, id est corpus, quinque locis perforatum est, et manibus cruci affixis
de demonibus palmam quam affectauerat assecutus est. Mortuus est ergo Cristus[11] in cruce ut quem[12] uiuum mundus non
dilexerat, saltem mortuum diligeret.

---

[1] equitatui] *corr. from* equitatiui T   [2] Ambrosius] *not in fact by
him; Walpole*, Early Latin Hymns, *Hymn 78, lines 5–9*   [3] uiuida]
inuida L   [4] subdens dedisti] sub. de. L sub de T   [5] ditati]
ditari T   [6] eis] ei L   [7] hominis . . . uisio] *om. but supplied in
margin by original scribe* T   [8] libri] liber T   [9] reseratus] *corr.
from* reseratur T   [10] ipse subuertit] subuertit ipse *but marked for
transposition* T   [11] Cristus] *om.* T   [12] quem] qñ (*for* quando?) L
qm̃ *corr. to* quem T

[Subheading] *Quod Cristus nos plusquam socius socium et plusquam mater filium diligit.*[1] O ineffabile dilectionis signum quo Cristus, in dilectionis sue augmentum[2] quam erga[3] nos habuit, pro nobis mortuus est. Plus igitur nos dilexit quam quiuis socius socium. Socius pro socio librum uel aliquod[4] tale impignorat in iudaismo; Cristus semetipsum pro nobis Iudeis uice pignoris exposuit. Euangelium: 'Ego sum; si me queritis, sinite hos[5] abire.' Cristus nos plus dilexit quam mater filium. Mater filium in aquis balneat, Cristus in sanguine. Apocalipsis: 'Qui dilexit nos et lauit in sanguine suo.' Amat nos[6] Cristus plusquam uir uxorem suam. Uir propter adulterium[7] uxorem dimittit; nec nos propter adulterium Cristus uult dimittere. Ieremias:[8] 'Uir si dimiserit uxorem numquam reuertitur ad eam; tu autem fornicata es cum amatoribus multis;[9] tamen reuertere ad me et ego suscipiam te, dicit dominus.' Amat nos Cristus plusquam anima corpus. Anima numquam uellet separari a corpore; Cristus autem animam suam a corpore suo pro nobis permisit separari . . .

Participii lectionis proposite uersus sequentes sunt memoriales:

> Munera dat, breue mittit, ad arma recurrit; in hostes
> Deseuit. Clipeus Cristi penetratur, obitque,
> Vt qui[10] uiuus[11] erat odio, defunctus[12] ametur.

(73) *A.W.* f. 105a/18–105b/20 (exemplum of the king who lost his life for the sake of a hard-hearted lady besieged in an earthen castle). The details (except for f. 105b/13–16, for which see under no. 72 above) appear to be the author's own invention, but a similar allegory occurs in *Mor.* III. 21 (L f. 124, T f. 193):

[Subheading] *Quod peccator obsidetur peccatis suis sicut*

---

[1] diligit] dilexerit T   [2] augmentum] argumentum T   [3] erga] *corr. from* ergo L   [4] aliquod] aliud T   [5] hos] eos L   [6] nos] *followed by* et lauit *subpuncted* T   [7] adulterium] *corr. from* adulterum T   [8] Ieremias] *om.* T   [9] multis] tuis L   [10] Vt qui] Vtque T   [11] uiuus] unius T   [12] defunctus] diffunctus T

castrum hostibus.[1] Peccatum enim obsidet hominem et circum-
stat ne faciat bonum siue admittat bonum (id est, graciam et
uirtutes). Sicut castrum aliquod obsidetur a militibus uel ab[2]
aliis, si homo defluit[3] luxuria, si [distrahitur][4] auaricia, et sic
de aliis uiciis, quasi obsessus non permittitur bonis uacare operibus, et ideo dicit apostolus, 'Circumstans nos
peccatum'.

(74) *A.W.* ff. 105b/21–106a/1 (Christ as a champion in a tournament who has his shield, i.e. his body, pierced). See the end
of the first paragraph of the passage from *Mor*. III. 47 quoted
under no. 72 above. The idea comes also in *Mor*. III. 5, 'Quod
Cristus multiplici ratione diligendus sit' (L f. 112[v], T f. 171[v]):

Athleta[5] etiam Cristus est, qui scutum, id est carnem in
cruce habuit perforatam.[6]

Christ is again represented as a champion in *Mor*. IV. 17 (L
f. 198[v], T f. 332[r–v]):

Quis autem homo tam crudelis esset ut, si aliquis athleta[7]
pugnasset[8] pro hereditate[9] illius et multis uulneribus
sauciatus esset,[10] eum expelleret ab hospicio suo quousque
saltem[11] illius uulnera sanarentur?[12]... Et quis est adeo[13] fortis
et tantus athleta[14] quantus dominus noster Iesus Cristus qui
tot uulnera et tanta obprobria pro nobis sustinuit—sputus,
alapis, cesus, flagellatus, tandem crucifixus mortuus.

[1] Quod ... hostibus] *om.* L   [2] ab] *om.* T.   [3] defluit] de-
fluxit L   [4] distrahitur] distrahatur L detrahatur *faintly altered to*
distrahatur T   [5] Athleta] adletha L   [6] perforatam] foratam L
[7] athleta] adletha L   [8] pugnasset] pugnascet T   [9] pro heredi-
tate] propheditate T   [10] esset] esse *struck through and replaced
in margin by* esset L   [11] saltem] saltati *imperfectly altered to* saltem (?) T   [12] sanarentur] sanaretur L   [13] adeo] *corr. from* a deo T
[14] athleta] adletha L

The conception of Christ's body as a shield comes also in *Mor*. III. 1 (L f. 109ᵛ, T f. 166ᵛ):

Simplicitati proposite serpentis prudentiam decet esse annexam, qui[1] id moris habet quod ad caput conseruandum illesum totum corpus perditioni exponit. Num[2] ab re est quod cum in caput aliquid nociuum uibratur, manus, quinque digitis insculpta, ad ictum excipiendum uice scuti obicitur? Absit![3] Per hoc quidem intelligitur quod cum[4] iacula temptationis ad capitis nostri, id est Cristi, lesionem a demonibus contorquentur, ipsis uice scuti corpus illud, quinque uulneribus perforatum, in quo de demonibus triumphauit obicere tenemur, ut sic caput nostrum, Cristus scilicet, qui cum patimur in nobis patitur, seruetur illesus.

(75) *A.W.* f. 106a/1–3 (Christ's body on the cross was wide as a shield above, narrow beneath, with 'the one foot, according to many a man's opinion, set upon the other'). This disposition of the feet is mentioned in two similitudes in the *Moralia*. The first is in *Mor*. III. 61 (L f. 154, T f. 254):

Hic est Cristus qui per[5] comptum[6] affixum posti, in quo utensilia domus suspendi solent, exprimitur. Et[7] merito: comptus in parte inferiore unico clauo, in superiore[8] duobus clauis posti[9] affigitur; ex parte uero superiori a poste auertitur[10] et tendit superius. Sic et Cristus secundum humanam naturam confixus est cruci uno clauo in pedibus et duobus in manibus superius.

The second is in *Mor*. III. 66 (L f. 158, T f. 261):

Hostium in tribus partibus aperitur: superiore[11] scilicet, in-

---

[1] qui] Qui LT   [2] Num] Non T   [3] Absit] Ac sic T   [4] cum] tam*en* T   [5] per] *om*. L   [6] comptum] comptum conterim T   [7] Et] Ex T   [8] superiore] super⟨i⟩ore T   [9] posti] *om*. T   [10] auertitur] reuertitur T   [11] superiore] *followed by* parte per fixuras *but with* va . . . cat *written above* T

feriore,[1] et a latere. Sic et Cristus cruci appensus in superiore parte per fixuras clauorum in manibus impressas reseratus est; in parte etiam inferiore, pede uno alteri supposito et ipsis unico clauo confixis, ad illius impressionem apertus est.

(76) *A.W.* f. 106a/13–19 (Christ could easily have redeemed us with less suffering but did not choose to; he paid a great price so that we should have no reason to refuse him our love). So in *Mor.* III. 56 (L f. 150ᵛ, T f. 247):

Qui uero facile potuit hominem creare, potuit eundem sine difficultate redimere. Sed noluit[2] dominus, quod[3] facilitas nostre creationis posset[4] esse aliqua—etsi non[5] uera—excusatio nobis quare non multum diligeremus[6] eum. Non enim multum solet diligi qui dat quod non multum constat sibi. Posset autem cogitare homo quid constiterit deo nostra creatio: sicut de ceteris, ita de homine dixit deus, 'Faciamus hominem', et factus est homo. Vt autem hanc[7] euacuaret murmurationem, grauissimis hominem uoluit redimere tormentis.

(77) *A.W.* f. 106a/19–106b/2 (the symbolism of the three materials of which a shield is made; as a brave knight's shield is, after his death, hung up in a church, so is the crucifix in memory of the valour that Christ displayed on the Cross). The source is *Mor.* III. 3 (L f. 111ᵛ, T f. 170ʳ⁻ᵛ):

Ad memoriam[8] igitur passionem[9] Cristi scutum reducit.[10] Nec mirum, quia in scuto[11] tria sunt: affectio, pellis, et asser. Asser crux Cristi, color est cruor, et caro pellis. Sicut igitur in memoriam militis mortui scutum in ecclesia suspenditur,

---

[1] inferiore] et inferiore L   [2] noluit] nouit T   [3] quod] quia T
[4] posset] possit T   [5] etsi non] et non si L et⟨si⟩ non T   [6] diligeremus] diligemus T   [7] autem hanc] hanc autem T   [8] memoriam] memorandam T   [9] passionem] *corr. from* passiones T   [10] scutum reducit] per scutum reducito T   [11] scuto] *the* o *over erasure* T

sic et in memoriam[1] Cristi, pro nobis mortui, in ecclesia signum crucis erigitur. Nouo pugnandi modo usus est dominus
cum, manibus cruci[2] affixis, de diabolo triumphauit; unde
in Iudicum dicitur, 'Noua bella sibi elegit dominus.'

(78) *A.W.* ff. 106b/2–107b/3 (the four chief loves). See under
no. 72 above (second paragraph).

(79) *A.W.* f. 107b/6–10 (love is to be given to Christ because
he surpasses other men in six qualities—beauty, riches, high
birth, wisdom, graciousness, and generosity). There is a similar
passage in *Mor.* III. 52 (L f. 147ᵛ, T f. 241), in which there are
unusual differences between the two early manuscripts, evidently
because the T scribe was trying to introduce into the text re-
visions and marginal additions which the L scribe ignored or
which (more probably) had not yet been added to the exemplar
when he copied it. That L's text, listing four qualities only, is the
original is shown by its agreement with a line of mnemonic verse
written at the foot of the page in both manuscripts:

> Nobilis et pulcher deus est, diuesque potensque.

My text follows L at the main points of difference, with T's
variants recorded in the footnotes.

Felix ergo anima[3] que ad hoc suspirat, ut cum Cristo[4]
matrimonium[5] contrahat. In ipso etenim quatuor[6] que in
sponso carnali affectari[7] solent reperiet: diuicias,[8] potentiam,
pulcritudinem,[9] et generositatem.[10] Diues[11] est dominus, utpote in quo, iuxta apostolum, 'omnes thesauri[12] sapientie et

---

[1] memoriam] memoria L   [2] cruci] crici T   [3] anima] *interlined* L   [4] Cristo] *corr. from* Cristi T   [5] matrimonium] -u*m
added at end of line in margin,* u*m subpuncted at beginning of next line* L
[6] quatuor] quinque T   [7] affectari] affectu*m subpuncted and replaced
by* affectari *in margin* L   [8] diuicias] diuicias sapientiam T
[9] pulcritudinem] et pulchritudinem T   [10] generositatem] *followed by*
Unde Ieremias xxiii, 'Regnabit rex et sapiens erit' T   [11] Diues]
Diues est. Sapiens (*for* Diues et sapiens) T   [12] thesauri] *preceded
by* a *subpuncted* L

scientie[1] reconditi sunt'; qui etiam de se dicit, 'Meus est
orbis terre et plenitudo eius, etc.' Potens est, utpote[2] qui
de se dicit 'Data est michi omnis potestas in celo et in terra';
nec est potestas eius temporalis, sed eterna: Ysaias,[3] 'Potestas eius potestas[4] eterna'. Pulcher est, utpote cuius pulcritudinem sol et luna mirantur; angeli autem, septies
clariores[5] sole, delectantur in pulcritudine[6] eius. Nobilis
est, utpote quia 'a patre luminum' genitus[7] est, 'apud quem
non est transmutatio nec uicissitudinis obumbratio'; nobilis
est etiam quia peccatum non fecit, nec inuentus est 'dolus
in ore[8] eius'. Hic est de quo in Parabolis, 'Nobilis in portis
uir eius'. Tanto ergo et tam generoso sponso sponsam tam
illustrem associari oportet ut de illa dicere possit, 'Tota
pulchra es, amica mea, et macula non est in te', supple[9]
mortalis peccati.

(80) *A.W.* f. 107b/10–11 (people say of a generous man who can
keep nothing that he has hands with holes in them). So in *Mor.*
I. 49 (L f. 46[v], T f. 62[v]):

Et sicut manus domini erant affixe, perforate, extente, sanguine irrigate,[10] ita sacerdotes et prelati ecclesie debent habere
manus extentas ad pauperes perforatas largitate. Qui enim
dapsilis est, dicitur habere manus perforatas.

(81) *A.W.* f. 108a/28–108b/3 ('Ignem ueni mittere in terram . . .',
burning love into earthly hearts). The text is several times cited

[1] sapientie et scientie] scientie et sapientie T   [2] utpote . . . Pulcher
est] *om.* T *but supplied at foot of page by original scribe in following form*
(*with repetition of* Potens est *at beginning*): Potens est, quia potestas [e
altered from a] eius potestas eterna. Ewangelium: 'Nolite timere eos qui
occidunt corpus etc. sed potius eum qui potest corpus et animam mittere in gehennam.' Pulcher est: Psalmus, 'Speciosus forma pre filiis
hominum'.   [3] Ysaias] *so* L *but in fact Dan.* 7: *14*   [4] potestas]
om. L   [5] clariores] clarior⟨es⟩ L   [6] pulcritudine]-inem L   [7] genitus]
om. L   [8] in ore] *om. but supplied in margin by original scribe* L
[9] supple] suple LT   [10] irrigate] irrigante T

in the *Moralia*, e.g. in I. 30, 'De penitentia' (L f. 33, T f. 41),
where there is no resemblance to its use in *A.W.*; but it is applied
as in *A.W.* in *Mor.* II. 4 (L f. 68ᵛ, T f. 98ᵛ):

Abigit igitur ignis frigus[1] spirituale—nec quiuis passim ignis,
sed ignis de quo scriptum est, 'Ignem ueni mittere in terram,[2]
et quid uolo nisi ut ardeat?' Ignis propositus caritas est.

(82) *A.W.* f. 108b/3–10 (lukewarm love is hateful to Christ:
'Vtinam frigidus esses aut calidus; set quia tepidus es, incipiam
te euomere de ore meo'). The text is also cited in the *Moralia*
but is rather differently applied. There is some resemblance in
the way it is used in *Mor.* III. 48 (L f. 145, T f. 236):

Sic et prelatus: calidus esse debet, quia dicitur in Apocalipsi,
'Utinam frigidus esses aut calidus; sed quia tepidus es, incipiam te euomere[3] ab ore meo.' Calidus esse debet[4] calore
caritatis, scilicet gemine dilectionis dei et proximi.

More remote from *A.W.* is the use in *Mor.* III. 94 (L f. 182ᵛ,
T ff. 303ᵛ–4):

Has [*sc.* uitam et doctrinam] qui non exhibet, membra con-
trita uidetur habere. Tale animal offert uir theologus litteratus et prudens qui nec docet nec peccatum corripit,
contra quem loquitur Iohannes in Apocalipsi: 'Vtinam[5]
frigidus esses aut calidus; sed quia tepidus es, euomam te ex[6]
ore meo.'

(83) *A.W.* f. 108b/18–20 (the king of bliss spreads his arms towards you and bows down his head as if to offer a kiss). The idea
is a commonplace, but compare the passage from *Mor.* III. 45
quoted under no. 34 above, in which Christ on the Cross is likened

---

[1] frigus] *corr. from* friguus T
preceded by emo *subpuncted* L
[5] Vtinam] *corr. from* Vt**rum** T

[2] terram] terra L   [3] euomere]
[4] esse debet] debet esse T
[6] ex] ab T

to a nurse spreading wide her arms to embrace a child, and also one in *Mor.* IV. 16 (L f. 198, T f. 331):

Extensio[1] etiam brachiorum eius in cruce manifeste declarat quod paratus sit omnes ad se uenientes recipere et inter ulnas sue benignitatis admittere.

(84) *A.W.* ff. 108b/25–109b/27 (Greek fire can be put out only by urine, sand, and vinegar; i.e. the love of our Lord, or spiritual love, can be quenched only by the stench of sin, or fleshly love, by idleness, and by malice). In *Mor.* III. 18, 'Contra adulterium', Greek fire is the basis of a concise *exemplum*, differently applied (L f. 122, T f. 189ᵛ):

[Subheading] *Exemplum de igne greco et luxuria.*[2] Sicut igitur ignis grecus[3] aceto, sic et recordatione sanguinis Iesu[4] Cristi luxurie flamma extinguitur.

---

[1] Extensio] *corr. from* Extenso T   [2] Exemplum . . . luxuria] *om.* T
[3] ignis grecus] grecus ignis *but marked for transposition* L   [4] Iesu] *om.* T

DATE DUE

MY 26 '81			